An essay on Yugoslav Society

An essay on Yugoslav Society

Branko Horvat

 International Arts and Sciences Press, Inc.
White Plains, New York

Text translated by Henry F. Mins
Footnotes and references rendered
by Dorothy Pribićević

Originally published in 1967 as
Ogled o Jugoslavenskom društvu
by Jugoslavenski Institut za
Ekonomska Istraživanja, Belgrade

Library of Congress Catalog
Card Number: 79-77456
International Arts and Sciences Press, Inc.
White Plains, New York

Translation ©1969 by International Arts
and Sciences Press, Inc.

Contents

"Ideas are materialized in a nation to the extent that a need for them exists . . . . It is not enough that thought should strive toward realization; existence itself must enter into thought."

Karl Marx

Foreword

An epoch of our postrevolutionary development seems to have terminated. This realization leads us to a critical reexamination of the road we have traveled, as well as to an examination of future possibilities, the unfolding of prospects of development. It is a fascinating but risky enterprise.

The present *Essay* was not written in haste, and probably cannot be read through in haste either. It is the result of my thinking about our society for the last sixteen years. The section "The Transition Period" was written and published as long ago as 1951; the last section, on the theory of the party, was written only after the Brioni Plenum of the Central Committee of the Communist Party of Yugoslavia, when study of these problems had become socially relevant, in the sense of the quotation of Marx that has been adopted as the epigraph of this book. Part of the text has been published in *Ekonomist, Pregled, Gledišta* and *Naše teme.* Part I and Chapters 11 and 14 are taken from my book *Towards a Theory of Planned Economy.* Although these fragments came into being in the course of a decade and a half, final revision showed that their research results did not require amendment. At the same time, numerous additions and reformulations have been made. And, of course, completion of the work called for a series of new researches.

The title chosen is no accident: the *Essay* is not a systematic study. It aims at nothing more than the elaboration of some factors that in my judgment are strategic, merely giving the basic outlines of an overall picture of our society. A great deal had to be omitted. In the economic section, for example, there is no analysis of the functioning of the economic mechanism. In the sociological section there is no treatment of the sociology of self-government, of the sociological effect of the exodus from the village, and of many other matters. The political section lacks an analysis of the parliamentary system, of elections, of the organization of the government apparatus, of the functioning of the communal system, and of the place and role of Yugoslav trade unions. These gaps could be filled only by a *team* of scholars.

In places, the text is burdened with footnotes. Footnotes are disagreeable things in and of themselves; moreover, they make the text less readable. Although I was aware of these facts, I was compelled to adopt the "footnoteological" alternative for the following reasons. As a Marxist, I wanted to remove some inveterate vulgarizations and revisions of Marxist economic and political theory. One striking instance is the theory of productive labor, which has important consequences in practice. In such cases a "protective covering" of relevant citations was necessary. I know, from personal experience with this case, that the omission of even a single citation leads to charges of "intentional distortion," "lack of principle," etc. Moreover, as a Marxist, I was interested in pointing out those predictions of Marx that had proved, in the context of our society, to be mistaken. One such prediction concerned the economic organization of socialist society. Arguments on this point are supplemented by quotations, as in the previous instance. Finally, in scientific work, as distinguished from journalism, citations are sometimes needed in order to draw a clear line of demarcation between accepted ideas and one's own contribution and, in particular, to bring out authoritative ideas with which the author is not in agreement.

Dobrila Mićković and Anica Savićević took upon themselves the disagreeable task of converting my manuscript into a legible text. I thank them for their patience and care.

Branko Horvat

CHAPTER I

Historical Presuppositions
of the Yugoslav Type of Society
(Associationist Socialism)

1. SCHEMATIZATION OF SOCIOECONOMIC DEVELOPMENT

In beginning our analysis, it will be of value to recapitulate, in schematic form, the basic propositions of Marx's and Engels' theory of social development. In all probability this will be merely a review of things that are well known in the Yugoslav milieu. But it seems to me that this conceptual framework should be defined in advance, as clearly and precisely as possible, in order to bring out unequivocally the continuity of our extrapolation of the Marxist analysis and its applicability to the new social phenomena with which we are dealing, for the first time, in this work.

For a long period of time, much longer than that of written history, human communities could hardly manage to produce enough to survive. In the then-prevailing social relations there was no room for "class exploitation." [1]

However, as innovations gradually accumulated, the productivity of labor rose. In many communities it became possible to produce regularly more than was absolutely necessary for survival. Thus, an opportunity arose to live on other people's surplus product. When this economic opportunity became apparent, it was seized upon by some members of the community. And since the others (within or outside of the community) were not willing to part with their surplus product, they were compelled to do so by brute force; they were made *slaves*. Society became a *class* society, with the ruling class appropriating the surplus product of the exploited class and using it for its own purposes. In this sense, i.e., on the basis of controlling the means

1

of existence, class exploitation has continued to be exercised in all societies until our times.

A slave is a man owned by another (free) man, owned in the same sense as cows and plows. This formal similarity led Aristotle, in antiquity, to classify slaves — as economists are today tempted to classify wage-earners[2] — in the same economic category with cows and plows, distinguished only as tools that speak as against those that low or are mute. This was a delusion on the part of a man who conceived of the then-existing social relations as natural and therefore eternal. Plows and cows work equally well in all social systems, but human beings do not. For one thing, slaves were very inefficient workers. For another, their reproduction costs were high. On both scores, improvements were possible, and this is what made *feudalism* a more efficient social system.

The new ruling class had come to realize that, in order to extract the surplus labor, it was not necessary to resort to slavery. Feudal lords found it quite sufficient to own land, to be able to compel serfs to work for them a certain amount of time. The possibility of working for some time on one's own land, and of paying the feudal rent not only in terms of labor but also in terms of product, and later in terms of money, was conducive to the rising labor productivity.

In feudalism the worker was no longer the property of the master, but was still personally dependent on him, i.e., he was still made to work for him by means of noneconomic institutions. The land was not only a means of production; it was also a means of direct political power because a feudal estate was a sort of small state headed by a landlord exercising political, military, and administrative powers. The serfs were tied to the land, and hence were not only workers but subjects of their feudal lords as well.

The next obvious possibility was to replace personal dependence by market dependence and still have a smoothly working socioeconomic mechanism. After a certain number of violent clashes of antagonistic social forces in various countries, this proved possible. Workers, possessing no means of livelihood, have no other choice but to sell their labor power to the owners of the means of production, i.e., to the owners of capital. A new social system, *capitalism,* came into being. At the beginning, the workers had no political rights. Moreover, fines and corporal punishment in the factory, so common in those days, represented a direct continuation of master-serf relations. But after the new system had become more settled, this practice could and had to be discontinued; political rights were granted, with no ill effects for the stability of the system. Political and economic power was held firmly by the propertied class, while the free market system provided an efficient barrier for preventing a mass invasion of the higher social strata by members of the propertyless class.

Personal freedom and a *relatively* high social mobility had a tremendous impact on labor productivity. The slave and feudal economies, not to speak of primitive society, were almost stationary. Capitalism meant a dramatic change in human history. In the last two centuries — the approximate period of time that the organization of production may be described as capitalist — the production of material wealth has expanded more than in all the previous thousands of years. This is bound to have had a profound effect on the course of social development.

It need hardly be said that the sketch presented in the preceding paragraphs is nothing more than a scheme. Its sole purpose has been to point out the crucial factor in social development: the relationship between people in production. Ancient society was characterized by slave labor; feudal society, by serfdom; and capitalism, by wage labor.

Clearly, these relations are not a matter of choice, a matter of ethics, or of likes and dislikes. There is nothing "natural" about them; Aristotle thought that slavery was natural, while others think the same of wage labor in the service of private capital or of the government apparatus. If history teaches us anything, its lesson is that social relations change, that production expands, and that there is a correspondence between these two changes. This correspondence is very complex, but, schematizing again, it may be reduced to the following. The development of productive forces makes a new social system feasible; once the social change is made, it helps production to expand further. In class societies, social changes do not occur by friendly agreement or by means of rational legislation or anything of the kind; they are the outcome of the conflict of antagonistic social classes fighting for their interests. The class whose interests are tied up with the new and superior mode of production emerges victorious and reorganizes the society. In the most developed countries, class struggles at the end of a social epoch are likely to result in violent revolutionary overthrow of the old social systems. Once the new social system is more or less established in the most advanced countries, the ruling classes of other countries, unless they lag very much behind the general development, are likely to submit without civil wars. All this means two things: first, social development is gradual and stages cannot be skipped; second, since it is linked with the development of social forces, social development, i.e., the succession of social systems, is irreversible.

The process described is not a straight-line process. There can be temporary deviations and movements backward. Prior to the advent of capitalism, the world was not a unified whole as it is today, and so entire civilizations could perish without significant consequences for subsequent development. The scheme is primarily applicable to European history, which has been more or less autonomous and spontaneous, and therefore the process could work itself out fully. Once capitalism had taken firm root in Europe, it began to spread all over the world by means of trade and conquest. Capitalist institutions were imported into non-European countries, whose social systems encompassed the entire range from primitive society to feudalism; as a result, the most complex social processes were set in motion. Perhaps the only universal characteristic of all these processes was that everywhere capitalism was gaining ground against all rival social systems.

However, even in Europe, slavery, feudalism, and capitalism are not three rigid historical systems neatly separated from each other. In each, the institutions of the other two were known and developed to a certain extent. They are not "pure" systems, and they can be classified as separate systems only in terms of the predominant institutions. Determinism in development, i.e., in the succession of these systems, only means that, for instance, the uprising of Roman slaves under Spartacus in the 1st century B.C. and the peasant wars in Europe in the 15th and 16th centuries *could not* achieve the purpose of their initiators,[3] while the war of the Northern states in the USA for the abolition of slavery in the 19th century *could not fail* to achieve this goal (ultimately). As concrete events these are, of course, products of unique historical circumstances and, as such, unrepeatable. But once we abstract the irrelevant details, a regularity appears and provides a basis for generalizations. It is obvious that any single country may skip stages of development and that this is exactly what many backward countries are doing today. However, this fact does not affect the validity of the generalizations, for it is only *societies that lag behind* that are able to skip stages of development. This observation is intended as a reminder that purely rationalist blueprints of economic institutions — for example, the communist communities in America during the last century or the present-day communist village communes in China — are useless.

Finally, the two-class scheme focuses attention only on the main driving force of social change: the struggle between those who, as the ruling class, are united by their vested interests in the existing social system and wish to preserve it, and those whose

4

prospects are to benefit from the change and who therefore form the opposing social class. But ruling and exploited classes are not necessarily homogeneous; they are not necessarily rigid, and between them there usually exist a certain number of middle groups which, of course, must all be taken into account in an analysis of a concrete society. The two-class scheme is nothing but a convenient and very useful *abstraction* from social relations. An attempt to neatly classify all the individual members of a given society into two classes would only reveal extreme naiveté on the part of an overzealous empiricist. The purpose of the two-class scheme is to provide a simple analytical framework for studying polarization tendencies in the society, with their inevitable result — fundamental social conflict. By the term *fundamental social conflict* — as distinguished from social conflicts between individuals and groups that are part and parcel of life in every conceivable human society — I mean the situation in which the fundamental principle of social organization involves social conflict between groups that not only have divergent interests but are also related to each other as *upper* and *lower* groups, and as *minority* and *majority* groups. In all class societies it is easy to point out the existence of the fundamental social conflict, and, conversely, whenever we detect the potential existence of the fundamental social conflict, we may confidently expect the development of a class society. We shall shortly have an opportunity to make practical use of the last hypothesis.

2. STATE CAPITALISM

Social development did not end with liberal capitalism. This is obvious to us today, but it was known to very few when Marx and Engels began their analysis. In this context we cannot avoid discussing, if only in a very fragmentary way, the problem of the socialist revolution. It is well known that Marx and Engels, extrapolating the historical trend, reached the conclusion that socialist revolutions would break out in the most advanced countries.[4] In fact, however, socialist revolutions occurred in relatively backward countries, with no particular signs that they will necessarily be repeated — at least not in a violent form — in the most advanced countries. How is one to account for the failure of this prediction, which seemed to be so much in accord with historical experience?

Let us first note that the failure of the prediction was not at all general. Marx and Engels proved to be right in predicting violent socialist revolutions,[5] and they were right, too, insofar as they expected that it would be the most developed capitalist countries where the working class would be able to realize the first objectives of its program. At the time of *The Communist Manifesto* these objectives were, among others, the eight-hour working day, universal suffrage, working class political and trade union organizations, progressive taxes, free elementary education, social insurance, and a rising standard of living.[6] Today in all advanced capitalist countries these requirements are more or less satisfied;[7] moreover, in a certain number of countries, private ownership of productive means has been partly abolished, with certain industries passing into state ownership through nationalization. But all that was accomplished without a great socialist revolution — although in various countries there have been a certain number of bloody class clashes of the 1848 type. And this brings us to our second point.

Revolution is not a product of development as such, but of unbearable social tensions. In the pioneering countries, pre-1848 capitalism frequently generated social tensions approaching the explosion point. For an illuminating description of the workings of a capitalist mechanism in those days, one should look up the historical chapters of Marx's *Capital.* However, at that time conditions were still not ripe for the new social system. Later on, socialism became theoretically feasible, but social tensions were not generated to the extent necessary for a violent revolution. Why? I think that two crucial, closely related, and mutually reinforcing causes may be adduced as an explanation. First, unlike previous economies, the capitalist economy was not static; it was expanding relatively quickly, providing a possibility *both* for the toiling classes to improve their lot and for the propertied class to accumulate wealth. Second, the free market proved to be a very successful organizational principle; since it operated impersonally, apparently no one could be blamed for the existing miseries. For both these reasons the ruling class found it possible to give political rights to the toiling class without endangering its own position. This meant the further easing of social tensions. Gradually, the working class succeeded in organizing itself into trade unions and political parties, and the stronger the labor movement became, the smaller the gulf between the propertied and working classes became. For better or worse, the well-organized labor movement saved advanced capitalist countries from socialist revolutions.

The situation was different in the backward countries. Here, primitive accumulation of capital, with the accompanying social conflicts, was contemporaneous with the relatively high standard of living in the advanced countries and with the socialist ideologies professed by strong labor movements in those countries. As the Russian Revolution of 1905 showed, there was reason enough for a revolution. And once the great revolution had begun, it was very natural that it would not stop short of attempting to accomplish the most radical program the epoch had produced, the program of socialism, for revolutions are "the locomotives of history." They break the bonds of tradition, remove the obstacles of vested interests, and clear the ground for a free movement toward limits defined only by existing revolutionary ideology, which reflects the material and cultural conditions of the epoch as a whole, not merely of the country carrying out the revolution. Although subsequent implementations of the revolutionary ideology are modified to a great extent by the historical peculiarities of the country concerned, the essential fact stands out clearly, as is demonstrated by the two most momentous national revolutions. In the 18th century, the French Revolution did away with feudal relations, thereby paving the way for the more efficient capitalist form of organization; in the 20th century, the Russian Revolution removed the next obstacle, private ownership, and improved the efficiency of the economic machine still further. After the Russian Revolution had proved successful, it was likely that it would be followed by a number of socialist revolutions in other backward countries. Marx expected that capitalist development would lead to the polarization of wealth *within* the most advanced countries and that this would multiply class contradictions to the point of revolution. That, indeed, did happen in the earlier stages of capitalist development, but the rapid expansion of productive forces helped to check the polarization process before it had gone too far. Hence, in its later stages, capitalist development led instead — to the accompaniment of monopolization and imperialist wars — to a polarization of wealth on an *international scale,* as a result of which the class conflict in the backward capitalist countries was magnified and eventually led to socialist revolutions.

We must next investigate further possible changes in productive relations. We have seen that these relations (except in primitive society) have passed through three stages: that of complete personal dependence of the worker on the master; that of partial dependence; and that of complete personal independence of the worker, who, in working for the master, was compelled only by the impersonal force of the market. We have seen that the successive stages had increasing economic efficiency.

7

The whole process represents, in fact, a gradual liberation of the individual from social bonds, an equalization of men, a mastering of social relations in a manner similar to that by which nature and its forces were being mastered. If this generalization is meaningful, the next stage may consist in an elimination of all individual private owners of productive means, whose role as organizers of production will be taken over by a single owner, the state; this will lead to an equalization of individuals in their relations to the state. This expropriation of private capitalists by the state was what the socialist revolution was intended to accomplish. The economic advantages of state capitalism [8] over private capitalism are tremendous. In organizing production according to a rational plan, the state is able to speed up economic growth two or three times [16: Ch. 10].

The characteristic feature of capitalism is the alienation of human labor [17: 196-208]. In order to live, the proletarian is obliged to sell his inner being, his labor power, and he has no control over the product of his work. This observation implies two things: first, the worker is primarily an appendage to the machine; he is used to make capital yield fruits; second, the fate of the final product is governed by the blind forces of the market. In state capitalism, self-alienation reaches the ultimate possible limits, because the entire society is proletarianized. But at the same time, total alienation provides the means for its own total destruction. For while an individual cannot, the society as a whole can control the product of its work with the help of the state. And this is the point that attracts the main attention of socialists. State control is justified not for its own sake, but because it is thought to be the only alternative to the chaos of private capitalist production. However, if it can be shown that a planned economy can dispense with state control, it will become apparent that state capitalism is only a transitional stage in the development toward another and more efficient social system — socialism. Control of production without the state as intermediary means control by direct producers, which in turn means that the equality of proletarians is transformed into the equality of masters. The process of human alienation, started in the first class society, comes to an end, and in the first *classless* society it is reversed. Labor gradually ceases to be "suffering," "unpleasantness," and toil, and becomes the primary need of man, the affirmation of human life. Of course, all this has nothing to do with the *ethical* desirability of such a system. It only indicates the possibility of superior efficiency on the part of such a system. And if one can establish the *possibility and economic superiority of a social system, this will be equivalent, in a Marxist framework, to proving its inevitability.*

Returning to the problem of state capitalism, we have to inquire into what the social forces and processes are by which liberal and private capitalism is being transformed into monopoly and state capitalism. One of them, an (incomplete) socialist revolution, has already been mentioned. The other, gradual transformation, is by now so well known that a brief review will suffice.

The free play of market forces in competitive capitalism leads to a gradual concentration of production in the hands of a smaller and smaller number of firms, whose size correspondingly increases. One of the reasons for the greater efficiency of larger firms is purely technological: up to a certain point, the increase in output reduces production costs. The other — and by far more important reason — is related to the market. A large firm controls a certain portion of the market and can therefore undertake planning; a large firm is financially strong, which in a market economy means that it commands credit; hence it can exert pressure on weaker partners and in general can manipulate the terms of buying and selling in its own favor; it is able to survive periodic crises when smaller firms go under. Thus, competitive capitalism constantly generates tendencies toward monopolization.

Faced with the economic power of employers, workers begin to organize themselves into trade unions. In order to be effective, trade unions must become large organizations, and they grow until they reach the absolute limit of a nationwide association. At that stage monopoly labor confronts monopoly capital.[9]

A similar process takes place in politics. In order to have a stable government, the number of political parties is reduced until all political life is dominated by two major parties.[10] In addition, there is a strong tendency for these two parties to link themselves with the other two monopoly groups and to represent their interests. Thus we are likely to get a "conservative party" favoring the interests of private capital and a "labor party" supported by the trade unions.

Four giants dominate the social scene in monopoly capitalism: organized capital, organized labor, and the two political parties. Insofar as the political parties clearly identify themselves with two antagonistic social interests, the oligopoly of four reduces to duopoly. The Marxian vision of the two-class structure of society materialized (although with some important modifications due to the bureaucratization process) in the concrete social organization of a modern advanced capitalist country. Capital and labor fight for supremacy. The immediate outcome of this battle is not necessarily known. An extraordinary event — say, a serious slump

— may suddenly increase the possibility of the abolition of private ownership or, at any rate, seriously disturb the old balance of power in favor of labor. In this case, capitalists may resort to fascism, as they did between the two wars. On the other hand, the ruling class may stubbornly refuse to settle political issues by political means — say, by banning socialist parties. Finally, various countries will be able to preserve the precarious equilibrium between two antagonistic social forces, traveling slowly along the road of gradual nationalization in one form or another (first, perhaps, nationalizing "unprofitable industries in need of complete reconstruction"; then, "industries vitally important for the nation"; next, "unorganized industries in need of coordination"; and then again, "monopolized industries in which private monopoly cannot be tolerated"; and so forth, until the last possible candidate for socialization is taken up) and along the path of increasing state control. The widespread absentee ownership prevalent in modern capitalist economies makes the process relatively painless. Every new "labor" government will have to take another step in the direction of extending public ownership, and so private capitalism will be gradually replaced by state capitalism.

At this point we may summarize the above results. The problem of the system of production relations corresponding to a planned economy has been put into perspective. State capitalism is such a possible system; it is so not only as a logical possibility but also as an empirical reality. But this knowledge is not sufficient for the solution of our problem. We must ask: is state capitalism an *optimum* system under the given conditions? "In the early days of socialist thought," the West Indian socialist W. A. Lewis writes, "it was almost an axiom that once property passed from private hands to public ownership, all the major social problems were automatically solved; it would be put to purposes conforming more to the public interest, income would be more equitably distributed, economic power would be democratized, efficiency would increase, and the class struggle between owners and workers would end. This view has not survived the experience" [20:181]. Professor Lewis was referring primarily to British experience, but the conclusion may be easily generalized. The main reason for the inadequate functioning of state capitalism should be sought, I suggest, in the distinguishing feature of its economic and political organization: the rule of bureaucracy. Thus, our next task is to analyze the economic consequences of a bureaucratic organization of the economic process.

3. BUREAUCRACY AND "OFFICE FETISHISM"

In analyzing the functioning of private capitalism and the ideology it generates, Marx laid great emphasis on what he called "commodity fetishism," i.e., a tendency to treat relations between men as relations between commodities. A closely corresponding phenomenon in state capitalism may be called "office fetishism." It means hiding actual human relations behind impersonal bureaucratic rules, a mystification of the activities of office-holders. The judgments of the market are infallible, as are the judgments of an official with respect to his subordinates. The holding of office confers upon the incumbent the quality of being cleverer, more honest, more reliable (politically or otherwise) — in short, *superior* to all individuals placed lower in the hierarchy of office. The parallelism goes even further. Both the free market and the bureaucratic structure have their separate lives that cannot be brought under conscious control. In the case of the free market, the contention seems fairly obvious. In the case of bureaucracy, it may appear somewhat puzzling and therefore requires a more detailed inquiry.

Weber's Theory of Bureaucracy

Bureaucracy, as a social institution, has three fundamental characteristics:

1. When administrative tasks are simple and undifferentiated, no specialized apparatus is necessary for their execution. In a small social organization, the person in authority is able to control social activities — economic, political, and military — more or less directly. As the community grows in size, the need will arise for an apparatus to mediate between the source of power and the mechanism for carrying out orders. As the needs of the community become more diverse and social life becomes more complex, the need will arise for increased specialization of the members of the mediating administrative apparatus. Thus, quantitative expansion and complexity of administrative tasks provide "technical" preconditions for the development of bureaucracy. But this is not the whole story.

2. Like money, the institution of bureaucracy has been known in all social systems, with the exception of primitive society. However, the institution (again, like money) reached its fully developed form only in the capitalist system. The relation between the development of the money economy and that of bureaucracy is not only that of parallelism, but also a relation of mutual

11

causation. As Max Weber, the founder of systematic study of bureaucracy, [11] pointed out, money is a normal presupposition of bureaucracy; it makes regular pecuniary compensation possible and desirable. In feudalism, the administrators — the feudal lords — were in possession of the means of administration. Similarly, the soldiers possessed their own arms. In capitalism, the members of the administration and the army are separated from the means they manipulate, and this appears to be related to the separation of the means of production from the direct producers. [12] Money, in the sense of capital accounting, became an institutional basis for both rationalization and depersonalization of human relations. Bureaucratic structures fitted perfectly into this social framework.

3. The third characteristic of bureaucracy is that it is a product of a particular type of authority. Following Weber in his classification, but setting his scheme in a different theoretical framework, we can distinguish three fundamental types of authority. *Traditional authority* rests on an established belief in the sanctity of immemorial traditions and in the legitimacy of the status of those exercising authority under them [21: 301]. The loyalty of subordinate members of the community is given to the incumbent in office and not to the legal order. Hence there is a tendency to appropriate the means of administration. When economic development is slow, as it was before the advent of capitalism, changes in social institutions are very small and all of social life, including the institution of authority, is likely to be strongly traditionalized. The existence of traditional authority minimizes the possibility of gradual adaptation to the changing conditions of life; as a result, the existing institutional structure — economic, political, religious — tends to come into conflict with the social needs it is expected to serve, and the contradictions between the two tend to accumulate. Since there is little possibility of solving these contradictions within the traditional framework, a social explosion usually demolishes the traditional authority and replaces it, for the time being, by the *charismatic authority* of the leader of the revolutionary movement. Charismatic authority rests on devotion to the specific and exceptional sanctity, the heroism or exemplary character, of an individual person and of the normative order revealed or ordained by him [21: 301]. The essence of a charismatic movement is emancipation from the routine, and therefore the corresponding type of authority is bound to be short-lived and transitional in character. Charismatic movements either fail and perish, or succeed and through the "routinization of charisma" build new, traditionalized systems. Then the cycle may repeat itself.

With the advent of capitalism the mechanism just described ceases to operate — not in the sense that traditional and charismatic authority cannot appear any more, but in the sense that they cease to dominate the social scene. The impersonal market and expropriation of the means of production and administration destroy personal loyalties to the incumbents of offices. Rapid economic development requires flexible adaptations of the social framework, which, implying changes, exclude traditionalized solutions and, recurring in quick succession, make charismatic solutions unlikely. A new type of authority develops, the type Weber calls *rational legal authority*. Legal authority rests on belief in the "legality" of the patterns of normative rules and in the right of those elevated to authority under such rules to issue commands [21: 300]. The rules are universal, cover all possible cases of conduct within the jurisdiction of those in authority, and define the limits of that jurisdiction. Obedience is owed to the legally established impersonal order, which thus becomes the fundamental source of authority. As T. Parsons comments on Weber [21: 51], the authority extends to individuals only insofar as they occupy a specifically legitimized status under the rules, an *office,* and their powers are limited to a "sphere of competence" as defined in regulations. Outside this sphere they are private individuals with no more authority than anyone else. Thus a possibility arises for a new and more subtle "fetishism of office" to be added to the traditional "commodity fetishism"; an aspect of exploitative relations hidden behind the market is supplemented or replaced by the other, hidden behind the office. The individuals with split personality, as it were, masters in the office and clients at home, owning nothing and deciding on everything, public servants by title and public masters by position, are *bureaucrats.* The administrative staff, whose constituent members they are, takes the form of a *bureaucratic structure.*

Weber distinguished seven fundamental categories of rational legal authority. These categories are nothing but technical or formal characteristics of a bureaucratic structure. They are as follows: a continuous organization of official functions bound by rules; a specified sphere of competence; the organization of offices follows the principle of hierarchy, i.e., each lower office is under the control and supervision of a higher one; the rules regulating the conduct of an office may be technical rules or norms; the administrative staff is separated from ownership of the means of administration; the incumbent does not appropriate his official position; administrative acts, decisions, and rules are recorded in writing [21: 303-304].

These technical features of bureaucracy make it an extremely efficient tool for handling mass administration. Administrative functions can be specialized according to purely objective considerations, and then discharged by functionaries who have adequate specialized training. Business is conducted objectively, according to calculable rules and without regard to persons. From the point of view of those who hold the supreme authority, the bureaucratic machine works with unrivaled precision, stability, and reliability. Stringency of discipline makes possible a high degree of calculability of results. Finally, the scope of operations of the bureaucratic type of administrative organization appears practically unlimited, and this organization is formally capable of application to all kinds of administrative tasks [21: 309]. All this leads Weber to conclude: "Experience tends universally to show that the bureaucratic type of administrative organization . . . is, from a purely technical point of view, capable of attaining the highest degree of efficiency and is in this sense formally the most rational known means of carrying out imperative control over human beings" [21: 309].

But there is a snag in this ideal-type analysis of a social institution. Bureaucracy is perfectly suited for an imperative — i.e., coercive — control, but it does not insure that the interests of the controller and the controlled are identical. Moreover, there is a strong tendency for these interests to be polarized. A typical bureaucratic structure looks like a pyramid with a tiny top and a large base: with a flow of communication in only one direction, from the top downward; with these communications having an imperative character; with both ends loose — at the top, where hierarchical relations disappear in the sense that there are no more superiors, and at the bottom, where they disappear in the opposite sense, namely, there are no more inferiors, and with no direct communication between the top and the bottom of the social pyramid. The "purely bureaucratic type of administrative organization" begins to assume the ominous aspect of potential social conflicts. Clearly, Weber's ideal-type analysis appears to be dangerously simplified and misleading. If we are to evaluate the efficiency of the system when developed to its ultimate consequences, we must take into account the human relations the system is likely to generate. In addition, we must consider the dysfunctional effects of the system that are determined by its technical characteristics.

14

Dysfunctional Effects of Bureaucracy and Inefficiency of the Bureaucratic Mode of Operation ("Bureaucratism")

We have seen how strong the forces of integration are in a modern mass-production economy. In executing its administrative functions, the nationwide bureaucracy does not behave capriciously. In fact, there are marked regularities, which may be classified under three main headings.

1. Ideally, the bureaucratic apparatus is expected to carry out the commands of the authorities without questioning their validity. This makes for the calculability of results, which is one of the essential preconditions for the superior efficiency of a bureaucratic organization. In practice, however, bureaucracy does not operate in a social vacuum. The calculability of behavior in a bureaucratic organization rests on the premise that official policy will be faithfully carried out by subordinates. But why should it? True, there is stringent discipline backed by the threat of punishment. But this safeguard is operative only when individual members of the apparatus are involved. It breaks down when the interests of the bureaucracy as a social group, or even only the interests of the higher strata of the hierarchy, come into conflict with the policy to be executed. Various consequences follow.

The administrative staff is an apparatus of political rule or of economic management. In either case, if reliability and calculability are to be achieved, the interests of the bureaucracy and the ruling class must coincide. It is therefore natural that in a class society the upper strata of the bureaucratic hierarchy will consist of members of the ruling class or of those aspiring to enter its ranks. [13]

Hence we reach the conclusion that a bureaucratic organization, in order to be viable in a class society, must be a class-oriented organization. This at once destroys the foundations of rational legality on which Weber built his thesis of the maximum formal efficiency of the bureaucratic organization. Being class-oriented, bureaucracy generates social conflict and thus prevents the achievement of maximum efficiency.

Empirical illustrations for the foregoing conclusions can be found without difficulty. The recent history of the most important and most developed capitalist countries furnishes them readily. In Weimar Germany, to quote J. D. Kingsley, "an attempt was made to impose parliamentary control upon a Civil Service but partially committed to the ends the Republic sought to pursue; and the attempt failed disastrously. In France, too, reactionary officials successfully sabotaged the efforts of the Blum Government in finance and foreign affairs; and the Roosevelt Administration was forced to assemble almost a whole new set of officials to carry out the New Deal reforms. No comparable situation has arisen recently in England, but that is clearly because the bureaucracy in its upper ranges has been representative of the ruling class as a whole and because its aspirations have been those to which successive governments were committed" [25: 219]. The last statement stands in need of correction. British bureaucracy has also had an opportunity to show its class bias; one case occurred during the general strike in 1926, [14] and another during the second Labor government (1929-1931). [15]

It becomes clear that bureaucracy hinders social progress by its very nature. This fact is extremely relevant in the case of socialist revolution. The conclusion reached by Marx that socialist revolution, in order to be successful, must demolish and replace the old state apparatus, proves to be confirmed by historical events. [16] There is, however, a practical question: replaced by what? Suppose the ruling classes are dispossessed and the bureaucratic hierarchy is filled up with persons entirely unrelated to and even hostile to the old ruling classes. Is the new "classless" bureaucracy likely to behave differently from the old one? Before we attempt to answer this question, we must consider two technical features of bureaucratic action.

2. In order to insure precision, impersonality, and calculability, bureaucracy in action must be governed by rules that are, ideally, supposed to cover all possible cases. In practice, of course, no bureaucratic brain can anticipate and fix, by rules, the infinite diversity of life. Hence there is an inherent contradiction in the system: a completely bureaucratized organization would require that the number of rules be almost as great as the number of concrete decisions. Since this is impossible and the number of rules is much smaller, an important element of imprecision and unpredictability creeps into the organization. To cope with this defect, those in authority tend to multiply rules, whose sheer number and increasing inconsistency with each other have a strong negative effect on those who are required to observe these rules, and this drives them to inactivity. If the number of rules is reduced, the situation is not improved. Apart from the increased possibility of evasion, the typical functionary now feels less secure and hence consults the higher-ups more frequently. The behavioral effect of this contradiction is reflected in the tendency to avoid responsibility; by definition, bureaucracy is not responsible for its decisions (because they are preordained regulations) and is

irresponsible in behavior. The hierarchy of status amplifies this effect and adds a new one: not only responsibility but also work tends to be avoided, the former being passed upward, the latter downward. A considerable amount of intellectual and emotional energy is wasted in the process.

Nor is this all. The fundamental principle of hierarchy is conformity to rules and to the authority of superiors. Functionaries are trained to conform, for this makes the bureaucratic organization work. Conformity is clearly a means to the end that the organization sets out to achieve. But for the members of the hierarchy, conformity is an essential precondition for their own existence. The result is displacement of goals by means, a typical bureaucratic endeavor to satisfy rules and superiors, [17] and not to assist clients. The process is effectively summed up by R. K. Merton: "(1) An effective bureaucracy demands reliability of response and strict devotion to regulations. (2) Such devotion to the rules leads to their transformation into absolutes; they are no longer conceived as relative to a given set of purposes. (3) This interferes with ready adaptation under special conditions not clearly envisaged by those who drew up the general rules. (4) Thus, the very elements that are conducive to efficiency in general produce inefficiency in specific instances" [29: 366].

The dysfunctional effects of bureaucratic organization are magnified as the organization increases in size. In nationwide bureaucracies, the process comes to a logical end: the apparatus designed to facilitate control becomes uncontrollable itself. Technically, it is simply a consequence of what E. Jaques calls "a paradox of executive work": ". . . the higher the executive, the greater the number of people dependent on him, but the greater also is his dependence: for the carrying out of his wishes is in the hands of an increasing number of people" [30: 227]. Even if Plato's Philosopher stands at the summit of the bureaucratic structure, he will be able to realize his projects only within the limits of the performance possibilities of the apparatus at his disposal. For the reasons enumerated, the apparatus will tend to handle the tasks inappropriately and thus force the Philosopher to take decisions that may look fantastic to outsiders. But there is no necessity for a national bureaucracy to have a Philosopher as a leader. Perhaps it is more realistic to expect that, normally, the leader will have much more modest intellectual and organizational capacities. In this case the main task of the leader may reduce to a permanent struggle for preservation of his own position in the hierarchy — in which case the last trace of conscious control fades away. The probability that this will happen increases when we

17

take into account the next group of dysfunctional factors.

3. The process of administration is not timeless nor is it independent of the size of the organization. In a large bureaucratic organization, with many intermediary links, there will be a considerable lag between the moment in time when the command is issued at the top and the moment in time when the command is carried out by functionaries at the other end. This lag is doubled when the other-end officials initiate the process by first transmitting information upward and then await instructions on how to act. It is trebled or quadrupled if, for one reason or another, information is not properly understood at either end after the first transmission. Often, too, communications will travel the same distance a number of times because, at every link in the chain, bureaucrats, taking care of their own safety, will endeavor to clear up any controversial points. On their long journeys, information and instructions also get distorted for psychological reasons, and for all the other reasons we examined under (1) and (2). While the information and instructions are traveling up and down, circumstances change and the solution applied may prove grossly inadequate. Both cases reflect another inherent contradiction of bureaucratic organizations — namely, the contradiction of centralization and decentralization. If the aim is maximum efficiency, decentralized bureaucratic organization is a logical and psychological impossibility: logical, because it destroys coordination; psychological, because it is impossible to train a man to conform and to assume initiative at the same time. The "balance" is, then, normally struck in favor of centralization. Centralized organization produces results like those described by M. Chardon in France or by the author in Yugoslavia.

All branches of the public service, says Chardon, are so organized and staffed as "to produce words, papers, inaction. No technical consideration directs their efforts. Instead, there is an intricate network of routine mechanisms; constant dissipation of forces; chains of costly links on which business stagnates as successive verifications pile up; men consider, then reconsider; men verify, then reverify and counterverify; the least discrepancy gives rise to doubt, to supplementary inquiries, to commentaries, to pointless arid discussions" [31: 408]. As a concrete illustration of the ultimate effects: "To build a new bridge in place of one palpably unsafe, twenty distinct administrative steps were necessary, with the result that it took fifteen to eighteen months to initiate the construction" [31: 408]. My second example is taken from a completely different social milieu, but there, too, centralization gave similar results. It relates to the oil industry

18

during the period of administrative planning in Yugoslavia: "Even with their own management and accounting, enterprises were not independent. The Directorate [the Federal Government agency] interfered with even the most trifling businesses and problems of the enterprises, from the caloric value of food in dining halls to annual production plans. Frequent changes, complete dependence, wrong economic directives resulting from . . . ignorance of the problems of individual enterprises or from mere *Gleichschaltung* have transformed enterprises into unmotivated and initiativeless agents of an economic policy conducted by passing them by . . . . Failure to fulfill plans could always be explained by innumerable 'objective' difficulties . . . the number of employed personnel increased rapidly without corresponding economic effect; in the General Directorate, 360 employees were receiving about 170 reports and sending out circulars in the same proportion . . ." [32: 191]. The reports accumulated, forming volumes of many hundreds of pages, in which all the details of a damaged oil pump could be traced but from which it was absolutely impossible to evaluate the economic situation of the industry. Plans were changed several times a year; in one extreme case an oil refinery got the final version of its annual production plan in mid-December of the current year. [18]

The example of France is typical for the functioning of governmental bureaucracy in its traditional province. The Yugoslav example is typical for relatively modern cases of entire economies being run administratively. Similar examples could be multiplied at will and also indicate, among other things, that, as a rule, the more backward the country, the less efficiently bureaucracy works.

Bureaucratic Polarization of Society

Bureaucratic organizations may be, and normally are, invaded by elements alien to them. This may, and to a considerable extent does, mitigate the evils of bureaucratic administration. There are countless modifications possible, but they do not concern us here. What we are primarily interested in is discovering the inherent tendencies of the bureaucratic type of organization, and for this purpose the "pure" type is best suited. Let us suppose, therefore, that the social life of a country is organized and controlled by a huge bureaucratic apparatus. What sort of social relations are likely to emerge? We need only draw the conclusions of the above analysis.

The fundamental principle of bureaucratic organization is obedience. The behavioral consequence is obsequiousness toward (i.e., receiving orders from) superiors, compensated for by arrogance toward (i.e., giving orders to) subordinates. This behavior changes markedly at the top and the bottom of the bureaucratic pyramid; the top displays — or at any rate is able to display — arrogance; the bottom can choose only obedience. Interests are polarized because what represents maximum freedom of choice for the top represents at the same time minimum freedom of choice for the bottom. The closer the organization conforms to its logical ideal, the greater the span between the maximum and minimum relations, with the resulting maximization of potential social conflict. Hence there is a possibility for a sharp social differentiation to appear, the fundamental historical differentiation between the ruling and the exploited classes.

This potential conflict then materializes in overt signs of social stratification. In order to have a stable and efficient system, the rulers need a loyal bureaucracy. This loyalty upward is bought by economic privileges and reinforced by status differentiation.[19] Thus there will be a wealthy and powerful minority and a poor and powerless majority. Within the bureaucracy, Marx had already noted, the hierarchy serves to maintain the mysterious rightness of regulations, while toward the exterior the bureaucracy forms a "closed corporation" [35: 65]. As an administrative apparatus, the bureaucracy is inherently identified with the state. "Bureaucracy considers itself the ultimate aim of the state," Marx says. ". . .the aims of the state are transformed into the aims of bureaucracy, or bureaucratic aims are transformed into the aims of the state" [35: 64-65]. By taking the form of a closed corporation and using the powers of the state for its own purposes, the bureaucracy becomes a privileged minority contrary to the interests of the great majority of the members of society. This minority takes control of the means of production, while the majority must sell its labor power in order to live. The former will rule; the latter will be ruled. And that is nothing but the classical Marxian two-class structure of society.

We may now answer the question posed previously. *Even if the socialist revolution radically destroys the old state apparatus and in administrative jobs replaces the members of the old ruling class by members of the hitherto exploited class, the new society will not necessarily be a classless, socialist society. If the fundamental principle of bureaucratic organization — the principle of hierarchy — is left to operate, in the course of time two social classes with conflicting interests will again emerge.* In order to prevent this, the state, as an institution whose essence is coercion, must — to use the famous phrase of Engels — wither away. The emergence of class antagonism and of a ruling class does not depend on the *ownership* of the means of production by the *individual members* of that class, but on class *control* of the means of production, insofar as this control enables that class to exert political as well as power-backed control.[20]

4. ASSOCIATIONIST SOCIALISM

Complete state control means "the subordination of every individual's whole life, work, and leisure to the orders of those in power and office.[22] It is the reduction of man to a cog in an all-embracing machine of compulsion and coercion. It forces the individual to renounce any activity of which the government does not approve. It tolerates no expression of dissent. It is the transformation of society into a strictly disciplined labor army — as the advocates of socialism say — or into a penitentiary, as its opponents say" [38: 25]. If "state capitalism" is substituted for "socialism," the picture von Mises draws in the passage just quoted is not unlike that emerging from the analysis of the pure bureaucratic system in the preceding section. Where von Mises and other economists of the liberal school err is, of course, in their attempts to show that state capitalism should or could be replaced by liberal capitalism. It suffices to compare the capitalist countries of 1848 with the "welfare states" of our day to see at once that the idea is not very commendable. But this is not a correct way of looking at the problem. The essential point is that social institutions change together with the development of productive forces and that, therefore, 19th century institutions cannot be applied to a 20th century economy. State capitalism has proved to be markedly more efficient than the system it has replaced, and this means that the contradictions it generates will have to be solved in a new way.

I must repeat that the ill effects of state capitalism can be mitigated in various ways and that, therefore, there is no *necessity* for the picture painted by von Mises to come true. But there is the *possibility*. And I should add that this possibility increases, as the historical experience of our century tends to suggest, with the degree of backwardness of the society concerned. The need for economic development is felt most strongly in the most undeveloped countries, where the economy is nearly stationary and the tradition is often closer to feudalism than to capitalism. The first element — the need for development — points up the necessity for meager resources to be pooled, for available qualified personnel to be put under a unified command, and for the state to be made the responsible organizer of the economic process. The idea that, in this century, the state plays, or should play, a decisive role in transforming stationary economies into growing economies seems to command uniquely wide acceptance. But realization of this idea means the creation of a powerful bureaucracy. The second factor — semifeudal relations — indicates that underdeveloped countries have had no opportunity to pass through the rationalization and impersonalization process of the capitalist market (which creates the tradition necessary to make bureaucracy work properly,[23] but that there will be a strong tendency to transfer feudal status-consciousness to bureaucratic hierarchies and, similarly, a tendency to preserve the tradition of a unified political-economic power free of control from below. And that means a strong class polarization. Development requires state intervention, and state intervention has a potentially harmful effect; this is just an additional "vicious circle" with which an underdeveloped economy has to cope. The price of "skipping" a stage of development is the involvement in greater risk.

There are a number of policies that, in concrete situations, may limit the risks involved in bureaucratization. They are not our concern here. What we must do consists not merely in modifying the old system, but in outlining a new system that is most likely to replace the old one. The new system must satisfy the criteria of being both *possible* and *more efficient*. The essential characteristics of the new system follow directly from the preceding discussion and can be reduced to a single one: negation of the principle of class polarization. The new society, if it is to be more efficient, must be a classless one. It is easy to see that there are two aspects to the problem: one is economic, the other, political. We begin with the economic factor.

Von Mises correctly draws attention to one important difference between public administration and economic management of a business [38: 58-63]. In public administration there is no market price for achievements. An economic calculus cannot be applied to assessing the success or failure of a bureau. The efficiency of a police department or of a tax-collecting office cannot be established in the same way as that of a factory. Therefore the activities of bureaus must be guided by rules and regulations and by the directives of superiors. The more impersonalized the system manages to become, the closer it will approximate Weberian rational-legal authority.

Compared with public administration, economic management has a great advantage in possessing a yardstick for success and failure, in the form of surplus of return over cost, a yardstick that is fairly objective within the limits of inescapable market imperfections. This makes it possible to avoid bureaucratization even of very large organizations. Since net revenue "can be ascertained by accounting not only for the whole business concern but also for any of its parts, it is feasible to decentralize management and responsibility without jeopardizing the unity of operations and the attainment of their goal. Responsibility can be divided. There is no need to limit the discretion of subordinates by any rules or regulations other than those underlying all business activities, namely, to render their operations profitable" [38: 58]. This helps to resolve the centralization-decentralization contradiction and to stimulate individual initiative and collective entrepreneurship.

Economic surplus can be used not only as a check on efficiency but also as a direct motivational device. Under the conditions of economic welfare that we know, economic motivation is likely to have an extremely strong impact on the performance of individuals, and there is no reason for leaving this possibility unexploited.

Profit plus profit appropriation — does this not mean capitalism? Yes, if the institution of capital, in the Marxian sense, is retained as well. But there is no need for this to occur. The inner organization of a private (or state) enterprise represents a bureaucratic pyramid with two loose ends, the one-way flow of commands and the workers providing a base on which the structure rests. For reasons analyzed earlier, the interests of the "base" and the "structure" above it diverge. To protect their interests, workers are compelled to organize themselves into trade unions, i.e., to build new bureaucratic structures in the opposite direction. Thus the workers must support two bureaucratic structures that do the job on their behalf. It is a very roundabout method of organizing everyday life. It is easy to see that, insofar as the abolition of private ownership removes the source of antagonistic interests, the need for two bureaucracies fighting each other disappears. Instead, the base can be directly connected with the top through a line of upward-flowing specific commands: the board of directors is replaced by the workers' council. By connecting the two loose ends of a formerly bureaucratic pyramid, the economic organizations are transformed into self-governing associations and capitalism is replaced by socialism.

It may have been noticed that state capitalism implies, by definition, absence of private ownership and that, in spite of this, the "loose ends" are left unconnected in the organization of

23

production. This happens because of the internal logic of the bureaucratic organization. "Bureaucratic authority," Max Weber writes, "is carried out in its purest form where it is most clearly dominated by the principle of appointment. There is no such thing as a hierarchy of elected officials in the same sense as there is a hierarchical organization of appointed officials. In the first place, election makes it impossible to achieve a stringency of discipline even approaching that under appointed officials. Indeed, it is open to a subordinate official to compete for elective honors on the same terms as his superiors, and his prospects are not dependent on the superior's judgment" [21: 307]. In other words, the loyalty of the functionaries ceases to be linked upward and the hierarchical structure tends to disintegrate.

Application of the "principle of appointment" to the very top of a bureaucratic pyramid presents an interesting problem. The pyramid may be truncated, i.e., the organization may be run by a collegial body that co-opts new members. This collective body will normally have one member who acts as *primus inter pares* and who comes to hold this position by being *elected* by his colleagues (the initiative being taken either by them or by himself, or prescribed by rules). The truncated pyramid is a pure, technical type of a self-perpetuating bureaucracy. Experience suggests that all bureaucracies tend to develop elements of this type. But there are two further important modifications. In private capitalism, the owners of wealth nominate the top officials of economic organizations — legally and, to a large extent, actually. In state capitalism this function is performed by the wielders of political power. So we pass into the sphere of political organization.

Modern political systems, technically denoted as democracies, solve the "top appointment" problem by a fourth method: connecting the two loose ends at regular intervals of a given number of years. This procedure is called *elections,* and it produces parties, parliament, and government, i.e., the source of supreme authority. There is no doubt that the more efficient this procedure, the greater the chance that the operation of the hierarchical principle will be subjected to some social control. But there is also little doubt that the potential efficiency of the procedure is severely limited. To be effective, the government must hold office for some time, i.e., it must be stable. To be stable, the intervals between elections must be long enough and the number of parties reduced. The former, by definition, excludes frequent communication of commands; the latter implies the formation of huge party bureaucracies. Weber has already pointed out that the bureaucratization of party organization makes the member of parliament "an agent of the leaders of the party organization" [21: 387]. The point was expanded on by R. H. S. Crossman, who in a few words generalized modern experience by noting that the responsibility of ministers to the parliament "is rapidly becoming a constitutional fiction," going on to say: "Along with Ministerial responsibility, the responsibility of the individual Member of Parliament has withered away. . . . Now the prime responsibility of the Member is no longer to the elector but to the Party. Without accepting the discipline of the Party he cannot be elected; and if he defies that discipline, he risks political death" [18: 18].

Due to the long distance, the upward line from the base to the top tends to constitute a connection between the two loose ends of the social pyramid that is more formal than real. The obvious remedy appears to lie in cutting this distance, in forming independent self-connected structures throughout the system, in forming (to use Yugoslav political parlance) self-governing communes. In more familiar words, the remedy is decentralization of power. There are very few social activities that require rigid central control. Strictly speaking, only activities aimed at the protection of the interests of the community against the outside world belong in this category. Foreign policy is one such; defense is another. Practically all other executive functions can [24] be left to the jurisdiction of the communes, which are elementary units of economic-political associations. It is hardly necessary to point out that the technical solution, decentralization, becomes possible only under certain social conditions, namely, under conditions conducive to eliminating the causes that generate fundamental social conflict.

A federation of self-governing associations — political, economic, and any other — was Marx's vision of socialism, as inspired by the short history of the Paris Commune [40]. As the foregoing analysis shows, this is a possible and more efficient alternative to bureaucratic social organization.

It is important to realize that bureaucratization means more than a mere coordination and differentiation of administrative functions. Bureaucracy is an instrument of *imperative coordination* — to use a term of Weber's once again — based on coercion and, when nationwide, embodied in the state. Given the existence of the fundamental social conflict, coercion is an essential element of social organization, indispensable if disintegration is to be prevented. The function of coercion is performed by a special apparatus whose loyalties are linked on the basis of interests that are divergent from those of the majority against whom the coercion is to be applied. The process is, clearly, self-reinforcing. Rationalizing the experience of the Prussian state, Weber (like his countryman Hegel before him) implied that it represented the end of the possible development of social institutions. Once put in this form, the mistake becomes obvious. Not *every* authority has to be based on coercion. T. Parsons has pointed out that professional authority, that of a doctor or of a university professor, is not [21: 52]. And this provides the clue to the solution.

In governing a commune, as well as in running a factory, there are two types of decisions to be made. One of them represents policy decisions, decisions concerned with valuations, that is, with setting up a hierarchy of social values. The other type represents technical decisions; once the policy (the "end") is decided upon, technical experts set out to implement it in the most efficient way (the "means"). Bureaucratic authority, actually and often formally as well, makes both types of decisions *uno actu*. If, however, the two types of decisions can be separated, then, without any loss in efficiency, the coordination of technical performance will be based on professional authority. And elected self-governing bodies will be engaged in finding out the systems of values that best conform to the existing valuations of the members of the community. There is no need for coercion in this scheme, for the alternative to coercion is not anarchy but a system commanding undivided fundamental loyalties. Common agreement on fundamentals makes possible free disagreement on everything else. Men cease to be "representatives" of bureaucratic organizations and instead begin to represent themselves as freely developed personalities. The destruction of concentrations of power makes it possible to create a society "in which the free development of each is the condition for the free development of all" [Marx, 36: 63].

The "withering away of the state" is a slow process, which depends primarily on the rate of expansion of material wealth at the disposal of the community. But once it is started, the class polarization process will be stopped and reversed. Class society came into existence as a result of the rising productivity of labor. The same cause will make it perish.

5. WORKERS' SELF-GOVERNMENT IN HISTORICAL PERSPECTIVE

After the sweeping generalizations in the preceding sections, it would seem necessary to give some consideration to *concrete* historical events. However, despite this restriction, the discussion will prove to be sufficient for our purpose. In a second section we shall proceed to an analysis of the contemporary situation.

The First Three Waves

Examined within the frame of reference discussed in the preceding sections, the amorphous historical continuum of the last two centuries begins to assume a definite structure, and the regularities of paramount interest for our subject become apparent. We can distinguish four waves of events, which are partly successive and partly superimposed on each other. Our story begins with the first wave, which produced a group of prophets of a new social order.

The second half of the 18th century witnessed the advent of a new, capitalist society. The new society generated new class conflict, and very soon the exploited class acquired its first intellectual defenders — not quite conscious defenders, to be sure, because, as Engels observes, they did not claim, at first, to emancipate a particular class, but all humanity at once. The most developed countries of that time supplied the most remarkable of these prophets. For my purpose it will suffice to mention three of them, the three whom Schumpeter [4] aptly characterizes as Associationist[2 5] Socialists. They are Robert Owen (1771-1858), a Briton of Welsh origin, and Charles Fourier (1772-1837) and Louis Blanc (1811-1882), two Frenchmen. All three advocated social reconstruction through producers' associations.

Owen, the most famous of the three, conceived of future society as a federation of communes governed by producers. He came to this view after spending two decades as manager of a large cotton mill in the Scottish village of New Lanark, where he improved the houses of his workers, organized education for their children, reduced working hours, and, in general, anticipated by over a century the treatment that workers were to receive on a national scale. Owen's ideas inspired the cooperative movement. And in the early 1830s he was the leading figure in the growing trade union movement, which had only just emerged from illegality and which came to stimulate the formation of self-governing workshops. Under Owen's influence the new Builders' Union was turned into a Guild to carry on the building industry, thereby anticipating the future schemes of French Syndicalists and British Guild Socialists. However, after the Grand National Consolidated Trade Union was formed (1833-1834), employers and government acted quickly, and in a few months

Owenite unionism came to an abrupt end.

Fourier designed *phalanstères* in which capitalists, workers, and scientists were to live together in a harmonious community based on work so organized as to correspond to the personal likings and capacities of individuals. Louis Blanc, the least original but the most realistic of the three, proposed that the state undertake to establish social workshops *(ateliers sociaux)* that were to be run by the workers. When the 1848 revolution made him unexpectedly a member of the Provisional Government in Paris, Blanc tried to put something of this program into practice. But, naturally, his bourgeois colleagues tricked him out of the government and skilfully sterilized his activities. Blanc's ideal was an egalitarian society, with personal interest merged in the common good. This he summed up as: A *chacun selon ses besoins, de chacun selon ses facultés* — the idea that later in Marx's hands became famous as the formula of communism.

The Associationists were utopian socialists: instead of analyzing the actual conditions of development, they were concerned with devising ideal plans for social reconstruction. Consequently, when actual realizations were attempted (and a number of Owenite, Fourierist, and similar communities were organized), failure was more or less inevitable. But the Associationists' ideas left a lasting effect on the developing culture of the new society.

The appearance of the gigantic figure of Marx on the intellectual scene marks the beginning of the second wave in the historical process under consideration. Marxism is primarily a social theory (or ideology) of the already *emancipated* working class. Thus the essential feature of the new wave is that isolated individuals and their followers are replaced by broad movements: the developed capitalist production of the second half of the 19th century generates trade unions and working class political parties. These differ in details, but their programs are basically the same; they call for elimination of private capitalist control of the production process.

The profound influence of Marxian thought (which, however, was interpreted in various ways) on working class movements is well known, and there is no point in describing it here. But with respect to my main purpose, that of tracing the development of the institution of workers' management, I should like to mention three movements separately, one of which professed Marxism, while the other two did not. Although they had serious shortcomings, sometimes propounded nonsensical ideas, and occasionally were quixotic in their adjustments to reality, these movements well express the fundamental strivings of the working class.

At the end of the last century, the French trade union movement, then still in its infancy, came to be strongly influenced by the idea of *revolutionary syndicalism*. The Syndicalists wanted to place the management of industry in the hands of the trade unions. Trade unions were to be federated locally into *bourses de travail*, which would establish a monopoly of labor, presently take over ownership of the industries, and run them under local self-governing communes. Syndicalists repudiated parliamentary action, relied on a "conscious minority" instead of on thoroughly organized big unions, and hoped to achieve their aim by the general strike. These four characteristics of the movement explain at once why Syndicalists came to be detested equally by employers and by orthodox trade union leaders; why, by disorganizing the working class movement, their action inflicted damage on it;[26] and why they failed to achieve the goal of workers' management. The industrial militancy of the French syndicalist unions reached its peak in 1902-1906; later it receded, and after World War I their ideas were basically modified. In this process, a not insignificant role was played by the fact that, as a result of the war, the unions multiplied their membership and developed into big bureaucratic organizations.

Syndicalism spread from France to the United States, where it developed under the U.S. Socialist Labor Party, led by Daniel De Leon, and became known as *industrial unionism*. The American movement advocated the organization of all workers into one big union with sections for each industry. Industrial unionism thus overcame two basic weaknesses of syndicalism; it made use of political action and of strong union organization. However, it had weaknesses in other respects; it never exerted great influence on the American workers and died out after World War I.

Revolutionary and industrial syndicalism spread to Australia, Canada, Mexico, and some other countries, including Britain, where its influence was reflected in the famous manifesto of the Welsh miners, *The Miners' Next Step* (1912), which urged abolition of capitalist ownership in the mining industry and complete control over the industry by the workers. But in Great Britain at that time an autonomous British movement, *guild socialism*, began to develop as well. Guild socialists opposed state management of industry on the ground that it would lead to bureaucracy and that thereby the social position of wage-earners would not be changed. But they realized that the state is a very important institution that might be turned to very good use: the

29

working class should capture the state and use it to take industry under public ownership. After that, Parliament would hand over the task of administration to the national guilds (the former trade unions) within the terms of a parliamentary charter. Guilds, as well as communes and other political, social, etc., associations, were to be organized so as to allow every individual to participate and to have an effective say. All this was in sharp contrast with the current theory of democracy which, says G. D. H. Cole, the leading theoretician of the movement, "assigns to the ordinary citizen little more than a privilege . . . of choosing his rulers, and does not call upon him . . . himself to rule" [44: 13].

The National Guilds League, formed in 1915, exerted great influence on the shop stewards' movement and on several unions. During and after the war, a number of small guilds were created. Most important in this respect was the movement to reorganize the building industry as a national guild in which employers were to become salaried administrators, subject to election by the workers employed. In the ensuing depression of 1922-1923, this movement collapsed, and a year later guild socialism as an organized movement was dead.

If the first wave brought into existence individual socialist ideologues and isolated groups, and the second wave produced organized movements, the third wave brought the first realizations. Broadly speaking, the European revolutions of 1848 mark the time when the working class emancipated itself and asserted itself as a separate social class. It might be supposed that in the revolutions that were to follow, the working class would attempt to establish industrial self-government. Let us examine this hypothesis in the light of the events that actually took place.

The era of proletarian revolutions began with the Paris Commune in 1871. The Commune passed a decree by which industry was to be reorganized on a cooperative basis and enterprises were to be run by the workers.

The Russian revolution of 1905, the next in time, produced factory councils that attempted the management of enterprises. Both the Paris and the Russian revolutions were crushed, and workers' management did not survive them.

Different was the destiny of the second Russian revolution, the Great October Socialist Revolution of 1917. It was the first successful proletarian revolution. The resurrected workers' councils of 1905 played a leading role in anticipating and carrying out the revolution. [27] As early as November 1917, a decree on workers' control was passed, according to which the factory committees obtained the right of complete control of enterprises.

However, the ensuing civil war, with its concomitant shortages and sabotage, required strict centralization and a military organization of all the life of society, including industry. In 1918 the committees were transformed into organs of the trade unions, and in 1920 they lost the right of participation in management. After that the remnants of workers' control were alive for a number of years, first in the practice of appointing a *red director* (a worker) and later in the management triangle: director — party secretary — secretary of the trade union factory branch. In the late twenties, Stalin did away even with these remnants and in truly Weberian fashion proclaimed that the essential condition for discipline and efficiency was that the director had absolute and complete control over the enterprise and that he was subject only to orders from above. *Edinonachalie* [one-man management] was adopted as a basic principle of social organization. Significantly enough, after a short while the gap between workers' wages and managerial salaries was widened several times. Workers' control was eliminated.

The Russian revolution had a strong impact on revolutionary fermentation in other European countries, with the result that workers either extorted constitutional and legal reforms or, occasionally, assumed management of their factories (temporarily, or course). The most dramatic of all was the Hungarian revolution that gave birth to the Hungarian Soviet Republic in 1918. Here the workers' councils were first created as political organs that later concerned themselves with management in the nationalized undertakings. However, the revolution was crushed very soon, and instead of workers' control Hungary got fascist dictatorship.

The same was the destiny of the next revolution, the Spanish civil war, in which the attitude toward workers' management was the same. In Catalonia, enterprises with more than 100 employees (and some other categories of enterprises) were socialized. In 1936 a decree provided for workers' management in these enterprises.

If the revolutions generated by the social antagonisms of private capitalism so invariably[28] produced attempts to establish workers' control in the enterprises, it would be expected that in the countries in which private ownership has been eliminated, social upheavals would generate the same tendency even more clearly. The events in Poland and Hungary in 1956, with the very prominent role that workers' councils played, more than confirm this expectation.

It is frequently said (both in the West and in the East) that wherever workers' management has been attempted it has failed. In a sense this is true. But the inference that workers' management should therefore be regarded as an unrealizable utopia is manifestly false. In no historical period have new social institutions been successfully established at one stroke, without bitter fights against reactionary forces and without many failures. What is significant in the events we have reviewed is not the failure to achieve the goal, but their continual recurrence *despite* all their failures.

The Last Wave

The three waves described so far could not fail to exert a great influence and to modify that stable and sanctified pattern of social life we call the *establishment.* The establishment itself began to change, and this is the fourth and surface layer of the historical trend we set out to investigate.

Various kinds of workers' and works councils — the former are composed of workers only and are more prevalent than the latter, which include employers' representatives as well — are as old as the trade union movement. These councils or committees dealt with complaints, welfare work, and conditions of employment; they were always advisory, the employer reserving the power of making the final decision. But for a long time they were only sporadic[29] in occurrence and did not represent an institution. Similarly, labor legislation dealing with some form of workers' participation in factory organization, almost exclusively confined to welfare matters, can be traced back in several countries (Prussia and Austria, for instance) to the end of the last century.[30] These, too, were sporadic events, and the extent of workers' participation was insignificant. World War I and the Russian revolution represent the first landmark in the history of workers' participation in management.

During the war, in order to enhance war production, the British and German governments sought the cooperation of the unions and obtained it. As a result, various forms of management-worker cooperation were developed. The events that occurred in both[31] countries are so significant that they warrant a few more words.

The three years preceding the outbreak of the war represent one of the most disturbed epochs in British industry, says J. B. Seymour, the historian of the Whitley Councils. At the commencement of the war, 100 strikes were in progress [48: 9]. It was during this period that syndicalist influence was strongest in Britain and that (in 1912) the miners and the largest of the four railway unions adopted the demand for complete control over the industry by the workers. It was also during this period that the future shop stewards' movement was foreshadowed (Glasgow engineers' strike in 1912).

Before the war, shop stewards were minor officials appointed by the union from among the men in the workshop; they were to see that their union dues were paid and newcomers organized. They had no power to negotiate grievances; nor were they officially recognized by the management [48: 10]. Then came the war which, as C. G. Renold tells us on the basis of his firsthand experience as an employer, "was regarded by large sections as a capitalists' war and the restrictions, controls, and hardships were resented accordingly" [49: 16]. It suffices to add that in 1915, under the Treasury Agreement, after the trade union leaders had voluntarily pledged themselves not to sanction strikes during the war, the dissent of the rank and file was certain. The big Clyde engineers' strike early in 1915, when the strike committee disregarded superior union officials and won the strike, set the pattern and initiated what became known as the shop stewards' movement. [32] The movement brought works committees to a high point of development.

Syndicalism, guild socialism, the shop stewards' movement, the increasing number of workdays lost by strikes despite all restrictions (2 million in 1915, 2.5 million in 1916, 5.5 million in 1917) — this alarming situation called for government intervention. In October 1916 a committee (known as the Whitley Committee) was appointed to examine methods for securing permanent improvement in industrial relations. The following year, the Whitley Committee produced its scheme of employer-worker cooperation. For each industry a national joint council and district councils were to be formed, to bring together employers' organizations and unions, and in individual establishments joint works committees were to provide a recognized means of consultation between the management and the employees. But the scheme, on the whole, failed to work, except in government departments. "The employers, as a body, have never favored the scheme . . . . The trade unionists, frightened by the shop stewards' movement, appear to shrink from giving authority to any rank-and-file movement and away from the central organizations" [48: 191]. By 1929, out of about 100 works committees formed in response to the Whitley Committee recommendations, only one-half were still alive. After the war, the government rejected the miners' and railwaymen's demand for nationalization and self-government. The first postwar recession, which started in 1921, killed the shop stewards' movement and guild socialism. The situation was back to normal, and the capitalist machine could work again as before — but not quite: the seed had been sown.

Unlike Britain, Germany was defeated in the war, and events took the other possible form. The defeat, coupled with the tremendous influence of the Russian revolution, produced a German revolution (1918). Workers' and soldiers' councils sprang up all over the country. Frightened to death, employers were ready to go very far to escape full-scale socialism. And thus Germany became the first capitalist country to have a constitution (July 1919) that, among the "fundamental rights" of citizens, included the following one: "For the purpose of safeguarding their social and economic interests, the wage-earning and salaried employees are entitled to be represented in Workers' Councils for each establishment, as well as in Regional Workers' Councils organized for each industrial area, and in a Federal Workers' Council (Article 165 [46:10])".

On the basis of the constitution, a law was passed in 1920 making works councils [*Betriebsräte*] compulsory in all establishments with 20 or more employees. The councils were to supervise the working of collective agreements, enter into agreements on the conditions of work and on subjects not regulated by wider agreements, watch over hiring and firing, and also advise the employer on how to improve efficiency and organization. But constitutions and laws are dead letters if not backed by active social forces. The German working class movement of that time was deeply divided both in its trade union and in its parliamentary sections. The majority, who held the power, were undetermined, hesitating. The government bureaucracy was hostile. This gave the employers breathing space. The results of the revolution were gradually undermined (the slump of 1924 playing a not insignificant part) and then liquidated. The process came to an end in May 1933, when both trade unions and works councils were abolished, marking the advent of fascism. In our day, unsuccessful or half-successful socialist revolutions — this seems to be the lesson of Hungary, Germany, and Spain — end in fascism.

As to the other European countries, it suffices to mention that in the period 1919-1922, for the same reasons, similar laws were passed in Austria, Czechoslovakia, Norway, and elsewhere. In Yugoslavia, the law on protection of workers (1922) provided for election of workers' commissioners *[radnicki povjerenici]* from the shop floor, whose task it was to protect workers' interests and cooperate with the employer. The attitude of employers and trade unions very soon reduced this provision to a mere formality [10:22]. After a period of strikes, a similar solution was reached under the Popular Front government in France in 1936; it involved the recognition of workers' delegates *[délégués ouvriers]*, with the right to meet management every month. In the United States a somewhat different union-management cooperation on production problems began on one of the railways in the 1920s, when the union wanted to reduce costs in order to secure work for railway shops. Other firms and unions experimented with similar ideas until the 1929 depression, which killed experiments of this kind. A decade later the steelworkers' union developed quite successful cooperation plans in a number of small steel and steel products firms. The steelworkers' scheme survived the last world war and continued to be operated in some 50 firms [51: 55].

The second landmark in the development of workers' participation in management was provided by World War II. Like World War I, it initiated a cycle, though on a much larger scale. Again governments sought the cooperation of workers in order to increase war production, and joint production committees were set up in various countries (Britain, the United States, Canada). Again Britain was victorious and Germany was defeated, and there was a spontaneous development in the former and legislative measures were taken in the latter. Again British miners expected to get self-government; instead, they got joint consultation. But there were also several novel features, of which the most important were the large-scale nationalization in some countries and the full-scale nationalization in a number of others (East Europe and Southeast Asia). In all nationalized industries, joint consultation between workers and management was introduced as a matter of course.

In Britain, two national agreements during the war set the pattern for the establishment of works committees: the committees were to be advisory and were to provide an outlet for the regular exchange of views between employers and employees on welfare and production matters, subject to the qualification that terms and conditions of employment were to be dealt with by the unions on behalf of the workers. In 1947 the National Joint Advisory Council recommended to the employers' organizations and unions that joint consultative machinery be set up where it did not already exist. The recommendation was followed, and today there are several hundred works committees in existence in Britain. [33]

In Germany the legislation of the Weimar period was not only revived but also pressed a step further, from joint consultation to codetermination *[Mitbestimmung]*. In the two basic industries (coal, and iron and steel) the unions achieved parity for workers'

35

representatives on the supervisory board [*Aufsichtsrat*], a body which appoints the board of management. Moreover, one of the members (there usually are three) of the management board, the personnel director [*Arbeitsdirektor*], is nominated by the union (law of 1951). In other industries, workers' representatives are still in the minority, although this minority (one-third) may be larger than in the Weimar period. Workers' councils [*Betriebsräte*], representing both wage and salary earners, must be elected in all establishments employing not less than five permanent employees (law of 1952).

In France a law passed in 1946 made it compulsory for industrial concerns employing more than 50 workers to establish a works committee [*comité d'entreprise*], representing the manual workers and the technical grades. Every act of major management importance must be approved by the committee. If there is a disagreement, the case goes to arbitration. Similar laws were passed in Belgium in 1948, and in the Netherlands in 1950. In 1946, in Sweden, the unions and the employers' associations reached an agreement according to which enterprise councils were set up in firms with 25 or more employees. The task of these councils may be broadly described as joint consultation on all important matters. It is of some interest to record that when, in 1923, a Royal Committee proposed the formation of similar joint production committees, both unions and employers opposed the idea and nothing came of it. From World War II to 1950, enterprise councils were set up in 2,650 firms employing a total of over 600,000 workers [42: 56-58]. Similar joint consultation committees were introduced in Norway (1945) and Denmark (1947) on the basis of union-employer agreements, and in Finland by a special law (1946).

In a number of other countries the prewar practice of joint consultation was continued after the war or, where it had not existed, was introduced for the first time. In 1951 the International Labor Office registered more than 30 countries with *permanent* organs of workers' participation in management. While practices vary, they have a common feature: with few exceptions, they are confined to joint *consultation*.

Characteristics of Development After World War I

It will be useful to attempt a brief evaluation of joint consultation as it came into being and developed during the last four decades. The following five aspects of the problem seem important.

1. The *motivation* for setting up joint consultative machinery falls into three distinct categories. Revolutionary pressure from below compels employers and the government of the day to relax managerial authoritarianism. Since the struggle arises out of a strong clash of interests, its outcome must be legally sanctioned to remain permanent (although legal sanctions often prove to be a fiction). The German case is typical for this situation.

Next, during modern totalitarian wars, governments are vitally interested in stepping up production, and therefore devise and advocate schemes of joint consultation to bridge the gap between employers and workers. The case is typified by British and American practice. With respect to the latter, the International Labor Office study says: "The general purpose of the Labor-Management Production Committees was to raise the quantity and quality of output for war production by the joint effort of labor and management in each war plant" [53: 197]. The extent to which this purpose was achieved is seen from the following evaluation of the same study: "While there seems to be little doubt that the committees made a substantial contribution to plant output, a number of the committees did not aid to as great an extent as had been expected ..." [53: 257]. Some 5,000 committees were set up in plants with war contracts. Most of them disappeared with the end of the war.

The third type of motivation is that of individual employers who are not forced *by law* to adopt joint consultation. They adopt it primarily on economic grounds. This point is illuminated by the following statement by C. G. Renold, himself an employer with successful consultation in his firm: "In the first place the point should be made that the whole development had its origin in a very practical need — the need felt by the management for closer contact with its men in the interest of smooth working" [49: 100]. On the occasion of my visit to Renold, it turned out that he is not a socialist and does not regard himself as one, but that he is deeply aware of the fact that, under the new conditions, the old method of running the enterprise could only result in decreasing its success. The need for regular contact with workers' representatives appears when a concern outgrows one-man management. [34] It becomes urgent in the turbulent conditions of war and industrial unrest. And once the works council is set up, it is likely to continue to exist in the ensuing period of military and industrial peace. War has another effect as well: it increases the self-consciousness of the exploited classes and humanizes the members of the higher social strata, thus providing a psychological bridge between the two worlds. [35] Then there are also a small

37

number of employers [36] who are interested in joint consultation for its own sake, because they regard it as a humanizing institution. This Owenite type of employer, earlier practically nonexistent, is likely to multiply to the extent to which the adverse social pressure — of their equals and of the establishment as a whole — decreases. The example of individual employers, the recurrent interventions of governments, and the constant improvement of the workers' educational standard gradually create an atmosphere in which joint consultation becomes an indispensable part of managerial routines. Precisely this seems to be happening in Britain today, as demonstrated by the appearance of yet another type of employer. In the majority of firms visited by the National Institute of Industrial Psychology research team, "joint consultation seemed to be regarded as an up-to-date technique for improving management-worker relationships" [52: 59]. Competition is the essence of capitalism; accordingly, there is nothing to stop a capitalist firm from competition even in improving relations with workers. This sounds paradoxical, but these are the conditions of full employment under capitalism. Clearly, such competition, if pursued consistently, must eventually lead to the destruction of capitalist relationships, but this will be nothing more than a parallel to the phenomenon that Marx described so well: the destruction of profits by competition initiated to increase profits.

Nationalized industries and nationalized economies present a separate case. There, joint consultation is an indispensable minimum to make these systems work at all, that is, to make them socially acceptable. The only further development I can visualize is a constant increase of workers' participation in management, either granted by the governing bureaucracy or fought out by revolutionary means.

2. What happens to the *discipline* in an organization when executive authority is undermined by everybody's having the right and the opportunity to question the validity of the commands from above by reference to his own set of criteria? This is the very first question our Weberian-minded generation will ask in connection with the practicability of workers' management schemes. For is it not true that an efficient organization requires obedience, obedience being defined as following "such a course that the content of the command may be taken to have become the basis of action for its own sake" [Weber, 21: 300]?

In fact, however, the literature on joint consultation and workers' management, [37] including the most detailed field studies, shows no awareness of the "problem of discipline." I can do no better than quote the testimony of two employers.[38] "When I first took the step of introducing joint consultation on a very broad basis into my own works," writes G. S. Walpole, "I was told by most of my fellow employers that I was selling a pass to the enemy, and that the first result would be that works discipline would go to the devil. I have found, on the contrary, after two years' experience, that works discipline has improved almost out of recognition, and that every other legitimate interest of ownership has been catered to in a measure which four years ago I would not have believed possible: production is up, absenteeism is down; wastage is reduced and valuable time is saved" [54: 166]. C. G. Renold explains the mystery of this phenomenon: "The need to base managerial authority on reason rather than on arbitrary power — as is implied in the whole philosophy of joint consultation — has enhanced that authority" [49: 119].

It is hardly necessary to add that the same applies with even greater force to the system based on the philosophy of self-government. For want of references (no field study has been made so far) I may perhaps be excused in backing this contention by my own experience as a member of a workers' council. Self-government substitutes understanding for obedience, agreement for the exercise of arbitrary power. By eliminating capitalist or bureaucratic duality and the polarization of interests, it reduces tensions and improves coordination.

3. The *success* of joint consultation has been rather limited so far, and we shall examine the reasons for this in a moment. McKitterick and Roberts evaluate the success of the German works councils of the Weimar period by saying that councils "were useful in protecting the workers' interests, but achieved virtually nothing in the way of genuine participation in management" [60: 9]. As regards the postwar development, the same authors state: "Where workers' councils exist, the general experience has been that employees take a keen interest in their activities . . ." [60: 20]. In Britain, the broad masses of workers are still apathetic, but four-fifths of the workers' representatives in councils support the institution and show a keen interest in it [52: 64]. It is also significant that the experience in joint consultation has induced chief executives, senior management, and workers' representatives to take a more favorable view in 37, 48 and 58% of the cases, respectively, and a less favorable view in only 9, 5 and 1% of the cases, as compared with the view on joint consultation they had originally held [52: 65].

4. Next, there is the problem of the *fundamental relation* between capital and labor. These two opposing sides are reflected

in the very term *joint* consultation. The initiative on the part of the employer in introducing joint consultation in his firm is not infrequently a deliberate attempt to anticipate and check the development of unionism.[39] But even if this is not the aim, joint consultation increases loyalty to the firm, and this loyalty and loyalty to one's class are two different — nay, conflicting — loyalties.[40] It produces workers' leaders who are not trade union officials and so are outside the grip of the trade union machinery. Clearly, unions will not be enthusiastic about partnership proposals and frequently will be opposed to them.[41] On the other hand, if a union or shop stewards seek to participate in joint committees, employers will fear infringement on their own prerogatives. The hopelessness of the situation lies in the fact that *both* sides are correct in their fears. With the employers basically opposed to surrendering their arbitrary power and the unions basically unwilling to assume responsibility for the organization of production (because they gain nothing and lose their independence, along with their grip on the membership's loyalties), the status quo is likely to be prolonged and potential changes prevented. The logic of the situation is such that unions act in virtual collusion with employers against workers, a collusion that becomes overt in more turbulent times.[42] This sheds new light on the events we have surveyed; formidable social forces have opposed, and will continue to oppose, workers' participation in management.

5. The trade union paradox represents another illustration of the working of bureaucratic structures. In order to protect themselves in a world of polarized interests, the world whose institutions are against them, workers build strong bureaucratic organizations: unions and parties. Once these organizations are built, they acquire their separate interests, different from the interests of those who support the whole structure. There is nothing ethically wrong in this; it does not happen because the leaders are wicked; given the institution, the development observed is inevitable. The way out of the impasse is logically easy. The organization must first be used to eliminate the fundamental cause of the polarization of interests — in this case, to eliminate private control of production. And then the bureaucratic principle of organization must be replaced by self-government. However, actual unions and socialist parties are not likely to follow this course immediately, of their own accord. Having become a part of the establishment, with a clearly defined role in it, they are not prone to leave the life of routine and rush into the uncertainties of full-scale socialization. Self-government, on the other hand, is an

idea so alien to the spirit of bureaucracy that it is clear that it will encounter vigorous resistance.[43]

The situation, however, cannot remain completely unchanged. There is no reason to believe that business cycles have died out. But there is some reason to believe that the governments of industrial countries in the second half of our century cannot afford to tolerate heavy unemployment without risking major social upheavals. Curing the slump introduces the first decisive element of change into the process: the increasing degree of social control. The welfare state is its symbol. However, uninterrupted full employment has had a thoroughly anticapitalist effect: it generates competition in the improvement of management-worker relations, for the employers are vitally interested in avoiding labor turnover, in escaping strikes, and in overcoming resistance to the introduction of new processes, while workers feel secure and for this reason are actively conscious of their rights and potentialities.[44] By raising the status of the workers, employers gradually surrender their autocratic power; thereby their social function loses its content. In this way the second element, the increasing degree of workers' management, is introduced into the process. It is not likely that the process will always develop smoothly. In case of revolution, however, the trend is even clearer.

In the 150 years that have passed since the first Owenite experiment in New Lanark, relations between employers and workers have been constantly changing. These relations are reflected in the character of meetings between employers and employees which, as the British National Institute of Industrial Psychology describes aptly, "over the last 150 years show a historical development from deputation and negotiation to consultation" [52: 29], and, we may add, to direct management in the end. This last phase of development supersedes the bilateral character of the meetings and unifies the interests of all those concerned in the institution of self-government. The last four decades have already produced the first attempts to go beyond mere consultation. German codetermination is a case in point. And the first individual firms have already begun to move even further toward the state of genuine workers' self-government.[45]

We see that by the time World War II was over, the idea of workers' self-government was already in the air. It was not grasped as something distinctively new; it was not yet systematized or introduced into university curricula,[46] but it was nevertheless firmly established, like all those great ideas that mark an epoch and whose significance comes to be appreciated only afterward. In the light of what we have learned from the history of this idea, we may be induced to envisage the following hypothetical situation. Suppose a social revolution occurs somewhere, sweeping away all the traditional barriers and − like all preceding revolutions − raising the demand for workers' management. Suppose, further, that the country in question is fortunate enough to have workers' management developed before the bureaucratization process, resulting from the socialization of the economy, has proceeded so far as to polarize society, separating the revolutionary elite from the broad masses. If these circumstances obtain, it is very likely that workers' self-government will become a permanent social institution. Now, the situation described is in fact not so hypothetical; it materialized in postwar Yugoslavia.

The decisive period was the first five years after the revolution. A law passed in 1945 provided that workers' commissioners [*radnicki povjerenici*], as legal representatives of the workers, should establish contact with management, government agencies, and union branches, with the task of protecting the social and economic interests of the workers and helping advance production. In the following year the major portion of the economy was nationalized, and nationalization was completed in 1948 (with the exception of agriculture and craftsmen). In the meantime, the workers' commissioners ceased to exist; instead, trade union factory branches obtained the legal right to make proposals to the management. This was a retreat from control to consultation, a dangerous step backward reminiscent of Soviet development in 1917-1920. However, by 1949, there was already a new change: in a number of factories, consultation between the management (mostly people who had taken an active part in the revolution themselves) and workers came to be spontaneously introduced. Parallel with this, the fierce attack of the Cominform, launched in the middle of 1948 and continuing over a period of several years, acted as a force helping to check the polarization process. In the fall of 1949 the Political Bureau of the Central Committee of the Yugoslav Communist Party adopted an orientation aiming at immediate transition to self-government by producers in the economy. In December of that year, the government and trade unions jointly issued an instruction on the formation of workers' councils as advisory bodies. Councils were elected in 215 larger enterprises; but soon other enterprises asked to enjoy the same privilege, and by the middle of 1950 there were already 520 councils in existence. In June 1950 the National Assembly passed a law by which the councils were transformed from advisory into managing bodies. The working *collective* of every enterprise elects the workers' council [*radnicki savjet*] which, as long as it enjoys the confidence of the electors, is the supreme policy-making body in the enterprise. The council elects its executive committee, the managing board [*upravni odbor*], which is concerned with day-to-day implementation of the council's policy; the actual execution of the directives, as well as the job of routine coordination of the activities of the enterprise, is left to be performed by the general manager and the expert technical and administrative staff. This piece of legislation did not at once cause the perennial management-worker antithesis to cease to exist, but conditions were created for a solution. By 1950 it had already become abundantly clear that, in general, bureaucratic organization results in inefficiency and undesirable social relations, and thus the introduction of workers' management cleared the ground for a series of institutional changes that were to follow. [47] Subsequent developments in other spheres of social life strengthened the new organization of industry. Self-government of producers was extended beyond the immediate place of work, while all representative organs, from local councils up to the Federal Assembly, got a second chamber, the Council of Producers. In 1953 a change in the Constitution took account of the new social institutions. *Workers' management has become a part of the social system.*

FOOTNOTES

[*All quotations from non-Serbo-Croatian sources have been retranslated.*]

1. J. Schumpeter is one of those who disputes this statement [1: 146]. But a glance at any modern work on the anthropology of primitive communities suffices to show that Schumpeter is in error.
2. In this respect, Knight's article on capital in the *Encyclopedia Britannica* (1946) is characteristic: "Though for 'human' reasons, laborers are not usually referred to as 'means of production,' they are economically similar to other productive agents. The difference is 'institutional,' and in a slave economy laborers of all classes would be merely species of capital goods. This of course was once largely the case in parts of the USA. There usually are, indeed, important differences; sentiment and social usage, including religion, cause human slaves to be treated in a somewhat different way from work animals, or machines. Important economic differences arise in the control of reproduction and the rearing of children. However, all these things are matters of detail and of degree, and similar distinctions exist between many categories of capital goods. . . . In short, the meaning of capital and its yield is essentially unconnected with the general organization of the social economy . . . . The distinction between human beings and property and that between personal and real property are important in law and human relations, but no fundamental economic differences correspond to them."
3. This is true even in the case of military victory, as with the Bulgarian peasant uprising of 1277; after the victory of its leader, the shepherd Ivailo, he became the Tsar. And, as in fairy tales, the shepherd Ivailo married the widowed Empress.
4. For example, the young Engels wrote (1847), in a document that formed the basis for *The Communist Manifesto:* ". . . the development of the proletariat in almost all civilized countries is being suppressed by force, and thus the opponents of the Communists themselves work with all their might on the outbreak of the revolution. . . . For this reason the communist revolution will not be a national revolution; it

will be carried out in all civilized countries at the same time, that is, at least in England, America, France and Germany. In each of these countries the pace of its development will be faster or slower, depending on whether this or that country has a more developed industry, greater wealth and a bigger quantity of productive forces" [2:356 and 358].

5. In fact, shortly before his death, Marx came to expect that it would be precisely Russia that would set the example. "Now . . .," he and Engels wrote in 1882, "Russia is the advance unit of the revolutionary movement in Europe" [3: 601]. On another occasion, Marx, at a meeting in Amsterdam following the Hague Congress of the First International in 1872, singled out America and England as countries "in which the workers could achieve their aims by peaceful means." Twenty years later (1891), Engels wrote: "It is possible to imagine an old society growing peacefully into a new one in countries where the national representation concentrates all authority in its hands, where, by constitutional means, you can do whatever you wish so long as you have the majority of the people behind you; in democratic republics such as France and America, in monarchies such as England . . . where . . . the dynasty is powerless against the will of the people" [4: 67]. A comparison of this quotation from Engels, then near the end of his scientific career, with the stand of the twenty-seven-year-old Engels quoted in the preceding footnote, shows that Engels, in the course of his life, passed through a certain evolution. That evolution was also conditioned by the accumulated historical experience of half a century.

6. See, e.g., *Forderungen der Kommunistischen Partei in Deutschland* [Demands of the Communist Party in Germany] (1848), by a committee of six, including Marx and Engels; the program of the Social Democratic Workers Party of Germany adopted in 1869; the *Gotha Program* of 1875; the minimum program of the French Workers Party, 1880; the 1883 draft program of the Russian social democratic group "Osvobozhdenie truda"; the program of the Social Democratic Workers Party of Austria, 1888; the program of the Serbian Social Democratic Party, 1903; etc.

7. E. F. M. Durbin made the following instructive comparison: "One hundred and one years ago — in 1841 — Britain stood at the beginning of the 'hungry forties.' Let us suppose that the representative member of the toiling and starving industrial proletariat had been told, 'In three generations your great-grandchildren will work for eight hours a day (instead of twelve) for an average real wage of three pounds a week (instead of twenty-five shillings); there will be universal adult suffrage (instead of a tiny electorate composed entirely of the rich), and universal and free elementary education (in place of your illiteracy); most of the unemployed will be supported by a state insurance and assistance scheme (instead of being humiliated, as you are, by the Poor Law); there will be regular provision for the sick and the aged (instead of the private charity and starvation from which you suffer); the sons of poor men will go to Oxford and Cambridge at the expense of the state, and working men will enter the House of Commons in large numbers and occupy the highest offices in the state; the recognition of Trade Unions will be the rule, and not the exception; and most members of your class will possess little property.' What would the poor man of 1841 have had to say to all that? He would, I suggest, have laughed bitterly. The prospect would have seemed preposterous to him — unrealisable in its optimism, a foolish dream" [5: 25].

8. By "state capitalism" I mean state ownership and direct control and management of all means of production, or at least their dominant part. Such a system is sometimes called state socialism. In the *general* case, state capitalism or state socialism may be considered as the final stage of capitalist development or the initial stage of socialist development, where an accomplished revolution would demonstrate whether it is one or the other. However, the social content of a revolution does not result from its label, but from its real effects on social existence. The French Revolution proclaimed brotherhood and equality, but brought a bourgeois society with the right of the economically stronger, and with exploitation. Further, what about those societies that do not go through a **violent** revolution? The position might be taken that socialism should not be idealized, and that in an analogy with capitalism, which produced fascist Germany and cantonal Switzerland, there is the socialism of Stalinist Russia and self-governing Yugoslavia. Then, too, state or state-bureaucratic socialism is in some respects a distortion of socialism, but in other respects it is a first crude phase, out of which the self-governing phase grows [Fiamengo, 6, pp. 11 and 18]. At this point the question arises: to what degree can socialism "be distorted" and still constitute socialism? For example, if there are prison camps, is there or is there not socialism any longer? And then the question arises again: from the point of

44

view of Marxism, is not "state socialism" a *contradictio in adjecto?* Must it not be either not *state* or not *socialism?* What has been said leads to the conclusion that it is preferable scientifically to use a single term, namely, state capitalism. This term follows from Marx's description of capital as "power over labor and its products [96: 167], and is customary in Yugoslav economic literature. Thus, M. Novak says that the preservation of state ownership "would mean not an abolition of the proletariat but a transformation of all men into proletarians, not the abolition of capital but its universal rule, in which it may develop and necessarily develops an exploitation of its own kind" [7: 92]. Approaching the problem from another angle, N. Pasić comes to the conclusion: "Formerly, state intervention in the economy was mistakenly identified with socialism. If this criterion were applied to the last few decades, it would bring into the socialist camp all the prominent capitalist politicians of the time, from Baldwin and Roosevelt to Hitler and de Gaulle" [8: 11]. A. Dragicevič contends that "nationalization of means of production and planned economy are preconditions of socialism, but *only preconditions* and nothing more" [9: 218]. Similarly, P. Kovač and Dj. Miljević observe that "state ownership and state management by themselves produce little change in the position of the producer in production and in his right to participate in the management of the economy,. . . . In countries where the socialist revolution has been victorious, the state, instead of becoming an organ of the working people, may become and does become an organ of the government and party apparatus, which rules 'on behalf of the working people'" [10: 13]. I may add that in a certain sense this line of thinking was already anticipated by Engels: "The modern state, whatever its form, is essentially a capitalist machine, a state of capitalists, an ideal total capitalist. The more productive forces it takes over, the more it becomes the real collective body of all the capitalists, the more citizens it exploits. The workers remain wage-earners, proletarians. The capitalist relationship is not abolished; rather, it is pushed to an extreme. State ownership of the productive forces is not the solution of the conflict, but it contains within itself the formal means, the key to the solution" [11: 293]. A similar judgment was arrived at by L. Fabria almost half a century ago, in connection with Lenin's *State and Revolution*; he drew the following logical conclusion: "Even if the state becomes the owner, we shall still have state capitalism, and not socialism . . . . With the state as owner, all the proletarians would become employees of the state instead of employees of private capitalists. The state would be the exploiter, and this means that the entire apparatus of major and minor administrators and the entire bureaucracy, with all its hierarchical orders, would constitute a new ruling and exploiting class. Apparently something like that is taking place in Russia . . ." [12: 164]. There has been a tendency among us in recent years to replace "state capitalism" by the emotionally neutral term of "statism" (which at the same time eliminates discussion as to the meaning or meaninglessness of the concept of "state socialism") (see, for example, M. Popović [13: 328-336], M. Pecujlić [14]). S. Stojanović is most radical in this respect: "Statism is the name that should be given to the system based on state ownership of the means of production and on state management of production and other social activities. The state apparatus represents a new ruling class. As collective proprietor of the means of production, it employs labor power and exploits it. The share of the individual member of the ruling class in the distribution of the surplus value is proportional to his position in the state hierachy. . . . The specific characteristic of the statist class, as compared to others, is that its economic power comes from its political power, while the converse is true of the bourgeoisie" [15: 33].

9. The two monopolization trends are not necessarily antagonistic to each other. As R. H. Crossman, a British socialist, puts it: ". . . it must be noted that, in modern large-scale industry, there are certain common interests uniting organized management and organized labor. For instance, it is obviously convenient for both sides that power should be concentrated in fewer and fewer hands" [18: 10].

10. "Two great monolithic structures face each other," says Robert McKenzie in describing the British scene, and adds, characteristically: "and conduct furious arguments about comparatively minor issues that separate them" [19: 586]. It is not difficult to agree with Crossman that McKenzie, in his *British Political Parties,* "has shown conclusively that the two great parties have developed in accordance with the law of increasing oligarchy which operates in industry, in the trade unions, and on Fleet Street" [18: 21].

11. In what follows, Weber's position will be developed in greater detail, in view of the fact that Weber initiated the systematic investigation of bureaucracy and that subsequent practice in the Soviet Union (which Stalin advertised as the Marxist dictatorship of the proletariat) coincides, to the greatest possible extent, with that

position. It turns out that it was Weber, and not Marx, who was the ideological precursor of Stalin and his successors. In this respect, as in many others, the vulgar pseudo-Marxists attributed an ideology to Marx that was not only foreign to him but was diametrically opposite to his views on the state, class struggle, and socialism.

12. If the phrase "other things being equal" is interpreted as meaning "under conditions of antagonistic class interests," the following passage from Max Weber may help to illustrate the point: "The expropriation of workers in general, including clerical personnel and technically trained persons, from possession of the means of production depends on the following principal economic factors: (a) the fact that, other things being equal, it is generally possible to achieve a higher level of technical efficiency if the management has extensive control over the selection and the modes of use of workers, as compared with the situation created by the appropriation of jobs or the existence of rights to participate in management. These latter conditions produce technically, as well as economically, irrational obstacles to efficiency . . .; (b) in a market economy, a management which is not hampered by any established rights of the workers, and which enjoys unrestricted control over the goods and equipment that underlie its loans, is in a superior credit position . . .; (c) from a historical point of view, the expropriation of labor has developed since the 16th century, both extensively and intensively, by the sheer technical superiority oriented to the particular market situations and by the structure of power relationships in the society" [21: 227]. In proposition (a) we see a theoretical ancestor of the Stalinist argument for centralized administration [*edinonachalie*] that was introduced in the USSR at the end of the 1920s (see Ch.5).

13. Cf. the illuminating empirical studies by T.B. Bottomore [22] on the French higher civil service, and by R.K. Kelsal [23] on its British counterpart. Before the last war, the French higher civil service was "a virtual monopoly of the Parisian *grande bourgeoisie.*" After the war, in the period 1945-1951, 65% of the successful candidates at the admission examinations came from families in the first two occupational grades (employers and independent professional men; higher civil servants, managers and technicians), which account for only 9% of the adult male population [22: 149]. In 1950, in Britain, people born to the propertied and professional classes (i.e., the families of landed gentry and other persons not gainfully employed, large and small employers, high and intermediate civil servants, managers, professional people) held 71.9% (79.9% in 1939 and 86.0% in 1929) of the highest posts in the civil service, while the same occupations constituted only 18.1% of the adult male population in the same year [23: 157]. American civil servants are more "middle class" in social origin, but in one significant respect the American bureaucratic elite resembles the other two: the exclusion of people of working class origin. Workers constitute more than half of American society, but produce only 10% of its highest administrators. Cf. Bendix [24: 29].

14. Cf. Gerth and Mills: "The general strike of 1926 showed that British bureaucrats will stand socially and politically with the ruling class" [26: 175].

15. S. M. Lipset quotes George Lansbury, a member of that government and subsequently leader of the Labour Party, as saying: "All through the life of the late Government, Treasury officials obstructed and hindered the Ministers in their work. No one can deny this" [27: 259].

16. S. M. Lipset observes: "Since the days of Karl Marx, some socialists have maintained that a successful socialist state must destroy the old state apparatus and erect a new administrative organization. In recent times persons who have served in, or studied, socialist governments have suggested that one crucial reason for their failure to proceed more vigorously toward the attainment of their goals has been the 'bureaucratic conservatism' of old civil servants" [27: 258].

17. In studying the behavior of a section of American military bureaucracy as participant-observer, A. K. Davis notes:"Bureaucratic personnel suffer from chronic status-anxiety. Everyone focuses his attention on his superior, whose slightest display of pleasure or displeasure is magnified and distorted downward. The mildest criticism from a superior is often viewed by the recipient as a crushing attack" [28: 389]. The same, of course, takes place in every bureaucratic organization, perhaps in a slightly less pronounced form; everyone will know this from personal experience.

18. For the British wartime experience in administrative planning, similar in many respects to the Yugoslav experience, see the illuminating book of Professor E. Devons [33]. Cf. also W. Eucken for the German experience [34]. The most interesting would be the experience of Soviet planning because it has been in existence long enough to eliminate some, or many, of the defects apparent in the first few years of Yugoslav planning. But I do not know of any good critical account

of the Soviet experience, written by Soviet authors, that I could quote. Scattered evidence suggests that the picture is essentially the same.

19. Status differentiation is achieved through ranks and uniforms, through exclusive clubs and other similar means of ostentation. Privileges in living quarters and vacation resorts reinforce the differentiation. A more subtle method is reflected in the absence of criticism upward: a private is not supposed to criticize a colonel, not even outside the barracks. There are, of course, a number of other processes conducive to the perpetuation of bureaucratic polarization (family ties, for instance, play a significant role), but we cannot discuss them here. However, one is worth mentioning because it represents an inevitable extension of status differentiation to international relations. It is the development of a strong nationalism with a tendency to domination. By its very nature, bureaucracy is "patriotic." As such, it spontaneously proceeds to build up the myth of national grandeur, for it is germane to its way of thinking to attribute to various nations various degrees of merit, naturally reserving the *highest*, or *next to the highest*, rank for its own nation. This serves two useful purposes: by crediting itself with the actual and hypothetical achievements of the nation or, which comes to the same thing, of the social organization, domestic bureaucracy proves its own indispensability; by assuring the rest of the population that they belong to a superior nation or live under a superior system, bureaucracy tries to provide fictitious strata beneath the bottom stratum, i.e., to transform the loose bottom end of the social pyramid into a pseudohierarchical stratum similar to all the others above it, in order to prevent the development of consciousness of antagonistic interests. In this way the operation of the hierarchical principle transcends national boundaries and brings about bureaucratization on an international scale.

20. Some economists might prefer to use the term *property* or *ownership* for what I call *control over means of production*. Thus, instead of speaking of private and bureaucratic control, one may speak of private and state ownership. I have chosen my phrase because it describes the essential relation simply and straightforwardly and because, being free from juridical connotations, it is not as ambiguous as the alternative term. Cf. the following dictum of Marx and Engels: "Communism deprives no man of the power to appropriate the products of the society; all it does is deprive him of the power to subjugate the labor of others by means of such appropriation" [36: 51]. The meaning of the statement depends on whether we place emphasis on "the power to subjugate the labor of others" or on "appropriation." Now, if put in this form, everyone acquainted with Marxism will recognize that the emphasis is on the former. But it has often been convenient to transfer it to the latter, and in this case surprisingly few people have been able to realize that the conclusion "the power to subjugate the labor of others vanishes when private property is abolished" is a *non sequitur.*

21. In Yugoslavia today we frequently use the term "self-governing socialism." Strictly speaking, the attribute "self-governing" or "associationist" is unnecessary. I use it only for didactic reasons because it provides a direct and unambiguous description of the social system in question. "Socialism," like all terms in extensive use, has come to mean such a variety of things — von Mises' usage in the quotation below being an instructive example — that it is seriously lacking in the precision requisite for a scientific term.

22. In fact, this already happens in private capitalism as an inevitable result of capitalist development. Compare the following data on the distribution of employed population in England and Wales before the advent of capitalism and at the end of its laissez-faire phase of development [37: 215]:

	Late 18th century	1921
Employers	14	4
Employees	34	90
Independents	52	6

It appears that under the system so dear to von Mises, the "life, work, and leisure" of 90% of the population are subordinated "to the orders of those in power and office." The figures in the two columns are not strictly comparable. The first column is an estimate based on the well-known figures of Gregory King; hence they are of doubtful accuracy. But this does not affect the general picture. The England of the 1700s can easily be replaced by, for example, the Yugoslavia or Russia of the 1920s,

47

and then the proportion of independents (peasants and artisans) rises to more than four-fifths of the employed population.

23. "The tradition and concept of a merit, nonpatronage civil service was related in many countries to the needs of the dominant business groups, who demanded cheap and efficient service from the state. J. Donald Kingsley has shown how in England the policy of a merit civil service grew with the increase in political power of the business class. Business groups desired an efficient state that would facilitate and protect the development of commerce" [27: 257-258].

24. This simple truth is almost entirely neglected in the modern political-economic literature, which is so profoundly influenced by the existence, and apparent inevitability, of colossal bureaucratic organizations. Everyone who dares to take it up is likely to be denounced as an anarchist or a visionary. A refreshing exception, and possibly a display of intellectual courage, is provided by W. H. Morris-Jones: "It is . . . our present thesis that the most powerful contribution to the solution of the problem of bureaucracy lies in a revival of local government through a reconstruction of its functions and a determination of its areas on the basis of the people's ties and loyalties" [39: 25].

25. The term was already used by F. A. Neff in 1950 [42] and by L. H. Haney in 1911 [43].

26. Consequently, syndicalism, or anarcho-syndicalism, as it is sometimes called, has become a derogatory word in the working class vocabulary. It is of interest to note how the opponents of workers' self-government invariably use this term to designate — and denigrate — those in favor of it, even if the latter have no connection with syndicalism. In this connection it is instructive to analyze the vocabulary of Soviet-Chinese criticisms of the Yugoslav workers' government, as well as the vocabulary of similar criticisms by orthodox trade union leaders in Western countries.

27. Soviets of Working People's Deputies, together with Soviets of Soldiers' Deputies, acquired political power and, in fact, gave the new Soviet state its name (soviet = council). It is interesting to note the testimony of G. Gurvich who, even before the October Revolution of 1917, took part in forming workers' councils in Russian enterprises (for example, in the well-known Putilov factory). Gurvich says that Lenin at that time took the position that planning and social revolution were impossible if they were not based on the direct participation of the workers, on workers' self-management. This position also went into the second program of the Bolshevik Party which, however, was destroyed after it was printed [66: 6].

28. This absolutely uniform pattern is characteristic for the European revolutions. Asian revolutions proceed in a somewhat different way. This can be explained by the small size of the working class in these countries and by the fact that they have a different cultural tradition.

29. The oldest works council still in existence in Britain is, as far as I know, that at the Bournville Works of the cocoa and chocolate manufacturing firm of Cadbury Brothers Ltd. In this firm, works committees were established at the beginning of the century. The aim of the management was defined as *rapprochement* of employer and worker [45: 2].

30. For the sake of completeness, an interesting early German attempt should be mentioned. The Industrial Commission of the revolutionary National Assembly, which met in Frankfurt in 1848, put forward a resolution asking that factory committees, consisting of employers' and workers' representatives, issue work rules subject to the approval of district factory councils elected by the factory committees in the district. The resolution was never enacted because the revolution collapsed shortly thereafter [46: 1].

31. The demand for workers' control in British industry was most acute in the twelve-year period of 1910-1922. For a detailed and thorough account of what was happening, see B. Pribićević [47]. For a standard work on the comparable German movement, see C.W. Guillebaud [46].

32. Characteristic of the mood of the workers was the following published statement by the Clyde strikers: "We hold the view that the trade union officials are the servants, not the masters, of the rank and file, and that they require some pressure at times to move them in the path the rank and file desire them to tread" [50: 131]. D. Kirkwood, one of the leading members of the Clyde Workers' Committee, told the visiting Prime Minister, Lloyd George, at a meeting in December 1915, that they had organized the strike "in defiance of you, in defiance of the Government . . . and in defiance of the trade union officials" [47: 568].

Comparable to the British shop stewards' movement was the German works councils movement after 1918. And comparable to the statements of the Clyde strikers was the following published statement of the striking metalworkers in Düsseldorf in 1924: "In a great number of towns, the trade unions had adhered to the general strike proclaimed by the works councils. Where this has not yet taken place, the workers must force them to join the movement. The leaders of the unions who refuse must be ejected from their offices" [46: 70].

33. Inquiring into the problem of joint consultation in British industry, the National Institute of Industrial Psychology sent questionnaires to 4,719 manufacturing establishments employing over 250 people; returns were received relating to 751 establishments, of which 545 had joint consultation [52: 21].

34. "In many instances the idea took shape in the minds of individual employers or managers faced with rapidly expanding personnel, and was originally intended as no more than a substitute, of sorts, for that direct personal contact which is so easily lost when the payroll lengthens and the ratio of skilled and semiskilled workers increases." This is the testimony of G. S. Walpole, also an employer [54: 39].

35. The research team of the National Institute of Industrial Psychology records: "A number of the younger executives told us that their favorable attitude to joint consultation had been acquired through experience in the services during the war" [52: 69].

36. In France they have formed their own organization called *Union des Chefs d'Entreprises — Action pour les Structures Humaines.*

37. Cf. W. H. Scott [55, 56], E. Jaques [30], G. S. Walpole [54], C. G. Renold [49], the two ILO studies [53, 57] and the NIIP study [52], for joint consultation; and P. Kovač and Dj. Miljević [10], the Congress of Workers' Councils of Yugoslavia [59], and an ILO study [58], for workers' management.

38. As far as Yugoslav experience is concerned, the conclusions of a very serious study by the ILO may be quoted: ". . . while the self-government machinery for labor relations has decreased the former power of managerial personnel, it does not appear to have impaired their authority . . . . It has undoubtedly reinforced the position of the collective with reference to the management, but does not seem to have undermined labor discipline" [58: 203].

39. Describing conditions in the United States, the ILO study cited above says: "A considerable number of prewar plans for joint committees in factories had been developed primarily by management in order to interest workers in the successful operation of factories, and in many instances had been aimed at undercutting the development of unionism" [53: 185].

40. The resulting deep psychological conflict of the workers is well analyzed by the already-quoted Tavistock Institute study: ". . . it seemed as though the only time the members of the Council could hold their heads high was if there was a management-worker fight on; if there was no fight they felt guilty, as if they were not doing what was expected of them" [30: 122]. ". . . the desirability of employment with the firm has led workers to look to the management rather than to the trade unions for security of employment, and has aroused in the workers' leaders an acute conflict over loyalties divided between the firm and the trade unions" [30: 179].

41. The following statistic seems significant. In Britain, the initiative for starting joint consultation has come from management in about three-quarters of all cases, and in only 4% from workers and unions, respectively [52: 161]. The percentages are not susceptible to a simple and straightforward explanation, but basically, I think, they show that unions are *not* interested in pressing for workers' participation in management.

42. The conclusion is generalized, but it is of course not difficult to point to concrete historical situations that reflect this type of process directly. I choose the German works councils of the Weimar period to illustrate the point. In this connection, C. W. Guillebaud, their historian, has the following to say: "To the German masses . . . the workers' councils stood for the democratization of the industrial system and the attainment, in the economic sphere, of the same rights of self-government and self-determination as they thought they had achieved by the revolution of 1918 in the political sphere . . . . But when it came to the practical working out of the basic and, to the individual workers, the most important part of the structure — the works councils — they found that the bulk of the political leaders of labor were in league with the employers to prevent any too wide extension of powers to these councils" [46: 212-213]. The unions were apprehensive of losing leadership [5: 41] and hence were anxious to insure that the works councils did not become really effective; they and their political allies, the majority Socialists, "were backed up to the utmost by the employers, who were at least as much concerned to fetter the works councils and

to confine them within the organization of the unions. Of the latter the employers were not afraid . . . ."

43. As an empirical illustration I choose two authoritative pronouncements of unions and party views in Britain, but equivalent examples could be found without difficulty in any other country. The following statement of Mr. Gunter during the parliamentary debate on joint consultation in 1950 is evaluated by the National Institute of Industrial Psychology as a "very well-expressed trade union view": "There has been an amazing revival of the old syndicalist idea of direct workers' control in certain sections of labor. In my opinion it is impossible to envisage any great development in the sphere of joint consultation if we imagine that this old, fuzzy idea of workers' control can operate. In the last resort management must be allowed to manage and to make decisions, and must accept the responsibility. What we seek is that their decisions and policy shall be translated to the workers so that they may understand their objectives, and thereby help to ensure that cooperation which can result in much better and higher production. I cannot leave the trade union side without expressing my belief that the majority of trade unionists do not desire to see the establishment of workers' control, as it is sometimes called" [52: 82]. The Labour Party's 1957 policy document on nationalized industries asks the question, in the chapter on workers' participation — "Direct Representation?" — and answers it in the negative: "The syndicalist view of industry run by workers, either through their trade unions or through elected boards, was rejected by the labour movement many years ago" [61: 39]. Note the reference to "syndicalism" in both instances.

44. Cf. H. A. Clegg: "Today industrial discipline is a different matter in all industries from the prewar period of heavy unemployment. This is often said to be one of the greatest difficulties of British industry today. At the same time, full employment has done more to make industry more democratic and to raise the status of the worker than any legislation or any machinery for joint consultation could do" [62: 78]. Note, however, that the concluding antithesis of Clegg is spurious; the causation is different from the one implied. Democratization of the industrial organization produced joint consultation, not the other way around. If so, another straightforward conclusion follows. Once generally applied, joint consultation becomes a social institution and cannot be abolished without social upheavals. But neither can it be petrified in its present form, in which the attention of workers is channeled toward welfare matters, while management reserves the right to make the crucial managerial decisions. Workers will very soon begin to insist that this "toilet democracy" be replaced by "real democracy." C. A. Myers unintentionally describes something of the sort happening in Sweden when he says: "But unless the committees begin to tackle real problems . . . the 'stagnation' may turn into disgust and revulsion. 'Toilet democracy,' as one person described the current concern for better washrooms, lighting, etc., may suffice for a time, but it is hardly the 'industrial democracy' that the labor movement said it was seeking " [51: 71].

Incidentally, if the above analysis is correct, it gives two simple conservation formulas for the protagonists of the status quo. In order to save private capitalism, the unions must be recognized and helped to develop into stable bureaucratic organizations. Further, large-scale wars must be avoided, since they destroy capitalist social discipline. Of course, a certain limited amount of unemployment must be maintained in order to preserve discipline. A similar group of conditions applies to state capitalist systems. In order to preserve such a system, the state must likewise avoid major wars and the dislocation resulting from them. It must then extend the bureaucratic structure to the inferiors in the large bureaucratic structure known as a "camp." Naturally, a safety valve must also be provided in some mild form of joint consultation. However, both remedies have only temporary effects.

45. Duisburger Kupferhütte, where the chairman of the workers' council is a member of the managing board, is a German example. Glacier Metal Company is an outstanding British example. The constitution of the Glacier Works Council says: "The functions of the council shall be . . . to carry the responsibility of deciding the principles and policies which shall govern the management of the factory in the light of opinions of producers and managers, in the light of the interest of consumers, shareholders, and the nation at large, and in the light of total company policy" [30: 155]. In seeking to achieve this aim (the management to surrender its arbitrary executive power, while the workers develop responsible and effective collective decision-making), both management and workers had to overcome enormous difficulties resulting from their own learned attitudes and from the totally uncongenial institutional setup in which they were to act. These difficulties are indicative of the profound changes in social

relations brought about by self-government. The social and psychological changes that took place in the Glacier Company are admirably described in the Tavistock Institute study with the telling title *The Changing Culture of a Factory* [30].

46. In fact, academic economists, of both the left and the right, are still unaware of its impact. Cf. a characteristic footnote observation by J.A. Schumpeter: "Wild socializations — a term that has acquired official standing — are attempts by workmen of each plant to supersede the management and to take matters into their own hands. These are the nightmare of every responsible socialist" [63: 226].

47. For industrial self-government, see Kovač and Miljević [10]. For a general discussion of the institution of self-government and a description of self-government schemes in the rest of the system, see L. Geršković [64].

REFERENCES

[1]   J. A. Schumpeter, *Imperialism and Social Classes,* Blackwell, Oxford, 1951.
[2]   F. Engels, "Principles of Communism," in *Early Works of Marx and Engels,* Kultura, Zagreb, 1953.
[3]   K. Marx and F. Engels, "Preface to Russian Edition of the Manifesto of the Communist Party," *Works,* Vol. XV, Partizdat, Moscow, 1935.
[4]   K. Marx, *Critique of the Gotha Program;* F. Engels, *Critique of the Draft Erfurt Program*; Kultura, Belgrade, 1959.
[5]   E. F. M. Durbin, "The Case for Socialism," in *Problems of Economic Planning,* Routledge, London, 1949.
[6]   *Social Self-Management in Yugoslavia,* Yugoslav Sociology Association, Belgrade, 1966.
[7]   M. Novak, Introduction to the Political Economy of Socialism, *Economski pregled,*[Economic Review], Zagreb, 1955.
[8]   N. Pašić, *Public Corporations in Great Britain and Other Western Countries,* Kultura, Belgrade, 1957.
[9]   A. Dragičević, *Necessary Labor and Surplus of Labor,* Kultura, Zagreb, 1957.
[10]   P. Kovač and Dj.Miljević, *Self-Management of Producers in Economy,* Savremena administracija [Contemporary Administration], Belgrade, 1958.
[11]   F. Engels, *Anti-Dühring,* Naprijed, Zagreb, 1946.
[12]   *Bureaucracy and Technocracy,* Book I, edited by V. Stanovčić and A. Stojanovic, Sedma sila, Belgrade, 1966.
[13]   *Bureaucracy and Technocracy,* Book II, edited by V. Stanovčić and A. Stojanovic; Sedma sila, Belgrade, 1966.
[14]   M. Pecujlic, *Classes and Contemporary Society,* Savremena administracija, Belgrade, 1967.
[15]   S. Stojanović, "The Etatistic Myth of Socialism," *Praxis,* 1967, No. 1-2.
[16]   B. Horvat, *The Economic Theory of a Planned Economy,* Kultura, Belgrade, 1961.
[17]   K. Marx, "Economic and Philosophical Manuscripts of 1844," in *Early Works of Marx and Engels,* Kultura, Zagreb, 1954.
[18]   R. H. S. Crossman, *Socialism and the New Despotism,* Fabian Tract 258, London, 1956.
[19]   R. McKenzie, *British Political Parties,* Heinemann, London, 1955.
[20]   W. A. Lewis, "The Administration of Socialist Enterprises," in *Overhead Costs,* Allen and Unwin, London, 1949.
[21]   M. Weber, *The Theory of Social and Economic Organization,* Hodge, London, 1947.
[22]   T. Bottomore, "Higher Civil Servants in France," in *Transactions of the Second World Congress of Sociology,* Vol. II, International Sociological Association, London, 1954.
[23]   R. K. Kelsall, *Higher Civil Servants in Britain,* Routledge and Kegan, London, 1955.
[24]   R. Bendix, *Higher Civil Servants in American Society,* University of Colorado Press, Boulder, Colo., 1949.
[25]   J. D. Kingsley, *Representative Bureaucracy,* Antioch Press, Yellow Springs, Ohio, 1944.
[26]   H. H. Gerth and C. W. Mills, "A Marx for the Managers," reprinted in *Reader in Bureaucracy,* edited by R. K. Merton et al., Free Press, Glencoe, Ill., 1952.
[27]   S. M. Lipset, *Agrarian Socialism,* University of California Press, Berkeley, 1950.
[28]   A. K. Davis, "Bureaucratic Patterns in the Navy Officer Corps," reprinted in *Reader in Bureaucracy, op. cit.*

[29] R. K. Merton, "Bureaucratic Structure and Personality," *ibid.*

[30] E. Jaques, *The Changing Culture of a Factory,* Dryden Press, New York, 1952.

[31] W. R. Sharp, *The French Civil Service: Bureaucracy in Transition,* Macmillan, New York, 1931.

[32] B. Horvat, *Economics of the Yugoslav Oil Industry,* Tehnicka Knjiga [Technical Books], Belgrade, 1962.

[33] E. Devons, *Planning in Practice,* Cambridge University Press, 1950.

[34] W. Eucken, "On the Theory of Centrally Administered Economy: An Analysis of the German Experiment," *Economica,* 1948.

[35] K. Marx, *Critique of Hegel's Philosophy of Right,* V. Masleša, Sarajevo, 1960.

[36] K. Marx and F. Engels, *Manifesto of the Communist Party,* Kultura, Zagreb, 1948.

[37] W. F. Oakeshott, *Commerce and Society,* Claredon Press, Oxford, 1936.

[38] L. von Mises, *Bureaucracy,* Hodge, Glasgow, 1945.

[39] W. H. Morris Jones, *Socialism and Bureaucracy,* Fabian Tract 277, London, 1949.

[40] K. Marx, *The Civil War in France,* Kultura, Zagreb, 1947.

[41] J. A. Schumpeter, *History of Economic Analysis,* Oxford University Press, New York, 1955.

[42] F. A. Neff, *Economic Doctrines,* McGraw-Hill, New York, 1950.

[43] L. H. Haney, *History of Economic Thought,* Macmillan, New York, 1911.

[44] G. D. H. Cole, *Guild Socialism Restated,* London, 1920.

[45] *A Works Council in Being. An Account of the Scheme in Operation at Bourneville Works,* Publication Department, Bourneville Works, 1921.

[46] C. W. Guilleband, *The Works Council,* Cambridge University Press, 1928.

[47] B. Pribičević, *Demand for Workers' Control in the Railway, Mining and Engineering Industries 1910-1922,* doctoral thesis, Nuffield College, Oxford, 1957.

[48] J. B. Seymour, *The Whitley Councils Scheme,* King, London, 1932.

[49] C. G. Renold, *Joint Consultation over Thirty Years,* Allen and Unwin, London, 1950.

[50] H. Wolfe, *Labour Supply and Regulation,* Clarendon Press, Oxford, 1923.

[51] C. A. Myers, *Industrial Relations in Sweden,* Technology Press, Cambridge, Mass., 1951.

[52] *Joint Consultation in British Industry,* National Institute of Industrial Psychology, Staples Press, London, 1952.

[53] *Labour-Management Cooperation in United States War Production,* International Labour Office, Studies and Reports, New Series, No. 6, Montreal, 1948.

[54] G. S. Walpole, *Management and Men,* Jonathan Cape, London, 1945.

[55] W. H. Scott, *Joint Consultation in a Liverpool Manufacturing Firm,* University Press of Liverpool, 1950.

[56] W. H. Scott, *Industrial Leadership and Joint Consultation,* University Press of Liverpool, 1952.

[57] *British Joint Production Machinery,* International Labour Office, Studies and Reports, Series A. No. 43, Montreal, 1944.

[58] *Workers' Management in Yugoslavia,* International Labour Office, Geneva, 1962.

[59] *Congress of Workers' Councils of Yugoslavia,* edited by A. Deleon and Lj. Mijatović, Rad, Belgrade, 1957.

[60] T. E. M. McKitterick and R. D. V. Roberts, *Workers and Management,* Fabian Research Series No. 160, London, 1953.

[61] *Public Enterprise. Labour's Review of the Nationalised Industries,* London, 1957.

[62] H. A. Clegg, *Industrial Democracy and Nationalisation,* Blackwell, Oxford, 1950.

[63] J. A. Schumpeter, *Capitalism, Socialism and Democracy,* Harper, New York, 1950.

[64] L. Gerškovič, *Social Management in Yugoslavia,* Savremena administracija, Belgrade, 1957.

[65] R. Čolaković *et al., Review of the History of the League of Communists of Yugoslavia,* Institute for Study of the Workers' Movement, Belgrade, 1963.

[66] J. Duvignaud, "Georges Gurvitch: A Sociological Theory of Self-Management," *Autogestion* [Self-Management], 1966, No. 1.

CHAPTER II

The Transition Period and the Dictatorship of the Proletariat

In the first part of this essay, an examination was made of the historical presuppositions of our society and of the broad outlines of general tendencies in its socioeconomic development. As we approach our situation today, our method of analysis must be changed. It must become more minute and detailed, and the broad generalizations must more and more be replaced by examination of the interrelationships of concrete events. In this context, it is first necessary to reconsider the theory and practice of the transition period and the dictatorship of the proletariat. Thereafter, in the light of our revised orientation, we proceed to an attempt to systematize the stages of our concrete postrevolutionary development, which, as we shall see, coincides with Marx's transition period.

6. THE TRANSITION PERIOD

Once a victorious revolution has destroyed the old capitalist order, it cannot be expected instantly to install the new socialist order. Between the two orders there comes a transition period during which, by a sequence of revolutionary changes, the capitalist system will be put aside, transformed, and replaced by the socialist system. This is Marx's celebrated *transition period.* The transition period should last a short time and encompass the most basic, crucial changes, such as the taking of power, the replacement of the apparatus of government, the abolition of private property, the establishment of a new system of law, etc. Of course, this would not signify that socialism had already been attained, but that a basis had been reached on which it could develop further. This system, to be built on a socialist foundation, would have to possess the characteristics of a socialist system as described by Marx and Engels: the withering away of the state, the disappearance of classes and exploitation, the free development of the human personality and the unimpeded creative manifestation of his individuality, and so forth. When the system that actually developed did not correspond to those characteristics, a bit of sleight-of-hand was performed, and it was proclaimed to be socialist not because it was so but because, for example, private ownership had been done away with. At the same time a tendency appeared to treat *socialism* as a *transition* period. On that basis it became possible to apply Marx's thesis of the revolutionary dictatorship of the proletariat not to the transition period but to socialism as a whole. The last act of this revision of Marx's thought consisted in interpreting the *dictatorship* of the proletariat as a form of exercising rule, i.e., as a violent, undemocratic, political dictatorship (and not as the class content of the state of that period). Thereby Marxism was definitively stood on its head, and anything that reinforced the power of the bureaucracy could be presented as a socialist measure; under the influence of these pragmatic actions, socialism often took on a content that was alien and, in many respects, antithetical to the original socialism of Marx.

For these reasons, it will be well to try to give a short account of the original position of Marx, Engels, and Lenin on the problem of the transition period.

Marx, Engels, and Lenin on the Transition Period

In order to have a correct interpretation of the position of Marx and Engels on the transition period, it would be necessary to give a full and exhaustive account of its historical development. Considerations of space compel us to limit our historical account to a sketch.

As early as in the *Deutsch-Französische Jahrbücher,* Marx designated the proletariat as the bearer of socialism. The idea of the conquest of power by the proletariat is expressed especially clearly in *The Communist Manifesto.* There it is shown to be a necessary consequence of the class struggle in capitalist society. Marx and Engels say:

". . . the first step in the revolution by the working class is to raise the proletariat to the position of ruling class . . . .

"The proletariat will use its political supremacy to wrest, by degrees, all capital from the bourgeoisie, to centralize all instruments of production in the hands of the state (i.e., the proletariat organized as the ruling class), and to increase the total of productive forces as rapidly as possible" [1: 27]. Here (as elsewhere in the *Manifesto*) nothing concrete is said concerning the future communist society, but only a statement, in the most general outlines, of the immediate problems and perspectives of the future development of society. The conditions had not yet come into being for anything more concrete.

Although the term "dictatorship of the proletariat" is not used in the above citation (or elsewhere in the *Manifesto*), that is what is involved. Meanwhile (in 1848) revolution had broken out in France and spread to all of Europe. Marx and Engels took an active part in the revolution and made a careful analysis of it. Now the concept, which had been wanting, finally crystallized. In his *Class Struggles in France from 1848 to 1850* (written in 1850), Marx wrote:

"The bourgeoisie forced the Paris proletariat into the June uprising. . . . Then . . . the bold slogan of the revolutionary struggle appeared: *Overthrow of the bourgeoisie! Dictatorship of the working class!*" (Marx's emphasis). "This socialism (revolutionary — B.H.) is an announcement of permanent revolution, is class dictatorship of the proletariat as an essential transitional stage toward the elimination of class differences in general, toward the destruction of all production relations on which these differences are founded, toward the abolition of all social relations that correspond to these production relations, toward the overthrow of the entire ideology arising from these socialist relations" [1: 133].

And in his famous letter to Weydemeyer, dated March 5, 1852, Marx said:

"What I did that was new was to prove: 1) that the existence of classes is only bound up with particular historical phases in the development of production, 2) that the class struggle necessarily leads to the *dictatorship of the proletariat* (Marx's emphasis), and 3) that this dictatorship itself only constitutes the *transition* (my emphasis — B.H.) to the abolition of all classes and to a classless society" [3].

Here for the first time the question is clearly and explicitly raised of the transition period and of the political organization corresponding to it, the dictatorship of the proletariat, and the content of that transition period is outlined in a general form.

Anything more concrete about the transition period could only be said on the basis of analysis of practical experience, if it were not to be mere speculation. Since 1848 was followed by a twenty-year period of relatively peaceful development of capitalism, Marx did not concern himself, during that period, with the problem of the transition period.

In 1871 a new revolution broke out in France, whose practical results (above all, those of the Paris Commune) provided a wealth of material for further theoretical generalization. Marx and Engels, of course, followed and analyzed the course of events with great care. The immediate result of this analysis were Marx's "addresses," published under the title of *The Civil War in France.* In that work, Marx describes the Commune as follows:

"Its true secret was this. It was essentially a working-class government, the result of the struggle of the producing against the appropriating class, the political form, at last discovered, by which the economic emancipation of labor could be achieved," that is, that all "become workers, and productive work ceases to belong to a certain class" [1: 481].

The decrees of the Commune show what concrete practical measures had to be taken in order to realize those ends: a communal administration of the state was set up, the factories were turned over to be managed by workers' associations, the old oppressive machinery of state had to be demolished and replaced by workers' officials and deputies, and protection against the new bureaucracy was needed by insuring that it was constantly under control by the masses, by having all officials replaced at fixed periods, and by having the highest salaries in the bureaucracy no higher than the wages of a worker. And the bureaucracy itself, all the authoritative machinery of state, becomes increasingly superfluous. "To the degree that anarchy of social production disappears," Engels added some years later, completing the analysis made by him and Marx, "the political authority of the state will also wither away" [1: 145].

With this, the problem of the transition period was fully solved. But it received its classic formulation some years later in Marx's *Critique of the Gotha Program,* written in 1875 and published in 1891. Quotations from this work are misinterpreted with remarkable persistence.

Marx's classical definition of the transition period is as follows: "Between capitalist and communist society lies the period of the revolutionary transformation of the one into the other. There corresponds to this also a political transition period in which the state can be nothing but the *revolutionary dictatorship of the proletariat"* [4: 35].

This statement is often interpreted as meaning that communism is a second phase following a period of socialism, intervening between capitalism and communism. However, by communism Marx means a socioeconomic system different from the capitalist system, so that socialism, too, is communism — in fact, its lower stage, as Marx defines it several pages earlier (p. 24). Communism and socialism differ in "the degree of their economic maturity" (Lenin), but are not different systems. It might be said, as a rough image, that they differ somewhat as free competitive capitalism differs from monopoly capitalism. Just as it would be ridiculous to contrast monopoly capitalism to feudalism, and to say that the capitalism of free competition constitutes a transition period from feudalism to monopoly capitalism, so it would be ridiculous to impute such a distinction to Marx with reference to communism. In his *Critique of the Gotha Program,* Marx invariably contrasts capitalism and communism with the utmost clarity, and makes it clear that two phases may be distinguished in the future system — socialism and communism — and that between that system and capitalism there lies a transition period in which the state takes the form of the dictatorship of the proletariat. It clearly follows, therefore, that under socialism there no longer is a dictatorship of the proletariat, there are no classes or class exploitation, etc., and Stalin's idea of the dictatorship of the proletariat under socialism is nothing but an anti-Marxist thesis, one more feature of his reactionary state-capitalist ideology, in which the term dictatorship of the proletariat really means the dictatorship of the bureaucracy.

However, some passages in the *Critique* may give rise to some confusion. Thus, on p.22 Marx says: "What we have to deal with here is not a communist society that has *developed* on its own foundations, but, on the contrary, that has just *emerged* from capitalist society and that is thus, in every respect, economically, morally, and intellectually, still stamped with the birthmarks of the old society from whose womb it emerges."

Even now this principle is interpreted as meaning: these traces in socialism have to be wiped out; hence socialism is a transition period. Several lines earlier, however, Marx speaks of the society "just emerging from capitalism" as being a society "based on communal principles," in which "producers do not exchange their products," in which the category of value no longer applies. And as regards the traces, they will persist even after society has progressed deep into communism. From a later text it appears that the economic vestiges of capitalism consist in the fact that productive capacity is not far enough developed to satisfy all needs. The moral vestiges consist in the fact that people will not "immediately learn to work for society without any standards of law" [Lenin, *Collected Works*], and that the existence of the state will continue for a long time under communism, having the function of maintaining "bourgeois law" ("to all according to their work"), which in turn signifies that for "the complete withering away of the state, complete communism is required" (*ibid.*). The spiritual vestiges consist in the fact that the contradiction between intellectual and manual labor will continue to exist, which is "one of the main sources of present social inequality" and which will only disappear in the second stage of communist society (*ibid.*: 440). It turns out that what is actually involved is communist society, and not a transitional period. In regard to this, Lenin says in his *State and Revolution:*

"What is usually called socialism was termed by Marx the 'first' or lower phase of communist society. Insofar as the means of production become *common* property, the word 'communism' is also applicable here, providing we do not forget that this is *not* complete communism. The great significance of Marx's explanations is that here, too, he consistently applies materialist dialectics, the theory of development, regarding communism as something which develops *out of* capitalism . . . . In its first phase . . . communism cannot as yet be fully ripe economically, entirely *free from traditions and remnants of capitalism* (my emphasis — B.H.). Hence the interesting phenomenon that communism in its first phase retains 'the narrow horizon of *bourgeois* right' " . . . etc. [Vol. 25: 442].

Then what of the transition period? Why is it not emphasized in Marx's general view, but is instead passed over, or has to be supplied implicitly? It will be seen from the quotations above, and from Lenin's interpretation, that Marx simply was thinking of socialism and spoke of a transition period prior to it.

It would seem that Marx and Engels thought of the transition period as much shorter than is the case in present-day practice. The difference is all the greater in view of the fact that the socialist revolution broke out in relatively backward countries, where this transition period objectively had to last longer in any case: it was necessary, under the dictatorship of the proletariat, to build up the industrial potential and organization of production which advanced countries had built up under the dictatorship of the bourgeoisie. That is why it is no accident that there should be the following difference between the terminologies of Engels and Lenin. In a preface, written in 1891, to a work of Marx, Engels says:

"A new social order is attainable, an order in which today's class differences will disappear, and in which, *after perhaps a brief* (my emphasis — B.H.) transition period which will be linked with certain deprivations but which, from a moral point of view, will be very useful, the means of life, of enjoyment, of development and of the application of all physical and spiritual capability will, in increasing abundance, be universally available. This will result from the planned use and further development of the already existing enormous productive forces of all members of society, along with the equal obligation of all to work" [1: 52].

While Engels says that the socialist economy, even if it should not be instituted in an instant, will still come to pass after a short period, Lenin gave the following interpretation in 1919, that is, after the transitional period had already been in existence for two years:

"This aim (socialism, that is, the elimination of classes and of exploitation — B.H.) cannot be achieved all at once; it requires a *sufficiently long* transition period from capitalism to socialism — and therefore, since the reorganization of production is a difficult matter, and because time is needed for a fundamental change in all fields of life, and because the great powers are used to a bourgeois and petty-bourgeois administration, it can be attained only in a *long* persistent struggle. Therefore, Marx speaks of the *entire period* of the dictatorship of the proletariat as a period of transition from capitalism to socialism" [6: 401].

And a year earlier, in January 1918, Lenin writes:

" . . . the transition from capitalism to socialism requires *long* birth pains, a *long period* of the dictatorship of the proletariat, the destruction of all that is old, the ruthless elimination of all forms of capitalism, the cooperation of the workers of all countries who must unite all their efforts to ensure final victory" ("Speech at Third All-Russian Congress of Soviets," *Collected Works,* Vol. 26: 429) (my emphasis — B.H.).

Lenin expresses himself similarly in other works; sometimes he even speaks of the "epoch of the dictatorship of the proletariat," as will be brought out later by further citations. The above statements by Lenin give both the definition and the duration of the transition period. Of course, all his expectations related to the backward country that Russia was.

This brief account of the principal statements of Marx and Engels regarding the transition period would be incomplete without special mention of Lenin's interpretation of those statements, of which we have already spoken in the course of the exposition. Lenin expressed his view on these premises most fully in his *State and Revolution,* which aims precisely at giving a correct interpretation of the position of the classics. It is unnecessary at this point to cite all of Lenin's propositions; some have already been noted and others will be given later. We will only remark that Lenin, by way of a correct interpretation, inverts Marx's statement in the *Critique of the Gotha Program,* speaking of the "transition period between capitalism and communism" (Marx's last formulation of this principle); there Marx only says that two phases may be distinguished in that future communism.

In other writings Lenin speaks very precisely of the transition period as the historical period between a capitalism that has been defeated, but has not yet disappeared, and a socialism that has begun but has not yet been attained. We cite some of the statements. In his article "Future Tasks of Soviet Authorities" (1918), he wrote: "Unless we are anarchists, we must accept the necessity of the state, that is, coercion, for the period from capitalism to socialism" [Vol. 26: 238]. In the already cited passage from "Greetings to Hungarian Workers" (1919), Lenin says that the abolition of classes and class exploitation "cannot be achieved at once" and that "it requires a sufficiently long transition period from capitalism to socialism!" [6: 401]. According to this, socialism is already a classless society, and the task of the transitional period is to liquidate class exploitation. This is also what Lenin says in his article "Economics and Politics in the Epoch (!) of the Dictatorship of the Proletariat," when he writes: "Classes remain and will continue to remain during the epoch (!) of the dictatorship of the proletariat. Dictatorship will be unnecessary when classes disappear. They will not disappear without a dictatorship of the proletariat" [6: 449].

At the Third All-Russian Congress of Soviets, Lenin said: "There is not a single socialist . . . who would not admit the obvious truth that between socialism and capitalism there is a long (!) more or less difficult transition period of the dictatorship of the proletariat, and that this period in its forms will depend greatly on whether small or large ownership, small or large cultures, predominate" [Vol. 26: 415].

And to conclude: one quotation in which he rejects as un-Marxist − with the utmost clarity − the assertion that there is no transition period between capitalism and socialism (which would have to be the conclusion if socialism is identified with the transition period). Criticizing Rykov, Lenin declared at a party conference in 1917: "Comrade Rykov says that there is no transition period between capitalism and socialism. That is not

60

correct. It is a departure from Marxism" [Vol. 24: 216].

Lenin is consistent in his treatment of this question. He presents the same conception in *all his works,* making further citation superfluous.

Current Questions

The preceding discussion has dealt chiefly with the correct interpretation of Marx's statements. We must now go on to discuss some problems arising out of present-day conditions.

We have already posed one basic question: what is Marx's transition period? It is the period of social development between the capitalist socioecomomic system and the communist socioeconomic system.

When does this transition period begin, and how long does it last? I think this question might be answered as follows: the transition period begins with the political revolution, in which the working class takes power, and it comes to an end with the economic revolution,[1] i.e., by the complete reorganization of the economy on "cooperative principles" (Marx). Of course, what we call the political and economic revolutions are two sides of a single process of "permanent revolution" (Marx and Lenin), the transformation of class society into classless society, of a chaotic anarchic economy into one that is consciously guided and planned.

When, as the result of socioeconomic development, the point of socialist revolution is reached in a country and the working class takes power there, it uses that power to conduct revolutionary changes in the economy of its country, creating the conditions for its own liquidation and for the creation of a communist society. This, then, is the task of the dictatorship of the proletariat. Lenin said the following on this subject in 1922:

"So long as classes exist, a class struggle is inevitable. In the transition period from capitalism to socialism, the existence of classes is inevitable, and the program of the RKP says quite definitely that we are taking only the first steps from capitalism to socialism. Therefore, both the Communist Party and the Soviet authorities, as well as the labor unions, have an obligation to accept openly the existence of the economic struggle and its inevitability until such time as there is at least basic electrification of industry and agriculture, until small farms and control by the market are cut out at the roots" [8: 746].

The transition period is one of fierce struggle with the residue of the old capitalist socioeconomic system, a struggle in which *the triumph of the new social order will only be assured after complete transformation of the society's economy. The seizure of power, by itself, does not assure the triumph of socialism and the impossibilty of restoration,* as is shown by the case of the USSR, a case the classics did not foresee (namely, the possibility that the workers' party would win power and *remain* in power, and yet arrive at a restoration or, more precisely, at perpetuation of the class system). It had seemed (and many still believe so) that counterrevolution could begin and go forward only by virtue of the old order and for the purpose of restoring that order. On that account, attention was devoted exclusively to the fight against the elements of the old order. It turned out, however, that the main danger to the successful revolution came from another direction. In that sense, as Lj. Tadič observes, "the history of Stalinism is the classic model of counterrevolution in *socialism"*(my emphasis — B.H.). And Maoism, we see, reinforces this model.

What, then, are the criteria for communism to be actually built after the political revolution in a given country?

If the dictatorship of the proletariat in a country shows a tendency to retain the state and even to reinforce it, to make a fetish of political authority, then it evidently is not performing its task, which consists in the withering away of political functions; it is transformed from the dictatorship of the proletariat to its opposite, the dictatorship over the proletariat, the dictatorship of the bureaucracy over the people.

Marx, and Lenin after him, speak of the transition period only in connection with the proletarian state — in other words, *only as much organized (i.e., government) intervention in the economy as is needed to remove the capitalist fetters.* This evidently leads to an economy in which that organized force is no longer necessary in the battle against capitalist survivals. After the successful conclusion of the political revolution, the state takes into its hands the fundamental portion of the means of production, and during a short period of state socialism creates the preconditions for turning them over to associations of direct producers for "transformation of state property into ownership by the people as a whole" [Kidrić, 9: 6]. At the same time, by means of a steady reinforcement of planning elements in the balances of the economy as a whole, a process is begun of rapid elimination of anarchy in production and of its result, economic imbalance inherited from capitalism. On this matter, Engels says: "To the degree to which anarchy in social production disappears, the political authority of the state is weakened" [10: 300]. The further this process goes forward, the less the state intervenes in the economic life of the country; the associations of direct producers begin to conduct the economy directly by means of higher associations of producers; class differences disappear; labor productivity increases tremendously; the entire economy is so organized that political coercion on the part of the state loses its goal and withers away.

"Society," says Engels in his classic passage on the withering away of the state, "which will newly organize production on the basis of a free and equal association of producers, will put the state machinery where it belongs: in a museum, along with the distaff and the bronze axe."

And this means that the economic revolution as well has been won, that the transition period is over, that the dominant factors in the economy are the elements of a new social order, a classless society, communism. Now the restoration of a society of class exploitation is as impossible as, say, the restoration of the system of slavery under capitalism.

The country in which the first socialist revolution took place, the Soviet Union, went along the path described above, but stopped at the first step, nationalization of the means of production, so that the transition period developed into a new class system. The party-government apparatus, which had initiated the reform, set itself apart, in a position of independence with respect to the proletariat and other strata of society. "The stronger the government executive apparatus becomes in general, the more independent [it is] of the working class and the working masses," E. Kardelj generalizes, "the more it will turn into a separate social force tending to maintain and further develop state-capitalist forms and relationships. In other words, *under these conditions the proletarian revolution itself produces a force that degenerates to the level of the despotism of the state-capitalist bureaucracy*" [11: 284]. Thus, in the USSR, failure to complete the economic revolution prevented the advance of the political revolution, and this fact is an excellent illustration of their interrelationship.

The foregoing account also settles the more or less scholastic questions of the construction of socialism, the transition to communism, etc. The socialist revolution gets rid of the power of the bourgeoisie, and society begins to build socialism. *The term of socialism may be extended even to this period, in the sense that it is no longer a matter of further developing the old social system, capitalism, but of beginning the institution of a new social system, socialism;* it is a socialism that is *only beginning*, to be sure, but that is why we speak of socialism and not of capitalism in

63

connection with it. In this regard, Lenin noted at the Third All-Russian Congress of Soviets:

". . . We have only begun the period of *transition* (my emphasis − B.H.) to socialism; we have not yet reached it. You will be correct if you say that our republic is a socialist republic of the Soviet. You will also be right along with those who call many republics in the West democratic, although everyone knows that there is not one of even the most democratic republics that is completely democratic. . . . That is how we are now. We are far even from the point where we would be ending the transition period from capitalism to socialism. We have never deceived ourselves with the hope that we shall end this period without the help of the international proletariat. We have never had any illusion about this and we know how difficult is the path leading from capitalism to socialism, and we are obliged to say that our Soviet republic is socialist because that is the path we have taken . . ." [Vol. 26: 422].

It was also in that sense, in my opinion, that Marx implicitly meant to include the transition period in socialism, as has been suggested in the form of questions attached to an earlier quotation. This is a conception that is, of course, completely different from the conception that socialism is reduced to the transition period, i.e., that they are identical.

As for the "construction of socialism," we have referred to this earlier. The same applies to the question of the transition to the higher phase of communism. Indeed, socialism is the same thing as communism, no more and no less, except that in socialism the insufficient development of productive potential makes it impossible to use the direct appropriation of objects of consumption, and it is still necessary to measure labor and confirm its effectiveness in order to obtain criteria for distribution of the means of subsistence. The more the production forces rise, the greater the extent to which conditions will be established − economic and others − for the transition to distribution according to needs, that is, communist distribution.

At this point another question arises: why do we speak at all about the transition period from capitalism to communism, while we do not speak of transition periods between other social systems?

The reason is that we consider the transition period without separating it from the question of the dictatorship of the proletariat. In all previous social systems the new class came to power only after it had become master of the country's economy, after it had become the owner of the means of production. But in

64

the socialist revolution the proletariat comes to power just because *it does not possess* the means of production. In all previous systems the political revolution precedes the economic revolution. Finally, the difference is that the presocialist evolution of society took place *completely* spontaneously, before consciousness was involved, whereas with the appearance of socialism people begin to control their social development. At the outset there are only unsure efforts, but the course of development is more and more in the direction of consciousness determining being, when, as Engels says, "people themselves, with full consciousness, make their own history," when "social causes that men set in motion will yield predominantly, and in increasing measure, the desired effect" [10: 300].

These basic differences must not be lost sight of in defining Marx's term of the transition period from capitalism to communism. In point of fact, there are always periods of transition between social systems; there is never a sharply delimited boundary. But it would be a serious mistake to identify this transition with Marx's transition period, which is not merely a transition but a very particular transition.

The theoretical sense of the Marxian transition period may be stated roughly as follows:

During the transition period, the step is made from class to classless society. But this does not mean that *all* the traces of class society are eliminated; this occurs only under socialism. And just because socialism is *already* a classless society, it is not a *transition* to communism but is itself communism, its first phase. Nor is the liquidation of the last residues of class society — "economic, moral, and spiritual" (Marx) — a higher step upward, since the basic class category, exploitation, is already liquidated during the transition period, just as the basic economic category of all precommunist systems is also liquidated, namely, the chaos and anarchy of production. *Total* liquidation of chaos in the economy, which would mean that consciousness totally determined being, will never be achieved, that is, it is an eternal process that will remain even under complete communism, and even after it; but we can speak of that liquidation to the extent that the process has *already* (and "already" refers to a period of a tendency) begun, and insofar as it means a step that is completed in the transition period.

One further remark: if communism is not regarded as the system that takes the place of capitalism, "which grows directly out of capitalism" (Marx), which is the next stage in the development of human society, but is regarded as the end of a period of development and as such is contrasted to the previous class epoch, then socialism also takes on a different meaning; it ceases to be the lower phase of communism and remains a transition period from class society to classless society. But these are static abstractions, which contrast *total* class society to *total* classless society, conceptions that in my opinion are foreign to Marx and Marxism. For a theory of development such as Marx's, the question of totality without exception and without traces of the previous state can never arise, since even when the new quality appears in the course of development, it appears while elements of the old and elements of the new are both present; the new is defined as the *dominant characteristic,* as what is basic. The change in this basic factor *already* means a change in quality, regardless of whether the traces of the previous conditions are *already* completely eliminated. Consequently, socialism, with its "traces," is *already* a classless society, communism, and not a transition to communism.

This Marxian conception of the transition period was supplemented by Lenin, who defined state capitalism (under Soviet rule!) as a transitional phase of the organization of social production, in the direction of socialism. How Lenin conceived of that state capitalism, which would be the economic aspect of the transition period just as the dictatorship of the proletariat was the political aspect, will be seen from some statements by him, cited below.

In polemicizing with Bukharin at the session of the All-Union Central Executive Committee, April 29, 1918, Lenin said: "Bukharin says that there cannot be state capitalism under Soviet authority. This is obvious nonsense. There is a whole series of enterprises and institutes that are under Soviet authority and belong to the state, which itself shows the transition from capitalism to socialism. . . . We cannot help raising the question of state capitalism and socialism, of how to behave in the transition period — here, with a Soviet authority we have a bit of capitalism and a bit of socialism existing together" [Vol. 27: 275].

Three years later, in an article "On the Tax in Kind," Lenin wrote: "The more we are unable to achieve a direct transition from small production to socialism, the more capitalism is inevitable in a certain measure as a spontaneous product of small production and trade, and the more we are obliged to use capitalism (specifically directing it along the tracks of state capitalism) as an intervening link between small production and socialism, as a means, a path, a manner . . . of increasing production forces" [8: 700-701]. In the same year, Lenin said that "private interest, private interestedness, economic calculation" must "be employed at first as an essential bridge, leading, in the lands of small peasants, through state capitalism to socialism" [8: 736].

It is characteristic that these statements by Lenin, in which he supplements Marx's conception of the transition period and makes it more concrete, come in the period *after* the October revolution. He makes the same point to us in his report at the 11th Congress of the RKP(b) in 1922: " . . . there (in the old books – B.H.) we can read about the state capitalism that occurs in capitalism, but there is not a single book about state capitalism that comes with communism. Not even Marx remembered to write a word on this and he died without leaving one precise quotation or instruction.... That is why we must now find our own way" [8: 765].

By that time even Bukharin had become aware of the possibility of the formation of state capitalism – and with it, class exploitation – under the Soviet power. The following excerpt is highly illustrative:

"Of great importance is the question of the *transition period* from capitalism to socialism, i.e., the period of the dictatorship of the proletariat. The working class, at the moment of its victory, is not a uniform mass. . . . It wins at a time when production has declined and the material insecurity of the broad masses has increased. This cannot but lead to the appearance of a *tendency* to 'degeneration,' that is, the formation of a managerial stratum in the form of a rudimentary class" [12: 182].

Bukharin expected that this tendency toward restoration of class society would be paralyzed by the growth of the production forces and the abolition of the monopoly of education. What happened, however, was that the bureaucracy consolidated itself much more quickly than the forces developed that could be able to control it or prevent its formation. Eight years later, in 1930, the well-known Soviet revolutionary, K. Rakovskii (who soon perished in the Stalin purges), could only observe:

"From a proletarian state – with bureaucratic deformations, as Lenin defined the political form of our state . . . – we are developing into a bureaucratic state – with proletarian-communist remnants. Before our eyes a large ruling class has been, and is still, developing which has its own internal subdivisions that constantly grow and multiply by co-opting those interested, and with the aid of direct and indirect appointments. . . . As the foundation of these original classes, there is also original private ownership, that is, ownership by the state authorities"[12: 196].

The foregoing citations are also of interest as evidence that prominent Soviet revolutionaries were aware of the danger of the degeneration of the dictatorship of the proletariat into a dictatorship over the proletariat, the danger of perpetuation of class society. They tried to fight against the danger, but were not successful. The pressures from an undeveloped economy and, corresponding to that, an undeveloped social consciousness were too great. The huge steamroller of objectively conditioned statism overcame the subjective forces that tried to control it.

The Transition Period and State Capitalism

Our survey could be ended here. History shows that state capitalism is in fact the "best material preparation for socialism ... the step ι on the staircase of history between which and the step called socialism . . . there are no intermediate steps" [Lenin,5,Vol.25:533]. And that is why countries that have carried out the revolution before they have passed through that stage go through the phase of "state capitalism under communism." On the other hand, countries that have passed through or are arriving at complete "state capitalism under capitalism" (at present, the most developed capitalist countries) have already gone through their "transition period" before the revolution and, under their capitalist shell, show many features of the future socialist society. In the first case, the political revolution precedes the economic revolution; in the second, economic evolution precedes the political. Characteristic of both phases is that the two components needed for the design of socialism *are* *not* co-existent. Accordingly, it is probably better, in both cases, not to speak of a transition period, but of the development of an auxiliary intersystem, state capitalism, etatism. However, in the event that a country has simultaneously attained the requisite economic and political maturity, it can in a relatively short time − certainly within the lifetime of a single generation − carry out simultaneously the political and economic transformation of the former capitalist system into the socialist system; and in that case we can speak of a transition period. I think it can be said that the postrevolutionary development of Yugoslavia is a classic instance of the transition period.

The test for distinguishing between state capitalism and Marx's transition period consists in the establishment of the process of the withering away of the state. Insofar as a given social structure develops in the direction of state capitalism, it is impossible, of course, to speak of the withering away of the state; on the contrary, the state grows stronger and penetrates every pore of social life. State capitalism, like every class system, has its ruling class. This is the bureaucracy. In our analysis of the origin of bureaucracy, we saw that the state bureaucracy is never confined only to the official apparatus. This is and was the basic weakness of Weber's analysis. Bureaucracy is always class-tinged; the officials are always *someone's* officials. In fully developed state capitalism, two otherwise diverse groups — the professional politicians, who are the bearers of power, and the officials — merge completely to form a single bureaucracy. This is the well-known process of the fusing of the state and party apparatus into a single total bureaucratic monopoly.

State capitalism, even if not in its extreme forms, seems to be a necessary stage in the development of social systems. For this reason the pioneer socialist revolutions (and capitalist evolution) ended up in that system, and only countries that appeared later — Yugoslavia, for example — had any chance of avoiding it. But state capitalism is not a petrified system. Like liberal capitalism, it bears within it the motor of its own destruction. It is not any new class that will be its grave-digger but the loss of functionality by the bureaucracy as the ruling class, as a result of which it will be simply eliminated or absorbed in the course of development. This fact of evolution was noted by Mihajlo Marković, who concludes in a powerful passage: "The battle of the bureaucracy to retain its privileged status in postcapitalist society creates, at the same time, the conditions for its disappearance. In order to give the illusion of speaking for the progressive forces of society, it converts into the main *purpose* of the revolutionary movement what were the *means* of carrying it out: industrialization, increased productivity, material welfare. But whatever deformations it leads to, it increasingly creates a state of society in which the bureaucracy will lose even the last excuse for its existence" [13: 65].

And after the disappearance of the bureaucracy, on the basis of nonprivate property that has been created, the only possible development is the self-governing society, that is, socialism.

7. DICTATORSHIP OF THE PROLETARIAT

We begin our discussion with the already cited classic statement by Marx in his *Critique of the Gotha Program:* "Between capitalist and communist society lies the period of the revolutionary transformation of the one into the other. There corresponds to this also a political transition period in which the state can be nothing but the *revolutionary dictatorship of the proletariat*" [4: 36].

69

This statement constitutes a condensed restatement of the analysis made by Marx and Engels in *The Communist Manifesto,* from which we take two additional excerpts: "The proletariat will use its political supremacy to wrest, by degrees, all capital from the bourgeoisie. . . . In the beginning this cannot be effected except by means of despotic inroads on the rights of property and on the conditions of bourgeois production.

"When, in the course of development, class distinctions have disappeared and all production has been concentrated in the hands of a vast association of the whole nation, the public power will lose its political character . . . . When the proletariat . . . as a ruling class . . . sweeps away by force the old conditions of production, then it will have swept away, along with these conditions, the conditions for the existence of class antagonisms and classes generally, and will thereby have abolished its own supremacy as a class" [1: 27].

The citations given will recall to us Marx's theory of the dictatorship of the proletariat and the transition period, which may be formulated in the following four propositions.

1. Inasmuch as the destruction of the capitalist system is performed by violence, by a revolution (which seemed most likely to Marx), socialism will not come at once or automatically.

2. The transition period between capitalism and communism, of which socialism is a lower phase, characterizes a distinct type of state.

3. This is the state of the revolutionary dictatorship of the proletariat, which signifies that:

(a) the state represents the class interests of the proletariat, and

(b) it is a revolutionary regime, i.e., it is based on force, on "despotic inroads," on limitation of political liberty.

4. The revolutionary dictatorship of the proletariat is a temporary regime, whose sole purpose is to "abolish the old relations of production" and, thereby, the proletariat as a class with special interests.

In this analytical framework and in our historical context, we can now consider the corresponding section in the *Program of the Yugoslav Communist League:* "Antagonistic forces are not yet sufficiently weakened to cease to be a danger to the existence of socialism. Therefore the working class cannot give up the weapon of its class struggle — the dictatorship of the proletariat and the leading role of the League of Communists of Yugoslavia — in the struggle to overcome the social and material factors which, in various ways, still exert pressure on socialist relations in our reality in the sense of capitalist restoration or bureaucratic state

70

capitalism" [14: 235].

This judgment was made eight years ago, in the period after the first economic and social affirmations of workers' self-government. Eight years are not a long time, but in times of rapid social transformations it is a long enough time to justify a check on that judgment in the light of today's historical situation.

1. First of all, the Cominform antagonisms have been overcome to a certain extent. The socialist countries of Europe, with the exception of Albania, have partly revised their former attitudes.

2. Further, all those countries have for some time been intensively carrying out reforms that have many features of the path we have already followed. Undoubtedly, we have here a historic tendency toward getting closer.

3. The country's general position in foreign policy is favorable. On the internal plane, rapid economic development has led to a considerable rise in the standard of living, which is now *twice as high* as eight years ago.[2]

Economically and politically, the country is more stable than at any time in the past. This was brought out most evidently in the ease with which the political police was abolished. Obviously, the system enjoys *universal* support.

4. Workers' and social self-government has definitively established itself and become the essential originator of social actions in the nation.

On the basis of these four observations, the conclusion must be drawn that the restoration of capitalism in our country today is unthinkable. This does not mean, of course, that the road to socialism presents no obstacles now. On the contrary, development itself creates new obstacles. Bureaucracy is one, and a very dangerous one. But it is *a deformation that arises on a basis of socialism* and has no connection with the former class enemy. Consequently, *the dictatorship of the proletariat is powerless with respect to that danger.* The proletariat is not immune to bureaucratization, for its own state and party may be the vehicles of bureaucratic tendencies, as the experience of various nations shows.

Moreover, even on the theoretical plane it would appear that not everything is in order. The proletariat is the class of wage workers. Do wage workers exist in Yugoslavia today? Obviously not. Accordingly, under present Yugoslav conditions it is historically meaningless to use the term "dictatorship of the proletariat" without qualification.

It would seem that the continuance of the dictatorship of the proletariat is linked to the continuance of the leading role of the

71

Communist League. Such an interpretation is possible, but it is entirely outside the framework of Marxist analysis. But whatever the role of the Communist League may be, it does not consist in preventing a capitalist restoration, for we have already seen that such a possibility has ceased to have any present relevance. Hence, it would be well if the role of the Communist League were defined precisely in the future with reference to the tasks confronting us, and not with reference to the problems we have already solved.

Our conclusion with regard to evaluating the historical situation might be as follows. During the last quarter-century the transition from capitalism to socialism has been made in Yugoslavia. Political power has been won, the "despotic inroads on the right of ownership and on bourgeois relations of production" have been abolished, while "all of production is concentrated in the hands of associated individuals." [3] The dictatorship of the proletariat has completed its historic mission and will have to be replaced by something that we might call "the state of the working people" or "the state of all the people." [4]

The next task is to go a little deeper into the timing of this transition from capitalism to socialism.

8. THREE STAGES OF THE YUGOSLAV SOCIALIST REVOLUTION

It is customary to speak of a single revolution by which the transition is made from capitalism to socialism. But if we make a careful analysis of the last quarter-century of our social evolution, we shall find that we have gone through three revolutionary breaches corresponding to three stages of the revolution; more precisely, the third stage has just begun. Naturally, these revolutions were not entirely unexpected, and the changes proceeded continuously. There is no doubt, however, that there were three "qualitative leaps" in these changes.

The first revolution coincided in the main with the fight for national liberation. It cleared the country of the occupier, smashed the old socioeconomic order, and eliminated the exploiting classes. The enemy in this revolution was clearly defined. Its aims, too, were precise: state socialism of the Soviet type. Corresponding to this, in the political sphere, was a monolithic centralized revolutionary communist party.

Consolidation of this first revolution was suddenly interrupted in 1948 by the Cominform attacks. It turned out that Stalinism and socialism are not identical, and that state socialism, except as a brief transitional stage, is a *contradictio in adjecto.* It was

72

suddenly confirmed that there is no ready-made recipe for establishing socialism, and that we ourselves had to work it out according to our own needs. The enemy was no longer so clearly defined as formerly, but still could be determined fairly easily. They were the agents of Stalinist domination from without and the declared partisans of Stalinism from within; in the given situation, the latter were, objectively, traitors to their country. However, the *immediate* goals were all but clear; it was necessary to make a critical analysis of the entire preceding approach to the construction of socialism. In this process some erroneous actions were taken — for example, the administrative forcing of collectivization.[5] But very soon, on the basis of the revolutionary intuition of the masses, an orientation was made toward all further development, in the form of workers' self-government. The party of that period was a party of transformation. At the Sixth Congress in 1952, the historic decision was made to transform the classical communist party into the League of Communists. The change was a small one at first, but it grew with time. The party continued to be monolithic and not much less centralized than previously. At the base of the formation of a centralized party (and that is one of the contradictions of that period, a contradiction that constantly evoked disagreements and misunderstandings), there was the pledge of thorough and effective decentralization in all other spheres of social life. A system with workers' and social self-government had never been achieved anywhere in the world; there was no experience in back of it, no model, no guide. It was a voyage into the unknown. To eliminate the risks of excesses and chaos, the process had to be led by a well-organized, single, and authoritative political organization. This was the party or the League of Communists of the period of the second revolution.

It is not necessary to stress the fact that the pattern of development described above is an *ex post facto* rationalization. Certainly no one can say that he expected such a development in 1945, let alone in 1941. However, we have to discover the logic of events, even if *ex post facto*, in order to attain the elements of extrapolation for the future. That that logic, in an operative sense, was not discovered at the time is shown by the Fourth Plenum. And precisely for that reason we can take that political event as the beginning of our third revolution. Over a broad area of chains of events, the reform began that is now on the march. As intended, the reform began as *economic,* but rapidly expanded into a very far-reaching sociopolitical reform. The Brioni Plenum is only the most conspicuous political factor in the transformation of the economic reform into one covering society in general.

73

This third and, in all probability, most important of the three stages of the revolution differs essentially from the preceding two. The possible alternatives of subsequent development are highly complex, and it is not clear a priori which are the most desirable. Furthermore, the enemy is not clearly defined as of now. To begin with, it is not a class enemy or foreign domination. At the present time it is our own conservatism, reactionary dogmatism, and bureaucracy that have grown up on our own socialist soil.

Drastic manifestations of these dangers appeared in the abuses of the State Security Agency. Reporting on these abuses to the Skupstina, Avdo Humo stated: "All of its work and working methods were so set up as to contradict self-government and direct democracy in the formation of equality of rights between our nations and nationalities and the affirmation of industrial and social reforms. They disseminated suspicions concerning everything progressive and suspected everyone who did not think as they did. In this way many government agencies and sociopolitical organizations were destroyed, producing helplessness and demoralization, and thereby paralyzing the foci of progressive democratic thought and action."[6] The State Security Agency was set up as an organ of the *socialist* state, with the function of insuring the construction of *socialism*. However, in catering to the safety of the state, the Agency — as Humo's report shows — *undermined socialism*. Its subversive activity had no connection whatsoever with foreign intervention or the prewar bourgeoisie; it was an autochthonous product of *postrevolutionary* evolution. To be sure, the deformations of the State Security Agency were not accidental, nor were they the only ones. They can only be understood as part of a broad complex of social and political events in the nation, which we analyze in detail later.

Antisocialist tendencies and activities did not appear only within the government apparatus, as in the case of the State Security Agency. They were also manifested within the governing political body, within the League of Communists. The general idea of the League was that it was to be a monolithic organization with an undivided will, constructing socialism and, with equal unanimity, fighting against the enemies of socialist construction, who were of course *outside* the League. This conception proved to be defective. The League found itself inside a magic circle of formal unity [E. Kardelj, 16: 430]; conservative tendencies appeared at the summit of the party, with the proclaimed principles divorced from practice [K. Crvenkovski, 16: 238, 245]; the guiding political bodies had reached a crisis [V. Vlahović, 16: 729]; as a result, the confidence of the masses of people in the

74

League of Communists was shaken [Tito, 16: 136]. Such a situation is not arrived at suddenly; it was prepared by inadequate control of the course of events in recent decades. For the present, we shall only anticipate our later analysis and mention some of the most important factors.

From 1950 on, when workers' government was introduced, a fairly continuous line can be drawn of the construction of socialism in our country, a line oriented toward decentralization, self-government, and the affirmation of the human personality. At the outset the greatest emphasis was laid on the economic sphere. From 1958 on, with the introduction of the *Program* of the League of Communists — which, following *The Communist Manifesto,* proclaims the free development of each individual as the precondition of the free development of all — the accent of socialist construction has been placed more and more on the political sphere. At the same time, self-government reforms were intensified. An attempt at economic reform was made in 1961,[7] followed by the new Constitution of 1963; then at the Eighth Congress of the League a year later, with proposals for major reforms within the League, which were defeated,[8] however; in 1965 the 1961 reform was renewed, this time in a more thoroughgoing way,[9] and a year later the Brioni Plenum cleared the way for reorganization of the League. It should be borne in mind that there was a similar coincidence of the revolution with the battle for national liberation, and the process of self-governing construction coincided with the resistance to Cominform intervention. Both coincidences reveal the unity that has been forged in our party for a long time. Even bureaucratically oriented individuals carried out the self-government reforms. But when, after a decade of preparations and consideration, self-government began to show itself fully, foot-dragging and opposition began to appear. And when the self-government reforms of 1958 were intensified, by the logic of events, opposition was shown; *within the League of Communists there was a differentiation into progressive and self-government forces, on the one hand, and conservative, bureaucratic, and even openly counterrevolutionary forces on the other.* The battle was joined.[10] The outcome is known; at the Brioni Plenum, for the first time, it was stated explicitly in a party document: "There are forces in the League of Communists that openly stand for a policy of 'the hard fist,' forces that are trying to establish their rule over the League of Communists and, through it, over the government." Those forces were then defined more clearly as bureaucratic, guild, and monopolistic, even as far as openly counterrevolutionary forces [16: 11].

75

The question arises of how to fight effectively against such enemies, of what political system to employ to eliminate dangers from such enemies in the future. We still need to find the answer. Obviously, the political party of the period we are entering upon must differ radically from the party of the preceding two periods. It is no longer a party fighting to build socialism in a *nonsocialist* environment. It is a party (to give it that name conditionally) that, in a socialist environment, is fighting for the full assertion of socialism, and against all sorts of deformations and deviations. In this sense the liquidation of the political police at the Brioni Plenum symbolically represents the close of an epoch of presocialist development.

It is on this foundation that the general approach to the problems of Yugoslav society rests. We now proceed to a detailed analysis of each of the three aspects of that society: economic, social (in the strict sense), and political.

FOOTNOTES

1. That is the term Engels uses. In his letter to Turati dated Feb. 6, 1892, Engels says, in connection with this question: "How will this economic revolution end? That will depend on the conditions under which our party takes over power, on the time and the manner in which this is achieved" [7: 134].

2. It is worth spending a little time to consider just what this observation means. Decades, not to speak of centuries, passed until the country attained a social product of about 340 dollars per capita, which still left it in the group of underdeveloped nations. Now, in only eight years, the income has risen to about 650 dollars (in 1965 prices) and industry has assumed the characteristics of a moderately developed industry. Yugoslavia is today much more developed than the most developed countries in the time when Marx and Engels lived. Many will doubtless be greatly surprised to learn that the degree of industrial development in Yugoslavia approaches that of prewar France, that in some regions it has reached the level of France before the war, and that in Slovenia it has gone noticeably beyond it. According to the calculations of S. Stajić, the social product per capita was 650 dollars in Yugoslavia in 1966, and 880 dollars in France in 1938 (1965 prices). Some data on agricultural and industrial production will illustrate this fact more clearly:

	France		Yugoslavia
	1938		1965
	Actual	Comparative	
Electricity, billion kwh	20.8	9.9	15.5
Steel, million tons	6.2	3.0	1.8
Cement, million tons	4.1	2.0	4.0
Grain, million tons	17.7	8.4	10.6

The data in the second column for France have been reduced by a factor of 2.11, in proportion to the number of inhabitants, in order to make possible a direct comparison with Yugoslav data *(SGJ-1966* and *Statistical Yearbook of UN,* 1951). We could also point out that, as regards production, Yugoslavia is now where Italy and Austria were ten years ago.

3. It might appear at first glance that the individual production by farmers and craftsmen contradicts this. Actually, this is not so; no "alien" element is involved. See Section 15.

4. Once terms have become a part of daily usage, there is great psychological resistance to changing them, even when the contents they signify have changed in reality. People continue to *use the same terms,* but *have in mind* a completely *different content.* Thus, an attentive examination of the language of our daily press, inadequately critical articles by writers, and speeches by political personalities shows that three key terms have taken on new content: by the *working class* they mean all working people who are objectively or subjectively interested in the construction of socialist society in Yugoslavia, namely, the overwhelming majority of the population; the *class enemy* is the enemy of the construction of socialism, to wit, political emigres and bureaucratic and declassed elements in the country; the *dictatorship of the proletariat* is the state of the working class as defined above. It follows from these definitions that a one-class system has been created in our nation. That this is a contradiction in terms, and that the dictatorship of the proletariat is inconsistent with socialism within the framework of the Marxian system of thought, are logical difficulties that disappear in the face of the psychological equilibrium they give rise to.

5. In January 1949 the Second Plenum of the Central Committee of the Yugoslav Communist Party adopted a resolution that the center of gravity should be placed on the formation of rural labor cooperatives, and that this should be done with the utmost boldness and in a short time. Despite the Soviet experience, it was expected that this would result in increased agricultural production; it was regarded as the road to building socialism in the villages; and it was intended as a demonstration to the authors of the Resolution of the Informburo that they were wrong in saying that Yugoslav Communists did not intend to carry out collectivization [18: 473]. The harmful effects of this course soon became manifest, and it was radically revised early in 1953. "The criticism of practice," V. Bakarić observed ten years later, "was faster than our theoretical criticism" [19: 10].

6. *Borba,* December 10, 1966. The State Security Agency acted with particular destructiveness in Kosovo and Metohija. The report on the responsibility of the members of the provincial committee there states: " . . . the security agency . . . had . . . a negative attitude toward the life and cadres of Serbian and Montenegran nationality, who . . . were shadowed, slandered, and mistreated, and had police records opened on them, *especially in the case of people with progressive attitudes and ideas" (Borba,* October 14, 1966; my emphasis — B.H.).

7. By and large, this reform was unsuccessful, partly due to political opposition, but for the most part due to ignorance of and failure to realize the operation of the mechanism of a decentralized economy, so that the reform was inadequately prepared and badly executed. Cf. [17]. Failure of the reform led to repeated abandonment of the five-year plan and (a consequence that is often overlooked) to serious political complications.

8. K. Crvenkovski (to cite an authoritative witness) brings out the fact that in the course of the preparations for the Eighth Congress, there was "very sharp and, to a great extent, justified criticism, mainly of the work of the Central Committee of the League of Communists. In connection with the planned standards for the Statutes of the League . . . these criticisms were taken into account, but not fully. But later, as the time for the Congress drew near, other tendencies and other forces in the League of Communists began to be expressed, so that the platform of greater democracy within the League and the conception of its role in the next period have been cut down to a minimum." Crvenkovski goes on to say that principles are proclaimed in party documents, but something quite different is practiced, and concludes: "Needless to say, this condition can hardly be ascribed only to the manifestation of a conservative conception at the summit, although that conception and that opposition cannot be underestimated. It was powerful and influential. Because of this opposition, the summit could not be reorganized, and that had its effect subsequently. But conservatism has also penetrated the hierarchically constituted organization, and has made it impossible for the base to counteract those tendencies at the top" [16: 238].

9. But still with inadequate knowledge of economics, resulting in a sharp drop in the growth of production, and in 1967 to stagnation, which could not but evoke political complications.

10. "The battle could not but be sharp," V. Vlahović observes, "between the forces that demanded that working people should be kept as far as possible from the arena of decision, that they should be reduced to the status of clientele . . . and the forces that demanded far-reaching changes, beginning with the methods of forming governing agencies and guiding political life, down to explicit consideration of the essence of political leadership in the system of self-government" [16: 729].

REFERENCES

[1]   K. Marx and F. Engels, *Selected Works,* Vol. I, OGIZ, Moscow, 1948.
[2]   *Ibid.,* Vol. II.
[3]   K. Marx and F. Engels, *Selected Writings,* OGIZ, Moscow, 1948.
[4]   K. Marx, *Critique of the   Gotha Program,* Kultura, Zagreb, 1948.
[5]   V. I. Lenin, *Works,* 4th edition.
[6]   V. I. Lenin, *Marx, Engels, Marxism,* OGIZ, Moscow, 1946.
[7]   *Second International,* Rad, Belgrade, 1951.
[8]   V. I. Lenin, *Selected Works in Two Volumes,* 4th edition, Vol. II, OGIZ, Moscow, 1946.
[9]   B. Kidrič, "Thesis on the Economics of the Transition Period in Our Country," *Kommunist,* 1950, No. 6.
[10]   F. Engels, *Anti-Dühring,* Naprijed, Zagreb, 1946.
[11]   V. Stanovčić and A. Stojanovic, *Bureaucracy and Technocracy,* Book II, Sedma sila, Belgrade, 1966.
[12]   *Ibid.,* Book I.
[13]   M. Marković, "Socialism and Self-Management," in *Ideas and Perspectives of Socialism,* Praxis, Zagreb, 1965.
[14]   *Program of the League of Communists of Yugoslavia,* Kultura, Belgrade, 1958.
[15]   Lj. Tadić, "Current Theoretical Problems of the Communist Party," in *Marx and the Present Day,* Book II, IDN, Belgrade, 1964.
[16]   *League of Communists of Yugoslavia Under Self-Management,* edited by M. Nikolić, collected texts, Kultura, Belgrade, 1967.
[17]   B. Horvat, *Economic Science and the National Economy,* Naprijed, Zagreb, 1968.
[18]   R. Čolaković *et al., Review of the History of the League of Communists of Yugoslavia,* Institute for the Study of the Workers' Movement, Belgrade, 1963.
[19]   V. Bakarić, *On Agriculture and Problems of the Village,* Kultura, Belgrade, 1960.

CHAPTER III

Economic Organization

How should socialist industry be organized? Two organizational principles are in contradiction: centralization and decentralization. Discussion on these principles, which has been under way for a long time in our country, has recently begun in the other socialist countries of Europe as well. In a broader sense, a permanent discussion is in process within every social organization. Centralization and decentralization interpenetrate one another and have very diverse aspects; the apparent simplicity of the terms is deceptive. An obvious historical comparison is enough to bring out this fact. Under feudalism, for example, there was the strictest centralization for the fiefs of the feudal lords, and extreme decentralization and looseness in the economy of a country as a whole. Capitalist development completely reversed these relationships. The feudal centralisms were broken up and replaced by individualism, which found its characteristic expression in industry in the form of free competition. However, this individualism led, by way of the market, to strong concentration of production within national boundaries, and then more and more to worldwide industrial integration.

But the decentralization of liberal capitalism did not prove to be a permanent organizational form. Free competition leads spontaneously and steadily to the concentration and centralization of capital, and subsequently to extremely centralized industrial structures — monopolies. Society then protects itself from monopoly by the total centralization of industrial functions in the hands of the state.

The question arises: what kind of directions in development can be expected in a planned socialist economy? The answers to this question have been fairly uniform: centralistic. Socialists have explained the superiority of centralism by the economic efficacy of a centralized planned economy. The opponents of socialism have pointed to centralization as the disadvantage of socialism, since it denies the personality.

The differences between the socialist and the nonsocialist, accordingly, appeared in the realm of interpretation and values. From the point of view of economic facts, the agreement was practically total. The reasoning goes somewhat as follows. Autonomous economic units and free competition in the market lead to business cycles. The further the economy develops, the more complicated it is; and the more complicated it is, the worse the crises and the greater the need for state intervention. In order completely to avoid economic fluctuations, centralized planning has to be introduced. After the installation of a central plan, each economic unit is assigned production tasks on just about the same basis as integrated enterprises working on a program set up by the head office of some trust. The economy is viewed as a single enormous enterprise, and management of the economy as replacing the administrative functions of the enterprise.

When a planning system of this kind was introduced in the Soviet Union after the October Revolution, it was by and large taken by both the Left and the Right as something that was to be expected. And until the present, in fact, it remains one of the very few basic questions on which socialist and nonsocialist economists agree. There are two pure systems: capitalism, with private ownership, the market, and free competition; and socialism, with state ownership, planning, and central determination of the productive goals of economic units. In the last two decades various sorts of mixtures of these pure components have appeared. In the mixed systems there is, to a greater or lesser degree, state intervention (nationalization, universal social insurance, etc.) in the sphere of capitalist economic relationships, with the purpose of bringing about the "welfare state."

Of the three types of economy cited, we are interested only in the socialist type here and, within that framework, only in the question of the nature of planning. In discussions of this question, reference is frequently made to propositions from the classics of Marxism. Accordingly, it will be worthwhile to begin by adducing sections from the works of Marx and Engels relating to the point under discussion.

9. MARX AND ENGELS ON SOCIALIST ECONOMY

First Group of Propositions

We know that Marx and Engels firmly avoided giving any systematic descriptions of socialist economy. They felt (indeed correctly) that any attempts to answer the question at that time would be unscientific, utopian, "constructed after the manner of Hegel" [1: 421]. Their major works contain only isolated fragments relating to the question of socialist planning, which give only the most general of statements. It is characteristic, in addition, that the most extensive fragments occur in two explicitly polemic works, *Critique of the Gotha Program* and *Anti-Dühring*, indicating that the authors were led to the discussion by the theoretical mistakes of others, and not because they wanted to develop any definite theses. These limitations on the quotation and interpretation of citations are not always adequately taken into account.

In his "Basic Manifesto" of the First International, Marx contrasted capitalist and socialist economy in the most general of terms: ". . . the great dispute between the blind rule of the law of supply and demand, which comprises bourgeois economic policy, and social production directed by social planning, which is the essence of the economic policy of the working class" [2: 52].

At the same time, the capitalist economy prepares the way for the socialist economy, and this idea is developed by Engels:

"In trusts, freedom of competition changes into its opposite — monopoly; while the unplanned production of capitalist society capitulates before the planned production of socialist society . . . . With or without trusts, the official representative of capitalist society, the state, will ultimately have to undertake the direction of production . . . . The modern state, no matter what its form, is essentially a capitalist machine . . . the ideal total capitalist. The more it takes over of productive forces, the more it becomes the total capitalist. . . . Capitalist relations are not eliminated; they are rather brought to a head. But, brought to a head, they topple over. State ownership of productive forces is not the solution, but it conceals within itself the technical conditions, the key to the solution. This solution can only consist in the practical recognition of the social nature of modern forces of production, and therefore in harmonizing methods of production, appropriation, and trade with the socialized character of the means of production. And this can be achieved only by society openly and directly taking possession of the means of production that have outgrown all control except that of society itself" [3: 291-293].

Engels defines the meaning of this social appropriation a little more closely:

"With the seizing of the means of production by society, the *production of commodities* and, simultaneously, the mastery of the producer by the product *are abolished* (my emphasis – B.H.). Anarchy in social production is replaced by conscious organization" [3: 298].

This also determines the principles of distribution:

"With the final recognition of the real nature of the productive forces of today, social anarchy in production gives place to a social and planned regulation of production according to the needs of the community and of each individual. Then the capitalist mode of appropriation, in which the product enslaves first the producer and then the appropriator, is replaced by a method of appropriation of the product based upon the nature of modern means of production: on the one hand, direct social appropriation as the means of maintaining and expanding production; and on the other, direct individual appropriation as the means of subsistence and enjoyment" [3: 294].

It follows that the market and the category of value will be abolished and, with them, commodity production:

"The only value recognized by the economy is the value of goods. What are goods? Products made in a society of more or less isolated private producers, therefore, primarily private products" [3: 323].

Marx expresses the idea that exchange value is a form of appearance of the proportional distribution of social labor in the system of private exchange of individual products of labor [4]. If it is desired to avoid the anarchy of the commodity market, there must be direct control of the allocation of social labor:

"In fact, no form of society can prevent the regulation of production, one way or another, by the available working time. But, so long as this regulation is not carried out through direct conscious control over working time – which is possible only with common property – but rather through the movement of prices and goods, it remains what you quite correctly said in the German-French year books" [18:11].

In line with this, there is the following passage in *Capital:*

"In socialist society, monetary capital declines. Society distributes the labor force and means of production to the various branches of the economy. Insofar as I am concerned, the producers can receive paper vouchers for which they can obtain from the consumer reserves of society a quantity corresponding to their work time. These vouchers are not money. They do not circulate"[5a: 311].

When there is no market, there is no need for money either. But it is necessary and possible to exercise control over the proportions of expenditure of social labor time.

". . . after the abolition of the capitalistic method of production, while maintaining social production, specific values remain predominant, because the regulation of working hours and the distribution of social work among the various groups of producers and, finally, the bookkeeping become more important than ever" [5: 786].

The same thought is repeated in the *Critique of the Gotha Program:*

"Within the collective, on commonly owned means of production based on society, the producers do not exchange their products; nor does work spent on production appear here as the value of these products, as material property owned by them, because now, contrary to capitalist society, individual work becomes not indirectly but directly the component part of the entire work" [6: 15].

Then follows the well-known statement of the principle of distribution according to labor, including the following:

"Consequently, the individual producer gets back from society — after deductions — exactly what he has given. . . . He gets a certificate from society that he has done such and such an amount of work ... . With this certificate he receives from the public store of consumer goods a corresponding quantity of goods" [6:16].

These considerations have given rise to a violent polemic among socialist economists as to the existence or nonexistence of commodity production under socialism. These polemics, like Stalin's solution of the "transformation" of the law of value, are sufficiently familiar for me not to dwell on.

Engels conceives the process of social planning as follows:

"As soon as society takes over the means of production and uses them for production as direct socialization — all work . . . becomes in advance direct social work. The quantity of social work in some products does not now have to be established in roundabout ways; daily experience shows on the average the amount of work that is necessary. Society, therefore, cannot arbitrarily decide that the amount of work necessary for some products, which is now directly and precisely known, shall continue to be expressed in some merely relative, uncertain, inadequate measure which was formerly unavoidable as a necessary expedient . . . instead of in its natural, adequate, absolute measure of *work time* (Engels' emphasis). . . . The beneficial effect of the various consumer goods, compared with the amount of work required for their manufacture, will finally determine this plan (production). People will then complete everything very simply, without the intervention of the famous 'values' " [3: 326-327].

We can now give the conclusion of a previously interrupted statement by Engels:

"Anarchy in social production is replaced by systematic, definite organization. The struggle for individual existence disappears. Then, for the first time, man, in a certain sense, is finally marked off from the rest of the animal kingdom and emerges from mere animal conditions of existence into really human ones. The conditions of life which surround man, and which have hitherto ruled him, now come under the dominion and control of man, who, for the first time, becomes the real conscious lord of Nature, because he has now become master of his own social organization. The laws of his own social action, hitherto standing face to face with man as laws of Nature foreign to and dominating him, will then be used with full understanding and thereby mastered by him. . . . Only then will man himself, more and more consciously, make his own history — only then will the social causes set in motion by him have, in the main and in a constantly growing measure, the results intended by him. It is the ascent of man from the kingdom of necessity to the kingdom of freedom" [3: 298].

This proposition was used by contemporary Soviet economists to formulate the thesis of planning as the (basic) law of development of socialist economy and society.

In planning and carrying out the plan, the question of centralization and decentralization can also be treated as a question of the relationship of authority and autonomy. Discussion of this question was topical even in Engels' time; he devoted a short article to it, from which we cite the following statements:

"Some socialists have recently conducted a crusade against what they call the principle of authority. They believe that it is sufficient to call a certain act authoritarian for it to be condemned. . . . Authority in this sense means the imposition of an alien will upon our will and, on the other hand, authority presupposes subjugation. . . . Examining the economic, industrial, and agricultural relations on which the cited bourgeois society is based, we find that there is a tendency to replace isolated action by combined action. . . . Everywhere combined action, complicated by the process in which one depends on another, takes the place of independent action by individuals. But combined action means organization, and can there be organization without authority?

"Let us take it that the social revolution deposes the capitalists and that workers' authority manages production and the distribution of wealth. Let us take the completely antiauthoritarian view that the country and means of work have become the collective property of the workers who use them. In this case, will authority disappear or simply change its form? Let us see. We shall take, as an example, a cotton mill. Before it is turned into thread, cotton must go through six operations. . . . This must be decided upon by delegates who are at the head of each stage of the work, or it is settled, if that were possible, by a majority of votes. The will of the individual must be subordinate, and that means that the question is settled authoritatively. . . . A desire to destroy authority in a big industry means a desire to destroy the industry itself. . . . Another example: the railroad. Here, too, the cooperation of an enormous number of people is absolutely essential; this cooperation must be realized at precisely determined hours in order to avoid accidents. The first condition is the dominant will, which solves each subordinate question, whether that will is of one delegate or of a committee entrusted with the duty of carrying out the decision of the majority" [8: 580-581].

This might be taken as supporting the conclusion that authoritarian forms of organizing enterprises are inevitable. As we know, this conclusion was actually drawn and was known as the principle of one-man management. And in connection with organization of the economy as a whole, the conclusion might be drawn that centralism was indispensable. In fact, this conclusion was actually drawn, in both theory and practice.

Most of the cited passages are well known; they have often been quoted and have been the subject of many discussions. They have been assembled and arranged in a definite order, and thus give a definite picture of the organization of socialist planned economy. This picture does not seem much different from the organization of planning (including experiments with noncommodity economy) in the Soviet Union over the past several decades, and from our own vision of planned economy up to 1950.

It will be of value now, however, to present a choice of statements from the classics, statements which have been less frequently cited in the past and which illuminate another aspect of social planning.

Second Group of Propositions

What is the meaning of socialism? Undoubtedly it is, as every Marxist will say, the liberation of man from natural and social necessity, the departure from the "kingdom of necessity," the liberation of the alienated individual, and the affirmation of his human integrity.

As a twenty-five-year-old youth, a bourgeois radical[1] democrat at the time, Marx was enthusiastic over the idea of human liberation:

"Man, who would be a spiritual being, a free man — a republican. Petty-bourgeoisie will not be one or the other. . . . What they want is to live and multiply . . . that's what animals want. . . . Man's feeling of his own values, freedom, should be awakened in the breasts of these people. Only this feeling, which disappeared with the Greeks and which with Christianity is lost in the blue sky, can again make of society a community of men for the realization of their greatest aim: a democratic state" [9: 32].

The same thought, in its mature form, appeared several years later in the joint work of Marx and Engels, *The Communist Manifesto*:

"In place of the old bourgeois society, with its classes and class antagonisms, we shall have an association in which the free development of each is the condition for the free development of all" [10: 63].

This central proposition of the basic program of modern socialism was overlooked for some time. Its insistence on the development of the individual as the precondition for the development of society was in too great a contrast with the authoritarian conceptions of socialism, in which the relationship is exactly reversed. This proposition received the prominence it merited in the program of the League of Yugoslav Communists.[2]

In this connection, the key question is of course the relationship to the state. Marx observes:

"Freedom is when the state is transformed from an organ that is dominant over society into an organ that is completely subordinate . . ." [6: 24].

Engels wrote at length about the state. It is worth repeating one of his classic statements:

"When there is no longer any social class to be held in subjection; when class rule, and the individual struggle for existence based upon our present anarchy in production, with the collisions and excesses arising from them, are removed, nothing more remains to be repressed, and a special repressive force, a state, is no longer necessary. The first act by virtue of which the state really constitutes itself the representative of the whole of society — the taking possession of the means of production in the name of society — that is, at the same time, its last independent act as a state. State interference in social relations becomes, in one domain after another, superfluous, and then dies out by itself; the government of persons is replaced by the administration of things and by the conduct of the processes of production" [3: 294-295].

This reasoning, correctly interpreted, is a remarkable model of analysis. However, interpretations are possible, and actually do occur, which contain a dangerous *non sequitur*. "Taking possession of the means of production in the name of society" *potentially* eliminates the "collisions and excessess," but not *necessarily*. "Interference by state authorities in social relations" *may* become unnecessary, but for that additional preconditions have to be realized in addition to the basic one (state-social power). Otherwise, new partial interests can arise and the power of the state, far from being superfluous, can be engaged in protecting them. We know today that this is not an academic possibility. But Marx and Engels realized the danger of bureaucratic structures. They drew important conclusions in this respect from the experience of the Paris Commune.

"The Commune at the very beginning had to acknowledge that the working class, coming into power, could not rule with the old state machinery . . . that it had to secure itself against its own deputies and employees, proclaiming that all of them, without exception, were dispensable at any time" [11: 18].

This proposition was later introduced into our new Constitution, under the name of the principle of rotation. In addition, the Commune meant decentralization:

"The Paris Commune had, of course, to serve as the source for all the large industrial resources of France. As soon as Paris, and other centers, were brought into communal administration, the old centralized authority had to be replaced in the provinces by *self-managing producers* (my emphasis — B.H.)" [11: 62].

Decentralization does not mean particularism:

"The unity of the nation was not to be broken, but, on the contrary, to be organized by the Communal organization. It was to become a reality by the destruction of the state power which claimed to be the embodiment of that unity but which wanted to be independent of, and superior to, the nation itself" [11: 62].

That is the kind of communal system that is being set up in Yugoslavia.

Finally, the position of the worker-producer must also be

defined. Engels gives the following thesis of Marx:

" . . . the worker is free only when he becomes the owner of his own means of production . . ." [12: 351].

Notes and Commentary

The two sets of fragments of statements by Marx and Engels show what a complicated problem it is to interpret them correctly. The interpretation does not depend on the author alone but, probably, just as much on the interpreter. The same words, with the same grammatical meanings, have a different sense in different social situations.[3] This applies particularly to the selection of the relevant statements. Accordingly, it was not our intention, in selecting the passages and commenting on them, to arrive at any absolute truth, but primarily to outline two ways of reasoning — both, incidentally, based on those choices. Starting (grammatically) from Marx, it is possible (in terms of meaning) to arrive at entirely different results. It is very probable that Mao Tse-tung today sincerely believes himself to be the authentic interpreter of Marx's thought, and that many others regard him as just that. And it seems to me more than probable that Stalin and the majority of the delegates at the 16th Congress of the CPSU(b) regarded the following thesis as a masterpiece of Marxist dialectics:

"We are for the withering away of the state. And, at the same time, we are for the strengthening of the dictatorship of the proletariat which is the mightiest and strongest authority of all state authorities that have existed so far. The strongest development of state authority with the aim of preparing conditions for the withering away of the state authority — that is the Marxist formula. Is this 'contradictory'? Yes, it is 'contradictory.' But it is a contradiction of life and it completely reflects Marx's dialectics" [13:127].

This should not lead us into any agnostic relativism. On the contrary, we can say that we *know* that the theses of Stalin and Mao are not Marxist. But that is not the question. The problem is that citations as such are not a useful means of investigation. This applies particularly to citations from the works of Marx, undoubtedly the most difficult and complex author who ever wrote in the field of economics. When it comes to socialist economics, moreover, appealing to the classics is an empty procedure, with one or two exceptions. Since Marx and Engels always refused to erect any system of socialism, such an appeal would be a doubly hypothetical assertion: we know what they would have thought about the economics of socialism had they thought about it.

Nevertheless, every Marxist has to define his own position with regard to Marx's propositions. That is implicit in the concept "Marxist." On that principle, and with the limitations given, I have attempted to make an interpretation, a very crude one, of the fragments in the foregoing two sections. Two facts seem indubitable to me. First, experience has shown that the thesis of the liquidation, by means of planning, of the market, commodities, and money was incorrect. For one thing, this thesis shows a failure to overcome the influence of pre-Marxist utopian socialism; for another, it reflects a revolutionary optimism that greatly abbreviated the temporal and institutional distances to the future. Moreover, not all propositions are of the same theoretical and practical importance. In essence, what characterizes socialism is not the existence or the absence of commodities and money, but the existence or the absence of the free producer, the liberation of human individuality.

Another typical danger in interpretation is the logical fallacy of confusing necessary and sufficient conditions. We illustrate this by the interpretation of a well-known proposition from *The Communist Manifesto:*

"Communism deprives no one of the power to appropriate the products of society; all it does is to deprive him of the power to subjugate the labor of others by such appropriation" [10: 51].

Expropriation of the means of production puts an end to the possibility of exploiting others' labor by *direct* appropriation. From this the conclusion was drawn — for a long time and to this day in some places — that nationalization of the means of production puts an end to exploitation and automatically attains socialism, whose authenticity is measured by the percentage of nationalization. But this is a *non sequitur*. Exploitation cannot be done away with without doing away with private property, but doing away with private property does not mean that exploitation, too, is necessarily done away with. Expropriation is a necessary, not a sufficient, condition for socialism, for the withering away of the state, etc.

It should not be necessary to expand much more on this subject. To seek in Marx for a ready-made solution for socialist economy would not only be fruitless but, from everything we know of him, anti-Marxist. What is more, no system, neither socialist nor any other, should be looked for in Marx. He explicitly warned us against it:

"Techow further pictures to himself that I have constructed a 'system,' although I did exactly the opposite, and in the Manifesto, which was directly intended for workers, I rejected all systems, and put in their place a 'critical study of the conditions, course, and general results of the real social trends.' And such a 'study' can neither be modeled after someone else, nor put together like a 'cartridge belt' " [14: 73-74].

In keeping with his general methodological approach, Marx gave his analytical categories an expressly historical character; they were devoted to analysis of a single, very definite socioeconomic system and as a rule do not apply to analysis of the phenomena of any other institutional system. Consequently, it is un-Marxist to mechanically transfer the categories of *Capital* and to use them as the political economy of socialism. In his last theoretical work, just before his death, Marx ridiculed Wagner, the German economist, for trying to do just that:

"In the opinion of Mr. Wagner, Marx's theory of value is the 'cornerstone of his socialist system.' Since I never worked out a 'socialist system,' this is merely a fantasy of Wagner's . . . *i tutti quanti*" [15: 456].

A little later he ridicules the idea that the theory of value from *Capital* is applicable to socialism:

". . . all this simply leads . . . to the position that in 'Marx's socialist state' the important thing is his theory of value constructed for bourgeois society . . ." [15: 476].

However, even for categories that are correctly applied, in theory it is useless to seek for a definition in Marx, as Engels warns:

"These remarks (P. Fireman, 1892) are based on a misunderstanding that Marx wants to give a definition, and that in Marx one may at all seek a once-and-for-all established definition. Naturally, where things and their mutual relationship are not conceived as a permanent but as a changeable and thoughtful reflection of his ideas, they are also support for change and transformation; they are not compressed into a stiff definition but emerge in their historic or logical process of formation" [16: xxi].

And once again, Engels [4]:

"But all concepts of Marx (*Auffassungsweise*) are not doctrines but methods. They do not provide complete doctrines but starting points for further research and methods for that research."

Finally, it is of interest to cite the testimony of A. Bebel:

"By the way, nobody would reject the expression 'Marxist theory' but Karl Marx himself, if he were alive [17: 339].

One might ask: then what is there left of Marxism? Above all, there is the dialectic method of investigation. Precisely because this method has eliminated the limitations of a system, of rigid definitions of inapplicable concepts, the Marxist principles of investigation are flexible, adaptable, always modern, dialectical. It is not something that can be learned by memorizing citations and formulations from thick books; "it cannot be repeated after somebody." It can be mastered only by "critical study of the conditions and general results of actual social evolution," and certainly not by repeating the words of a teacher, but by repeating — so to speak — an active attitude toward the world in which we act. [5] That attitude is basically and, above all, critical. As the twenty-five-year-old Marx declared:

"If building a future and completing it for all time is not our affair, then it is all the more certain what we should do right now. We are thinking of reckless criticism of everything existing, certainly reckless in that the criticism does not fear its results, and also that it does not fear a conflict with the existing forces" [19: 38].

And that is what the mature man did in his life work, which bore a second title: *Critique of Political Economy*.

Accordingly, Marxist dialectics is incomprehensible to dogmatists, nor is it by any means easy to apply. But it provides us with a relatively simple and reliable criterion for distinguishing Marxists from "Marxists." Arguing by citations, disputing about definitions and construction of systems — these are the characteristics of the people of whom Marx once said: "I only know that I am not a Marxist" [1: 420]. Hence, what remains for us is a critical examination of our Yugoslav reality.

10. SELF-GOVERNMENT

Uniqueness of the Yugoslav Economic System

Up to about 1951, the agencies of the United Nations and other international bodies that made periodic surveys of world economics or of the economies of individual regions had no difficulty in classifying the Yugoslav economy. Yugoslavia was classified, along with the Soviet Union and the other East European countries, as having a planned economy. Later, some fluctuations set in. In both West and East, the Yugoslav economy was excluded from the "Soviet bloc" or the "socialist camp," but where it belonged was not certain. Sometimes the classification was made on a geographical principle, and Yugoslavia was assigned to Western Europe (a bit arbitrarily) or to Southern Europe (rather more accurately). Often, the Yugoslav economy was treated as a group by itself.

These dilemmas of the statistical and economic-analytical agencies of international organizations give us an opportunity to return to the question of the types of present-day economy with which we began. There are two pure types: the private capitalist type with the so-called free market, represented, for example, by the United States, and the centralized planned type with state ownership of the means of production, represented, for example, by the Soviet Union. Along with these are other, intermediate forms, accentuating one or the other component more or less, as is the case with the "welfare economies" of some countries of West Europe where Social Democratic parties are in power.

To which of these three types does the Yugoslav economy belong? It is interesting to note that it has been placed in each of the three, according to the circumstances of the classification and the classifier. The extreme protagonists of private property had little hesitation in stressing the bureaucratic-centralist character of the Yugoslav economy. At the opposite extreme, Chinese-oriented economists likewise did not hesitate to call the Yugoslav economy a capitalist one. Between these extreme groups, whose views are not of any special scientific interest, there are a large number of serious economists who are inclined to place the Yugoslav economy in one of the mixed types, viz., the types in which there is some kind of symbiosis between private initiative and government intervention.

Our thesis on this matter is that none of the three foregoing ideas has a scientific basis. The Yugoslav economy is obviously not a private-capitalist one, because private ownership of the means of production has been abolished. Nor is it a centralized planning type, because economic agents are autonomous in their decisions. Furthermore (and this is of decisive importance), it is not an eclectic mixed economy in which private[6] and state ownership coexist, because both capitalist private property and state ownership have been abolished (viewed as a process that has advanced far enough to have become irreversible). The Yugoslav economic system is not eclectic, but monistic; in all its aspects it is based on a single fundamental principle — social ownership — and this is the source of its unity. It is a type of economy that we could most accurately describe as associationist socialism.

In this context we must now consider the interrelationships of self-government, centralism, and planning.

Horizontal Decentralization

Economic connections are horizontal (on a definite territory, without regard to differences in economic activities) or vertical (according to economic activities, without regard to the territory).

Theoretically, four combinations are possible in the organization of the economy (and of society): (1) horizontal and vertical decentralization; (2) horizontal decentralization and vertical centralization; (3) horizontal centralization and vertical decentralization; and (4) horizontal and vertical centralization.

The first solution corresponds to a free-competition economy with such cantonal elements as we see in Switzerland, for example. The second solution, carried out consistently, is not very likely in practice. It would mean nationalization of branches of the economy, along with local autonomy. The third solution represents a centralized organization of the state, along with free competition of economic units, which is also unlikely in practice in any extreme form. The fourth solution corresponds to centralized planning on the basis of state ownership. It entails this system because vertical organization predetermines horizontal and, hence, total economic (and social) organization. Autonomous economic units are the precondition for territorial autonomy, and the abolition of autonomous economic agents would in all probability lead to bureaucratic centralism in general. This analysis, I suggest, is but an application of the general Marxist analysis, according to which the means of production determine productive relations and the latter determine all other relationships.

In the presocialist epoch, horizontal organization was predominantly political, and vertical organization was predominantly economic. In a socialist society, although emphases will probably continue to remain, the interpenetration of political and economic factors will be enormously greater, and this is a means of identifying and thereby eliminating the political and economic. The Yugoslav solution, like the Swiss one, belongs to the first of the categories named. However, there is a huge difference between the two, which in this context comes down to the fact that a Yugoslav commune practices much more economic intervention than a Swiss canton, and that, on the other hand, Yugoslav producers practice much more direct political intervention (Economic House of the Parliament) than those who control[7] Swiss economic organizations.

With the limitation stated, horizontal decentralization is a known historical phenomenon, and in this context we need not dwell further on it here. Vertical decentralization, in the sense of autonomous economic units, is a product of liberal capitalism. The aspect that interests us, the self-government of the producers, is a product of associationist socialism alone and requires further attention.

Vertical Decentralization

It will probably not be incorrect to say that until recently all Marxists were vertical centralists. The question arises: why? The following explanation seems plausible in the light of what has been said.

In the struggle for power, the decisive role is played by an efficiently organized workers' party. Accordingly, Marxists have always insisted on an organized working class — with a class consciousness of its interests and a class party that is politically organized — while any territorialization of workers' interests, by way of developing elements of self-government in economic units, would necessarily lead, in the framework of the capitalist system, to a weakening of class solidarity and thereby to a decrease in the striking force of the class party.[8] In this sense, Marxists waged a struggle against the anarchists and syndicalists while Marx was still alive and immediately after his death. The correctness of this position was historically confirmed beyond a doubt by the successful proletarian revolutions of the first half of this century. However, it was precisely this that led to intellectual inertia: what was true in the capitalist situation was transferred, mechanically and automatically, to the socialist situation. Until very recently many Marxists (and many non-Marxists)[9] regarded workers' councils as anarcho-syndicalist phenomena against which a bitter fight had to be waged.

Naturally, the statements of Marx and Engels had a great influence on the thinking of later generations of Marxists. Their basic interest lay in the analysis of the political preconditions for a successful proletarian revolution. When the first revolution, the Paris Commune, was accomplished in 1871, Marx's attention was drawn above all to the first political acts of the Commune. In that context, in statements cited earlier, he strongly emphasized the significance of horizontal decentralization. Marx did not leave unnoticed the formation of workers' councils in Paris [11: 65, 70], but neither then nor later did he ascribe any special importance to that.[10] In the sense of our pattern in the preceding section, Marx seems to have leaned toward the second solution: horizontal decentralization and vertical centralization. From this to the double centralization of the fourth solution was not a big step for insufficiently critical partisans.

Here it is important to mention a causal connection that will enable us to answer some questions that arise later in our analysis. Worker self-government was not arrived at for the sake of making vertical decentralization possible. On the contrary, decentralization was a necessary condition for genuine worker self-government.

Worker self-government has been attacked even from the ranks of workers on two different bases: (a) as being utopian and impossible in practice; (b) as injurious to the labor movement. The second judgment may be dismissed as a *non sequitur*; as we have seen, it assumes unconsciously (and quite unjustifiably) that what is harmful in a capitalist situation must be harmful in a socialist situation as well. The first judgment could be contested only theoretically until a few decades ago. Since that time Yugoslav experience has given us irrefutable historical evidence: worker self-government is not only possible in practice (it has been functioning in Yugoslavia for over a decade) but is economically efficient (since it was restored, the Yugoslav economy has reached the highest rate of growth in the world [21]).

At the same time, although worker self-government in its full force was realized for the first time in history in Yugoslavia, it is not something specifically Yugoslav. If an economic or social phenomenon is practically possible, if it passes the test of economic efficiency, and if the historical tendencies for its realization can assert themselves, then from the Marxist point of view it is not only possible but *necessary* as well. In this respect the genesis of worker self-government as a social phenomenon can be called a classic case. This genesis took place in four phases, as was depicted in Section 5.

On Authority

Discussions on autonomy and centralization bring to the fore, today as in Engels' time, the problem of authority. This is an extremely complicated problem which, as we know, goes beyond the bounds of *economic* analysis, but still cannot be passed over, because of its importance. We shall confine ourselves to indicating the basic features of the problem.

Without authority there is no effective organization; without organization there is no efficient economy. Often, however, the mistake is made of assuming that authority is authority, i.e., that there is only one kind of authority. This is a most serious error, leading to completely topsy-turvy conclusions regarding the necessary features of social and economic organization. We believe it necessary to distinguish at least four kinds of authority.[11]

The criterion for defining the first two kinds of authority is the presence or absence of prestige. In a democratically oriented society in the Marxian sense — that is, in a society that is an association of freely developed individuals — there is no basis for giving the prestige of certain individuals or groups more importance than that of other individuals (or groups). Consequently, in a socialist society, as regards prestige, every individual "has only one vote." However, there are social functions that lack prestige (or at least it is not predominant). When we are sick and go to the doctor and he prescribes a certain medicine, in the normal case we cannot dispute his decision. In this case the democratic rule is inapplicable, and we submit meekly to the authority of a specialist. The same sort of thing applies in school, in training for sports, in automobile service, etc. In a developed economy the division of labor is also developed, with professional specialization, and this grows as the economy expands and develops. Hence, the authority of specialists plays a greater and greater role.

This discussion is directly relevant to analysis of the functioning of the institution of worker self-government. The most frequent criticism of that institution is that the "authority" of the leadership is called into question and that this decreases the efficiency of the business. It is true that "authority" is called into question, but what authority? Not the authority of the specialist, but authoritarian decisions in the realm of prestige: arbitrary hiring, firing, and transferring, and, in general, arbitrariness with respect to personal relations; raising and lowering wages; decision of key alternatives in the orientation of the enterprise, etc. If authoritarianism, i.e., arbitrariness, is eliminated in this domain, it can only help the solidarity of the collective and hence the efficiency of control.

What causes difficulty in practice is the absence of any sharp line of demarcation between the decisions of specialists and democratic decisions, the domains of specialist and democratic authority. There is an area in which these two authorities and these two types of decision overlap. However, this is not a difficulty that is specific for this case alone. Nowhere in economics and society are there sharp boundaries, and this has to be taken into account in order to avoid the confusion that arises from identifying these interzones and areas where no overlapping occurs.

The criterion for distinguishing the other two kinds of authority is the presence or the absence of governmental compulsion. This leads us discreetly to an analysis of the problem of the state, a problem that is entirely outside the scope of this discussion. For our purposes it suffices to say that there is a political authority based on compulsion (in the usual sense of the word) and a social authority based on "social pressure," approval or disapproval, affirmation or boycott, etc., i.e., on potential sanctions arising out of life in a social unit. It is a notorious fact that in class societies, and in general in heterogeneous societies, political authority, although strong, is sometimes unable to prevent social explosions. In homogeneous societies the importance of social authority increases.[12]

This second differentiation of types of authority is directly relevant to the problem of centralization and decentralization. A nationalized branch of industry that is run by the state may be formally organized on the same principles as a system of worker self-government. Centralism here — and centralism there. But there is an essential difference. The first case involves a political authority that dictates; the second involves a social authority to which the workers' collectives submit voluntarily because they realize their economic and social interests.

This brings our analysis to the question of the enterprise and its role in an economy of the Yugoslav type or, a little more broadly, in associationist socialism.

11. THE COLLECTIVE AS ENTREPRENEUR

In an economy made up of self-governing bodies, the exercise of managerial functions is not the task of any special class of individuals, but of the collectivity of members of economic organizations, which we shall call *workers' collectives*. Social evaluation and risk-taking (also an aspect of evaluation) are explicitly functions of the collective. Supervision is a two-directional process in which every member of the collective takes part. The remaining function, coordination, is purely technical and as such is left to technical experts, who are themselves members of the collective. On this basis we arrive at the first important conclusion: *the collective is qualified to exercise entrepreneurial functions.*[13]

Coordinating activity is not *in and of itself* a purely technical activity; in other words, it is not independent of social relationships. When supervision is a one-dimensional process, i.e., in the case of bureaucratic supervision, the efficiency of coordination drops. And it is obvious that changes in efficiency are of enormous importance for economic theory. Let us therefore dwell for a moment on a closer view of the problem.

The efficiency of coordination comes down to the problem of centralization as against decentralization. Bureaucratic rule requires strict centralization. And this means (something that von Hayek made skillful use of in his plea for the free capitalist market) that existing and potential resources are dissipated from the mere necessity of not letting the facts be too generally known. For there are kinds of knowledge "which by their nature cannot appear in statistics and for this reason the central authority cannot be presented in statistical form. Statistical data which such central authority would have to use could be obtained only by abstracting the smaller differences between things, by grouping — just as in dealing with resources of the same kind — items that vary in location, quality, and other features, in a way that could be of great significance for a specific decision" [26: 524].

To insure maximum utilization of the resources and members of society, von Hayek proposes to use the functioning of the price mechanism. And undoubtedly, from a certain point of view, the market provides a much more effective communication mechanism than an administrative hierarchy. However, that is only one aspect of the problem; the other two are: (1) coordination of the market choices (in time and space), and (2) communication below the level of the enterprise. If we are effectively to solve the problem of coordination, we must solve it in its entirety.

If other factors remain unchanged, independence in communicating decisions enhances efficiency. In that case it does not signify disunity and disruption of the organization, and hence an uneconomic and anarchic disaggregation. On the contrary, it means maximum labor economy because of the cessation of immediate initiative and immediate responsibility on the part of the immediate performers, workers, and lower supervisors on the enterprise level, and of collectives on the level of the national economy. Administrative control and management are unable to react quickly and successfully to changes and problems arising directly out of work, and this tardiness and crudeness are the general causes of great losses. Within the enterprise, hierarchical relations have a depressing effect on individual performance; they check initiative, undermine the workers' drive, create opposition — in short, lower working efficiency.[14] Accordingly, the initiative and responsibility should be left to those who are in direct contact with the job to be done. Different social arrangements can meet this requirement in varying degrees. The system of worker self-government certainly must be better than any possible alternative in this respect. Compared to private capitalism, the state-capitalist organization has shown marked efficiency, as measured by the degree of growth of production, since it could utilize planning on a national scale. Compared to state capitalism, socialist organization will be more efficient, since it is in a position, by reason of eliminating class antagonisms, to make greater use of available knowledge, as well as of the intellectual and emotional energy of the members of the social unit.[15]

98

Although a collective may be autonomous to a great extent, it cannot of course be *fully* autonomous. In the case of evaluations that involve essential damage to the interests of other collectives, some higher representative body must hand down a decision. This is a very complex and little-investigated problem, but we cannot consider it here. In the matters that concern us primarily, the dependence of the collective will be chiefly technical in nature. The ideal solution would be to separate the regulatory and operative functions, leaving the former to representative agencies while the latter are settled by workers' collectives and their associations. On this basis, supreme coordination, including the social plan, along with the instrumentalities for its execution, would be left to the Skupština.[16] It should be emphasized that coordination will have to be partially accomplished on the spot with the help of specialized government machinery, in which case the regulatory functions gradually go over into operative ones. This interference on the part of the state apparatus may be very prominent in the first days of a new system. But as the process of standardization and institutionalization goes forward, the intervention can be gradually reduced to a basically routine activity. Banks play a special role in this general coordination by combining customary business criteria with the intentions of the social plan. Naturally, the planning agencies provide the enterprise with the relevant data, which become the elements for forming their economic policy. The firms report on their own important decisions, thus enabling the planning agencies to prepare new sets of data wherever required. The social plan, the banks, and the availability of information represent an effective coordination mechanism that enables the economy to function smoothly without central management. The final result of all this is to minimize risks and uncertainties, so that the functions of the enterprise appear in an entirely new light.

In carrying out economic plans, the main task of planning agencies consists in maintaining normal market relationships. Insofar as price fluctuations can be avoided, unwarranted profits and losses will likewise be avoided (the foreign market, of course, presents a serious problem). But to the extent that stability is achieved, *profits and losses of enterprises will depend on the productive efforts of their collectives.*

The next question relates to the distribution of revenue. There is no need whatever for the entire amount of profits earned by a given collective to be distributed uniformly to its members. Part of the profit that is to be distributed to the members of the collective has the function of an incentive. In the general case, we want to maximize the "supply of entrepreneurship," which we attain by institutionalizing a system of distribution that is universally accepted as "fair." Thus, the gross profit is split into two parts: the net profit, which is used as a reward to the members of the collective to stimulate the supply of the productive factor of "entrepreneurship"; and a remainder (if any), which is of the nature of rent, and as such must be absorbed by taxes. When we speak of profit as a price for entrepreneurial services, we mean net profit, i.e., that part of profit left to the free disposal of the collective.

A negative profit, or loss, calls for a similar approach. Within a definite interval it will be regarded as a market penalty for failing to provide the average quantity of "entrepreneurship." In this sense, and treating absolute loss as only a special case of general opportunity loss, the entrepreneurial function of the collective includes the assumption of risk as one of its components, as Knight reminds us somewhere. However, reducing the wage fund below a certain level would hardly appear to be socially permissible. Accordingly, the state, or the commune, will have to intervene and, in the same way that it took a superprofit by means of a tax, it will provide a subsidy for a superloss. It may also happen that some enterprise is not operating profitably, and that the collective was not subjectively responsible for this, so that a permanent subvention will be necessary, or even liquidation. In all these cases the risk is borne by the owner of the capital, i.e., the community; this reflects Schumpeter's example, in which assumption of the risk was excluded from the entrepreneurial function.

We now come to our second and final conclusion. *The collective-entrepreneur is constantly active in the process of technological, commercial, and organizational improvement,* that is, it considers itself as essentially an innovator. The supply of innovations is automatically regulated by the system of material rewards and penalties. Enabling people to follow their material interests, the institution strongly motivates (although, of course, it is not the *only* motivation acting in the same direction) constant increases in efficiency, which result in increased production, and this in turn increases the welfare of the cooperative in general. Analytically, this institution restores a powerful productive factor, a profitable price.

12. CENTRALIZATION

Misguided Polemics on Centralization

Centralization, like every word that is used a great deal, has

100

many semantic aspects that lead to confusion in discussion. Moreover, this term has a certain emotional connotation that increases the confusion still further. Today it is fashionable to be a decentralist, just as a short time ago it was fashionable to be a centralist. As we shall see, there are objective justifications for this. Nevertheless, just as some time ago not every centralization was positive and every decentralization negative, so today not every decentralism is the expression of an advanced position, nor is every centralism the expression of bureaucratic reaction. The naive conceptions of economic decentralization on the principles of liberal capitalism of the middle of the last century (of course, the protagonists of these conceptions were unaware of this doctrinal identity) are just as economically misplaced and politically harmful as was the emphasis on centralist solutions of the Stalinist period.

Very frequently the argument for the advantages of economic centralization takes the following form. The activities of a large number of economic units must be coordinated. This requires a central plan, the execution of which requires a central organ of power, namely, the state. Decentralization makes it impossible for the undeveloped regions of the country to catch up; it opens up a gap between the developed and undeveloped regions. Decentralization of the decisions of autonomous economic agents leads to wasting society's resources. Evidence: unused capacity, duplication of investments in some regions, and inadequate investments in others. Very often the answer to this reasoning is that economic organizations know for themselves what is more profitable for them, and that they will make use of their resources as profitably as possible. Accordingly, planned direction must be avoided because the plan may be faulty, and resources should be decentralized to a maximum in order to avoid faulty central interventions. Dissipation of social resources was much greater in the period of centralization. Evidence: political factories, low labor productivity, uneconomical investments.

Both lines of argument have a kernel of truth and accurate citations so far as statistically measurable phenomena are concerned. But they are also full of ambiguous use of terms and crude *non sequiturs*. Let us examine some of them. The centralist argument contains the need for coordinating economic activities and for a central — i.e., general — social plan. But it does not follow that this plan is obligatory (in the sense of administrative obligation) or that the state has to execute it. Obviously, there is a need for authority, but it does not follow that it must be exclusively a political authority. True, an uncontrolled market economy gives rise to a tendency to polarize the developed and undeveloped regions. But why should we leave such a process uncontrolled when effective instruments for regulating it, fully compatible with decentralization, are known? True, in the decentralization process in our country, there was and still is waste of the resources of society, but that was not and is not the result of decentralization as such, but of: (a) badly conducted decentralization, and (b) inevitable inconsistencies in transferring from one organizational regime to another.

In the decentralist argument, it is true that economic agents are subjectively motivated to exercise the most effective control when they are working with their own resources. But it does not follow that maximum profitability of the individual enterprise is at the same time maximum *social* profitability. The differences may be enormous. While it is true that the social plan cannot be forced on the enterprise and that the state cannot, by administrative measures, derogate from the autonomy of the workers' collective (for that would be the end of workers' self-government), nevertheless it does not follow that we should not insist on striving to achieve the social plan and to insure this by economic (hence, not administrative) means. It is very possible that the social plan may be faulty at the enterprise level[17] but it does not follow that adding up the autonomous plans of enterprises yields the best solution for the economy as a whole. On the contrary, a social plan on the level of the national economy is certainly better than what the individual firms can conceive.

The centralist-decentralist polemic was particularly animated among us in the period between 1961 and 1963. Those were the days of preparation for introducing the new Constitution, when significant reforms were made in the direction of further decentralization and democratization of our economic and social life. It was precisely during this period that there was heated disagreement over the tempo of economic development. Psychologically, it is understandable that this coincidence led a number of economists to another *non sequitur*: if there was a slowing down of growth after the decentralization reforms, then the decentralizations were a brake on economic development. Fortunately, these conclusions did not lead to a change in the course of the country's internal policy. An analysis of the mechanism of the slowdown of 1961-1962, in the so-called *Yellow Book* [23] in mid-1962 and at the Zagreb Congress of Economists in January 1963, showed that the slowdown of growth was due primarily to the following causes: (a) the preceding period of development had left behind it certain disproportions, which weakened the economic structure (stagnation of exports, agriculture, and heavy industry); (b) several radical economic reforms were instituted in this situation (regarding income distribution and the system of credit, banking, and foreign trade); (c) each of these reforms by itself would have been a major additional burden on the economic machine, all the more so in a situation where they were instituted all at once, the negative effects being heightened by the insufficient structural and organizational preparation of the reforms; and (d) there was general economic instability and uncertainty, with firms changing their production programs in the hope that the situation would clear up and economic conditions would stabilize, while the economic machinery wavered and its tempo fell to a half of what it had been. However, after the necessary lessons had been learned with reference to economic policy and adequate measures had been taken, the economy returned to its former developmental trend in 1963 and exceeded it in 1964. Accordingly, after the transitional difficulties had been overcome, decentralization did not hinder economic development; on the contrary, it created the potential preconditions for its being more rapid, in the following period, than it had been before. But it should be added at once that the actualization of these potentialities did not give rise to any data whatsoever to indicate a new delay in economic growth in the years from 1965 to 1967.

Centralization of Initial Economic Construction

In a certain sense the situation in socialist countries after the revolution, with respect to taking power, was like the situation in colonial countries after attaining independence. In both cases the old apparatus of power had to be destroyed and a new one erected. In both cases radical reforms had to be conducted (agrarian reform, nationalization), and, in the socialist case, social reforms as well. And in both cases there was an acute shortage of management cadres on whom the new regimes could rely. In such a situation the idea of decentralization would be a reactionary one, tantamount to liquidating the achievements of the revolution and of national liberation.[18] In such a situation the only correct solution is the strictest political and economic centralization. Centralization means, in this instance, great powers on the part of central government agencies, limitation of local autonomy, direct intervention by the state through economic-administrative measures.

The conditions just described prevailed in Yugoslavia for the first five years after liberation. During that time the agrarian reform was carried out, as well as the first and second nationalizations; ministries and agencies for branches of the economy, and their groupings, were organized; centralized planning was introduced and the first five-year plan put into execution; a new administrative apparatus was set up; and the first foundations were laid for the new social and political system. All this could be accomplished in such a radical fashion and in so short a time only by holding to strict political and economic centralization. That was a time when it was correct, as well as fashionable, to be a centralist.

The duration of the centralist period varies, of course, from one country to another. It depends on the depth of the preceding revolutionary transformation, on the degree of economic and cultural development, and on the international economic-political situation. But the period itself is inevitable and corresponds, in socialist countries, to Marx's well-known period of the dictatorship of the proletariat. The question arises: when the basic transition has been made from one system to the other, in the sense of the initiation of an irreversible developmental process, i.e., when the fundamental institutions of the old system have been crushed and replaced by adequate new institutions, what is to be done then?

Yugoslav practice has given a very definite answer to that question, an answer identical with the vision of Marx and Engels.

Centralization is not a goal but a means. The goal is the enactment of the transition from one system to another. After that transition has been made, a new means must be adopted, adequate to the new goal. This new goal is the construction of a socialist society. Practice in Yugoslavia and in other countries has shown that centralization is a very poor means for realization of that goal. The attempt was made to set up democratic centralism. But the course of development was as follows, without exception: *democratic* centralism, *democratic centralism,* democratic *centralism,* and finally *centralism* itself; this meant a dangerous and false bureaucratic road. What counts is not the good or bad intentions of individual leaders or groups, but the necessary consequences of bureaucratic structures.

Historical experience has shown the two fundamental defects of centralism: political and economic. They condition and penetrate one another. On the political plane, centralism inevitably leads to totalitarian bureaucratization of the social structure and to the well-known Stalinist excesses. In this situation the fundamental Marxist socialist postulate, "the free development of each individual is the condition of the free development of all," becomes incapable of realization. On the economic plane, because

104

of the shackling of individual and local self-initiative and the discouraging of development, the enormous (although latent) emotional and intellectual energies of society lose their efficacy, and the tempo of economic development and, above all, the standard of living of the worker drop below what they could be, objectively, in socialist society. [19]

Along with the new system, therefore, the process of economic and political decentralization must begin. This means the "withering away of the state," namely, the replacement of political authority by social authority, of the state machinery by social self-government. Sad historical experience was needed before this simple truth, which the classics foresaw, could be seen and carried out in practice. Actually, this should not surprise us. Great intellectual and emotional effort and a compact political organization are required to conduct strict centralization of the economy, only to proceed to its liquidation when it has attained its highest point of efficiency. It might be expected that some strong social pressure would be required for such a reversal of the process of social organization.

Centralization of Modern Economy

The seeming paradoxes of the situation are not exhausted by making the observation, as in the preceding section, that the only task of centralization is to prepare decentralization. The paradox is heightened by the fact that this decentralization must mean an efficient centralization. This is the source of fresh misunderstandings in discussions about centralization and decentralization. What is involved?

Of necessity, the nature of technological processes and the organization of production and distribution make the modern economy centralistic. Sismondism was impossible even in the last century, and certainly so today. It is not only the transportation and power systems that must be regulated, as is perfectly clear, but also foreign trade and exchange, the system of the internal market, the allocation of investments, the production of entire branches. If this is not done, the result is business cycles and crises or, at the very least, fluctuations and inflationary spirals. In this respect, nothing is changed by giving an economy the name of socialist. The market is inherently unstable, as Marx showed in his schemes of reproduction, as we can demonstrate by the modern technique of economic modeling, and as is known in practice on the basis of historical experience. Hence, an uncontrolled, decentralized market economy is inherently unstable and subject to business cycles.

The emphasis is on control here; how is it to be achieved? In trying to give an answer, we may again refer to Yugoslav experience.

After the early centralized planning had been increasingly eliminated and economic organizations had been given autonomy, there gradually came to be a loss of connection between the setting of plan goals and their realization. This became particularly obvious in 1961 and 1962. The plan suddenly found itself in a vacuum. The criticisms that at the time were directed at the makers of the plans were to a great extent unfounded. The essential thing is not that the plans were badly drawn up (in the sense of planned balancing of resources and production) or that they were overstrained. The plans were at least as good as in previous years. The essential thing was that the *system* of planning, taken broadly, i.e., as the preparation and *execution* of the plan, had not changed even though the conditions of the economy had changed. The gap between the planning system and the system of doing business was bridged by means of the *Official Gazette* and ad hoc administrative interventions,[20] which of course did not add to the efficiency of doing business. The lack of serious scientific work in this field had very serious consequences. But in the end practice once more came to the rescue. At that very time there began the serious development of a new organizational form, which was to contribute toward renewing the link between the planning and the execution of the plan: economic *integration*.

When *centralism from above* had weakened, it had to be replaced by *centralism from below*. This is the meaning of integrative movements in the Yugoslav economy. Integration is still one of those phenomena that evoke considerable misunderstanding. It is often regarded as a merger of enterprises. But merger is only one of the many possible, and actual, forms taken by integration. Often, integration (and particularly merger) is brought about by political pressure, which is harmful because it is a negation of the essence of integration as a de-politicized centralism. Practice has shown that such forced integrations show poor commercial results. However, if not theoretically, then by experience, the misunderstandings are eliminated and the integration movement leads to new and diversified forms of economic cooperation, whose spectrum begins at one end with a contractual relationship between the central enterprise and the cooperator and ends with fusion, and at the other end comprises the cooperation of two or more enterprises, up to integrative projects on the level of a branch of the economy.[21]

106

Integration is carried out for the purposes of specialization of production, rational distribution of supplies to foreign markets, and joint financing of capital formation. Integrative associations come into being in situations where it is necessary to centralize the taking of economic decisions on a broader base than that of the individual enterprise. On this principle, in contrast to central agencies of economic policy, there is, instead of a large number of individual and separate enterprises, a much smaller number of economic subjects. The economy is no longer atomistic, but acquires a definite organizational structure of its own. The formation of this structure fills the organizational gap between the social plan and the autonomous enterprises. To the extent that integrative processes develop, the need for administrative intervention by government agencies disappears. When these processes are in essence completed, regulatory mechanisms will have been built into the economy that reduce government intervention to a minimum.

The centralism of this system differs radically from the centralism of the system we spoke of earlier, of which, by a concatenation of historical circumstances, people usually think when they speak of centralism. The difference does not lie in the way in which decisions are arrived at; they are arrived at centrally in both cases. The difference does lie in the nature of the authority on which the decisions are based. In the first case, it is the political authority of the state; in the second, it is the social authority of associations of self-governing organizations. In this system, naturally, the system of planning also takes on essentially new features. In fact, the elaboration of this system still lies ahead of us. We discuss this in the final section of this chapter.

Two Dangers

Self-government and decentralization are not the universal panaceas to the problems of socialist construction. Centralism, which was unavoidable at a certain stage of development, contained the potential danger of bureaucratization and decreased efficiency. As we know, this danger did not remain merely potential, but it became actual in a number of countries. Decentralization, which is indispensable in the present phase of development, has its risks as well. We mention two: monopoly and the profiteering mentality.

After worker self-government had been inaugurated in 1950 and the general and principal directorates had been liquidated in the next two years, the decentralization process began in a very simplified and rigid pattern. One of the postulates of this pattern was: one enterprise, one workers' council. Organs of self-government at higher and lower levels were not contemplated. The desire was, on the one hand, to preserve the integrity of the enterprise from being broken up into shops and, on the other, to prevent huge economic organization from making it impossible for genuine worker self-government to function. The latter was in keeping with a second postulate: full competition. Competition was required, on the one hand, in order to put the economic agencies used in the administrative form of management on the road to businesslike independence and initiative, and, on the other hand, in order to avoid the appearance of monopoly. Cooperation was possible only via chambers of commerce; the individual branches of the economy (e.g., oil) held semilegal meetings for the purpose of doing business; trade was strictly separated from production; and only later did the possibility of legal cooperation appear shamefacedly in the ordinance concerning what were called professional associations. The economic arsenal consisted, in practice, of a single weapon: the so-called rate of accumulation and funds. This was roughly the picture in 1952 and 1953. It soon turned out that this rigid and oversimplified scheme had to be made much more flexible and complex. And life itself began to modify it. The organizational forms of self-government were broadened from below, on the level of the shop and the economic unit, as well as from above, on the level of economic formations capable of comprising enterprises located in various parts of the country. In keeping with this, the prohibition of associations yielded place to stimulating them, thereby marking the beginning of the integration process described earlier. The accumulation and funds rate was replaced by a varied and rich arsenal, later enlarged and perfected.

At the same time there is no doubt that, in a market economy, integration means not only increased efficiency but also increased economic power. The latter is what we had in mind in speaking of monopoly. Increased economic power can be used in socially beneficial or in socially harmful directions. Here again it is not good or bad intentions that are involved, but the logic of the situation. Accordingly, automatic correctives must be built into the economy. We already have such correctives: on the one hand, the Yugoslav League of Communists, the trade unions, and public opinion; and, on the other, the commissions of social supervision, the courts of honor, the chambers of commerce, and the price bureau. Whether they are adequate remains to be seen.

Monopolistic abuses do not seem, qualitatively, to be of great importance in the Yugoslav economy today. They appear primarily in the form of running up prices and of pressure on weaker competitors. However, no serious scientific study has yet been made of the problem, and it would be well worthwhile to undertake one as soon as possible.

The second danger is the formation of a profiteering mentality. Obviously, the financial profitability of a business and material stimuli are only means, and not the goal, of socialist construction. The goal is the fullest possible satisfaction of the needs of society. However, an insufficiently controlled insistence on the means may sometimes lead to an interchange of means and goal in the consciousness of people and in their motivations and ambitions. Such a *quid pro quo* would be very harmful, since it would check the formation of *socialist* social relationships and, combined with the negative effects of monopoly, might cause a demand for reinforcement of government intervention, with all its consequences.

The presence of this danger has been the basic criticism of the Yugoslav system made by some of its critics. One of the most interesting of these comes from P. Sweezy [24], the American Marxist. His argument is essentially as follows. The creation of material interestedness and exclusive orientation on market earnings must lead to the formation of a profiteering mentality. Hence, a system of aspirations is set up in society, and these aspirations are obviously not socialist. The evaluation of social desirability in terms of profit is characteristic of a capitalist system. Therefore, when the present generation, which made the revolution, transfers the dominant positions in society to a generation lacking the subjective factor that prevents a restoration, the new generation, brought up in a spirit of market individualism and egoism, will be in no position to resist degeneration toward capitalist social relationships. Sweezy already sees the beginning of the degeneration process in the absence of revolutionary socialist ideals among the youth and in the tendency for everyone to concern himself only with his own personal problems and a comfortable life. To remedy these deformations, Sweezy proposes a considerable reduction in the social esteem accorded to financial success, and the inauguration of nonfinancial forms of incentive, such as competitions, posters, and newspaper articles on the best workers, campaigns based on current political slogans, and, where necessary, government intervention to replace profiteering market regulation of production and in every way to combat the appearance of any kind of monopoly.

Apart from the arbitrary evaluations of Yugoslav

"deformations," Sweezy gives us a prescription we are quite familiar with, which comes down in practice to replacing the free decisions of the producers by bureaucratic orders and to the critical use of one's own thinking by the working out of directives. Certainly Sweezy does not personally desire these consequences; he speaks in favor of the establishment of workers' councils. At the same time, workers' councils are the same kind of foreign body in a government ownership system as they are in a system of private ownership. A workers' council is an institution that fits completely only into a system of social ownership, and it presupposes the degovernmentalization and autonomy of the immediate producers. Sweezy is Marxist enough to see the fundamental difference between the Yugoslav and the capitalist situations, the absence of private ownership. However, this only leads him to deny the Chinese assertions of the existence of capitalism in Yugoslavia, and to replace them by the thesis of capitalist degeneration. It is well to recall here that, according to Marx, capital is not the accumulation of profit (otherwise, the category of capital would exist in every market economy) but *"power* over labor and its products" [7: 167]. Is not autonomous worker self-government the most effective possible antithesis to "power over the labor of others"? And would it not seem that the substitution of government ownership for private ownership would not greatly alter the "power over labor and its products"?

Sweezy's criticism has enabled us to examine certain criticisms that can be made of the system of self-government. This criticism obviously does not hold water and is probably the result of very inadequate knowledge of actual events in our country on the part of the author. But the problem of the negative effects of the market on the ethical domain of socialist society still remains and merits careful and serious study.

Finally, one more remark, for the sake of completeness. All the foregoing analysis is based on Yugoslav experience. In some other country, or at some other time in this country, the historical situation will determine other solutions and conclusions. For example, in a country with a powerful democratic tradition and with labor habits that correspond to an industrialized environment, the stimulating effects of decentralization and the dangers of centralist deformations will perhaps not be as great as in the Yugoslav situation. Similarly, with a rapidly rising social standard of living, economic stimuli will gradually lose their efficacy in the attainment of social goals and will be replaced by noneconomic stimuli. In that situation, both the division of labor and specialization will be much greater, and, along with them, the extent of professional authority. It is likely that at that time central social administration will be able to occupy a much broader field of application without fear of abuse in evaluations or of bureaucratic deformations.

13. PLANNING

Faulty Dichotomies

Certain polemics with respect to the nature of planning in Yugoslavia may be reduced to the following three alternatives:[22]

1. Should a plan be a prognosis or an obligation to act?
2. In the case of planning on different levels, should the relationship be one of equality or subordination?
3. Should the social plan be derived from local and partial plans, or should the latter be derived from fragmentation of a central social plan?

It is evident immediately that these alternatives enter directly into the polemics on decentralization and centralization. Clearly, the first of the alternatives in each of the three pairs will occur in extreme decentralist positions, while the other three alternatives represent postulates of equally extreme centralist views. After what has been said, it will be clear that all these alternatives are *intrinsically* faulty. Instead of the formal-logical dichotomies expressed in "either-or" terms, the orientation has to be on the dialectical solutions that imply "both-and": both obligation and prognosis; both subordination and equality; both upward and downward flow of planning. We comment briefly on these theses.

1. A plan that was not binding on anyone for anything would not be a plan but an intellectual exercise. A plan has to be strictly binding on the agencies of economic policy: economic ministries (or ministries in general, as far as the *social* plan is concerned) and, in a definite, precisely defined sense, banks and chambers of commerce. All these are representative bodies, responsible for carrying out the goals of the plan. From the point of view of autonomous economic organizations, the plan is only a prognosis, and it is all the more probable, the better the planning system is worked out and the higher the professional level of the planning. A plan is also a prognosis in this sense: no one will insist on its performance 100 percent. New circumstances may call for changes in the plan that must then be made in conformity with established procedure, which may not bypass the representative agencies.

2. Equality of rights is a precondition of self-government. If we

111

destroy equality of rights, we should effectually liquidate self-government. This would be acceptance of Sweezy's inconsistent position, of which we spoke previously. On the other hand, this does not mean that *all* subordination must be anathematized. Subordination is a category that follows from authority. Nevertheless, political subordination (in the sense of administrative orders backed by the power of the state) is absolutely unacceptable; social subordination, which takes public opinion into account, is always in order. Likewise, it is not contradictory to emphasize the expert nature of the plans that have been worked out by the best experts in the country, and to give more social weight to the opinions of representative bodies than to individual economic subjects. In a word, insistence on social interests is not incompatible with the inviolability of autonomy. The deciding factor is the way in which this insistence is carried out. At the same time, even the standard administrative subordination is possible within individual state agencies.

3. The social plan is not a mechanical sum of local and partial plans, but it is not independent of them. In working out the social plan, there must be a constant flow of information upward from below, and vice versa, and a joint solution of the problems of real or presumed divergence of interests.

Mechanism of Planning

This is an enormous theme, which goes far beyond our field of vision here. For the present, we can only deal with a few basic factors and formulate them in nine theses.

1. It is of fundamental importance to realize that construction of the plan is not only a *job for experts* but also a *social act.* Both components are of equal importance for the efficacy of planning. As for the component of expertise (should we perhaps say, of science?), this is quite evident. In connection with the social act, one remark is essential. If the plan is to be not only put forward but also carried out, it has to contain motivation for its execution. That means that those engaged in the economy must actively comprehend the intentions of the plan, and at the same time their interests are not in conflict with those intentions. Accordingly, planning presupposes uninterrupted contact with economic subjects, consultation and exchange of ideas, and agreements and joint decisions. Consequently, integrative processes also facilitate planning to a large extent. A plan derived from this kind of work has considerably insured its execution.

2. The realism of a plan constitutes an additional motivation for

its execution. To the extent that the planned predictions fit into the facts (and these predictions need not be only the tasks imposed by law but the elements of documentation backing up the plan), the plan will inspire confidence in those engaged in the economy that what it predicts will actually come to pass. It will then be in their own interest to make a better adjustment to what has been envisaged by the plan.

3. The short-term and long-term aspects of the plan must be distinguished. The difference is that in the first case the capacities are taken as given, since they cannot change essentially, and economic policy concentrates on current production. In the second case, the basic problem is the change in economic capacities, i.e., in the amounts, structure, and allocation of investments.

4. When the capacities are given, effective regulation of production is attained by such customary economic-financial means as credits, interest, rent, quotas, turnover tax, bonuses and subsidies on domestic and foreign trade, foreign exchange parity, guaranteed prices, and government reserves. Where drastic intervention is required, measures of physical control are used: price fixing, import and export quotas, and allocations of materials in short supply. The stability and solidity of the economic system can be evaluated by the degree to which measures of the latter category are absent.

5. As regards economic growth, the question of investments is crucial. It is precisely in this respect that the socialist economy shows a marked superiority over the capitalist economy. Of the three aspects of investment, the one that is technically the easiest to solve is the matter of volume. If the investments are too large, they can be checked by taxation. If they are lower than required, the additional funds needed for financing can be collected from previous items by the most suitable means.

6. It is much more difficult to solve the problems of the optimal structure and allocation of investments. This set of problems has never had a satisfactory solution among us and, in fact, along with income distribution, is the basic subject of all our polemics on the economic system. At one time it was held that practically all investments should be centrally controlled in order to obtain their optimal structure and allocation, with maximal economic development. It was found, on the basis of Yugoslav practice, that it is sufficient to control directly, by various investment funds, about one-third of total investments (less than in France, for example, and it is still not the objectively possible minimum) to achieve an extremely high rate of growth. (We cannot speak of

optima; the reason is not the amount of investments controlled, for 100 percent would not do that, but because we do not know where those optima are.) The explanation is to be sought in the heterogeneity of the investment projects.

There are productive groupings whose minimum capacities are relatively large in relation to the social product of the country. For such projects, the only solution is financing from central funds; similarly, decisions as to the magnitude of capacity, technical procedures, and location have to be made centrally. In order to construct the Djerdap hydroelectric station and the Skopje iron and steel mill, several per cent of the annual product had to be committed, as well as picked teams of engineers and economists. On the other hand, there are productive groupings whose minimum profitable capacities are small (e.g., some units of the metal and lumber industries); in such cases, centralized decisions are out of place.

Some productive groupings are sources of economic development, e.g., the power industry, heavy industry, and, in part, communications and chemicals. In these domains more social intervention is called for. Most productive groupings, however, are heteronomous in nature and adapt to market demands without any great difficulties. This applies to the textile and footwear industries, and by and large to the production of consumer goods, for which gestation periods are short, profits usually high, and minimum profitable capacities not too large. This sector of the economy can take care of its investments itself.

Finally, (macro)location is decisive for the extractive industries and for groups engaged in processing bulk raw materials, for which social control has to be insured. For most productive groupings, the individual investors are adequately competent to insure location.

7. Just as there are means of short-term equalization, there are also means of long-term equalization: shares in investment financing, with which control is further extended to a portion of the resources from decentralized funds as well, favoring investments in industries that are lagging or applying the brakes to those that are overinvesting, doing this by more favorable taxation (in the former case) or by relatively prohibitive taxation of excessive investments (in the latter case). Building permits may be used as a means of physical control.

8. The development of undeveloped regions is a special problem. As a rule, investments in such regions are less profitable than in developed areas (because of the absence of adequate infrastructures, shortages of skilled labor, and the absence of

114

external economies). In a market economy there is therefore a constant tendency to channel investments to developed districts, thereby increasing the gap between the developed and undeveloped areas and disintegrating the national economy. These tendencies are corrected by setting aside certain quantities of society's investment resources under a special system (e.g., the Fund for Undeveloped Regions), to be expended exclusively in undeveloped regions. The means of (7) can also be employed.

9. When we spoke, in the preceding theses, of the need for social control, we did not necessarily imply control on the part of government agencies. In a socialist economy (in fact, the process has already begun under capitalism), banks can also act as organs of social control. In this way the system acquires greater flexibility and the economy is still further degovernmentalized.

Final Notes

Three comments must be made.

The first relates to the fairly frequent confusion concerning obligations and responsibilities. A decentralized economy is not an economy without obligations and responsibilities. On the contrary, these are in principle entirely clear, and they should be so in concrete practice as well. In this connection there is an argument that is instructive. Since the subjects of the economy are autonomous, they are responsible for *all* the consequences of their decisions. If a duplication of capacity takes place somewhere, then the collectives or management are not socially responsible enough and they have to be called on the carpet and brought back to the right path by political methods. If individual incomes are too high somewhere (and if, for example, labor productivity is high and resources are large), then that too is a sign of social irresponsibility and calls for political measures. If dislocations occur in some sector of production, then in all likelihood the producers are guilty. In short (and somewhat in caricature), inadequate consciousness is guilty of its misfortunes. Very close to these ideas is the position of the centralist, according to whom these sorts of dislocations are a *necessary* consequence of decentralization.

There is no need to go into detail on the voluntarism of these explanations in order to show how wrong they are. To be sure, when a system is still unfinished and not yet solid, subjective factors play an extremely important part. Accordingly, it is not only unnecessary to abandon the methods of control, political work, and the like, but, on the contrary, to make maximum use of them. That is one thing, but it is something entirely different to assert absolute responsibility for individual decisions and their consequences.

In principle, one can be responsible only within one's own sphere of competence. The workers' collective of *one enterprise* cannot be responsible for the *Yugoslav economy,* for it is not qualified, nor does it have the possibility of seeing what is best for the economy as a whole. What is expected of a collective is that it make use of existing working conditions to attain the maximum prosperity for its enterprise by legal means and in compliance with definite social standards. If in so doing it arrives at economic dislocations, the workers' collective is not responsible; someone else is. Hence, an individual workers' collective can only be held responsible for its individual errors (or successes). If certain branches work badly (or get extra personal incomes), someone else bears the responsibility. And those other people are the agencies of economic policy and, in the first place, the state apparatus.

The state apparatus is responsible for creating conditions for economic activity so that the normal interests of economic organizations will mesh with social interests, i.e., the normal business activity of economic organizations cannot elicit economic dislocations and waste of social resources. This is an extraordinarily difficult task and an extraordinarily great responsibility; in this respect, the state apparatus is in a much more difficult situation in the Yugoslav economy than under capitalism or in an administratively planned economy. In the former, by definition, the *state* apparatus is not responsible for the activity of *private* producers (although it should be noted that there has been a considerable evolution of ideas in this respect in the so-called welfare economies); in the latter, the hierarchical discipline makes direct intervention possible in cases of dislocation. In our economy, the state apparatus is in an economically paradoxical situation, since it is responsible for the actions of subjects whom it does not control because they are autonomous. The paradox is specious because the impossibility of *administrative, bureaucratic* control does not signify the impossibility of control *in general.* But the problem is that nonadministrative control (although potentially effective) is enormously more complex, and that it requires not only much greater expertise but also a major psychological strain to make an *administrative* apparatus exert *nonadministrative* control.[23] Further theoretical and practical investigations are needed in this field, and it is not impossible that major institutional changes will be made in the future.

116

In a broad sense, an adequate system of information is also a constituent element in economic activity. For economic decisions to be correct, it is not sufficient that the motivation be correct; it is also necessary that those active in the economy *know* accurately what is to their best interest. In this respect the existing system of information is far from adequate, either institutionally (who is competent to give what information, or from whom the given information can be obtained) or technically (keeping in mind the vast unexploited possibilities of modern information techniques).

The final remark relates to the observation of a deleterious disproportion in the present phase of development. All the above-mentioned analysis shows that the Yugoslav type of economy is much more complex than the types we had previously been acquainted with. In addition, it is a new type of economy, for which there is no foreign experience that can be copied. Because of both these reasons, the problems faced by responsible social-political and state agencies are extremely complex and fraught with consequences. Many problems of the present stage of development are still open and unresolved. With further rapid economic development, the problems of planned socialist coordination of society and of the economy will become even more complex. These tasks and problems can be solved effectively only on the basis of scientific research of the highest quality. The socioeconomic machinery is, of course, incomparably more complicated than any kind of mechanism in the field of technology. Yet this complex economy has available only the most primitively organized kind of research in the field of the social sciences, and particularly so in the field of economics. The experience of 1961 and 1962 is a warning that this disproportion is neither academic nor innocuous. And the more complex the economy becomes, the more serious are the potential consequences.

FOOTNOTES

1. For Marx, being radical meant "getting to the root. And the root of a man is the man himself" [25: 81].
2. It would be interesting to analyze how many programs of other socialist parties, which consider themselves Marxist, contain this proposition, and under what conditions it entered into and departed from party programs.
3. For example, Engels' work on authority is probably to be interpreted correctly as a reaction to irresponsible attacks on social discipline rather than as insistence on authoritarian government as compared to self-government.
4. Letter to W. Sombart, March 11, 1895.
5. The extent to which this basic element of Marxism is unknown is illustrated by the following incident at a recent international conference. I had been asked to explain the principles of the planning of the Yugoslav economy. The presentation was oriented toward showing how our institutional solutions result from our practical situation. This "pragmatic," "common-sense" Yugoslav approach obviously pleased

those present, but at the end of the discussion, an American professor, with many apologies and assurances that I did not have to answer if it was not convenient, asked, "What does this have to do with Marxism?" My answer — that for us this was pure Marxism — brought a wave of applause and laughter. It was taken as a triumph of academic humor; but it was the most accurate answer possible.

6. Agriculture and the artisanate each has a specific position, which has not been adequately formulated in theory nor effectively solved in practice. Hence our constant difficulties in these two areas of the economy. In analyzing the nature of the social organization of labor in these two areas, two facts must be taken into account: (a) the process of socialization has not been completed, and (b) the labor of an individual with his own means of production is not capitalistically organized and does not in any way represent a foreign element in a socialist economy based on social ownership. It is probably no oversimplification to say that although state ownership represents the negation of every form of private property, social ownership negates only capitalist private ownership.

7. Those who control — hence, owners and managers; there is no analogy in the Yugoslav social situation.

8. A similar analysis can be made of trade unions.

9. For example, some British trade union leaders.

10. But we need not overlook Engels' interpretation, in the Introduction to *The Civil War in France:* ". . . the most important decree of the Commune ordered the organization of big industries and even of manufacture, an organization that would be founded not only on associated workers in each factory but would unite all these associations in one big federation; in brief, an organization which, as Marx in *Civil War* quite correctly said, must finally lead to communism . . ." [11: 17].

11. It is possible to subdivide the concept of "authority" in other ways as well. For example, Erich Fromm distinguishes rational and irrational, and public and anonymous, authority [22: 108-112].

12. This should not be confused with social conformism, which is an entirely different phenomenon. The ideal socialist society is a union of nonconformist individuals who base their relationships on social authority. It is interesting to note that conformism (as Erich Fromm effectively demonstrates, it is the utmost alienation of the personality [22: 158 ff.]) sometimes claims socialist relationships as a model; it is not worthwhile "sputtering."

13. This conclusion can be illustrated by a statistical picture of the collective-entrepreneur in action under the particular Yugoslav conditions in 1958. In that year the regular daily meetings of the workers' councils contained these typical items in the following proportions: plans of production and investment, expenditures on production and sales, accounts of the executive committee, free use of funds — 40%; working relationships, discipline, economic delicts — 19%; wage rates, standards, and labor productivity, distribution of profit — 17%; social questions and cadres — 13%; miscellaneous — 11% [67: 11]. In 1956 the average net profit made and distributed among the members of the collective was about 10% of the standard wage fund (data from *Statisticki godisnjak FNRJ 1958* [Yugoslav Statistical Yearbook 1958], pp. 105-106).

14. Empirical studies have just begun in this field. What has been done so far shows that labor productivity probably decreases significantly under the customary conditions of autocratic business management as compared to what is possible when workers are able to participate in arriving at decisions that affect their work. The National Institute of Industrial Psychology (NIIP) reports an American experiment in a textile mill, where the differential productivity in this respect had been 54-61 (with the usual management principles) and later reached 76-86 units (with worker participation) [27: 217]. In another American experiment, in a clothing factory, Coch and French found that relative productivity went from about 50 to about 70 units, while "fluctuation and aggression were in inverse proportion to the degree of cooperation" [28: 524]. Mention should be made of the pioneer work, still of general significance today, of K. Lewin and others on the differences among "autocratic," "democratic," and "laissez-faire" leadership [29] (summed up, along with later investigations, in [30]) and of the work of K. Lewin on group decision [31]. Reference may also be made to the well-known Hawthorne experiments. The general significance of these experiments is aptly summed up by R. Bendix: "A controlled observation of small work groups over a number of years showed that increased production on the whole was linked more to moral groups than to any other variable (such as breakfast, higher

pay, variations in development, temperature, etc.). Morale, again, was linked to improved supervision, a prestige position of each member of the group, with increased attention given to individual problems, opinions, and suggestions" [32: 78].

15. The foregoing section is taken in large part from a study of Soviet, American, and Yugoslav organization of the petroleum industry that I made in 1952 for one of our large oil firms [33: 22]. Later I tested these theses by an analysis of the weaknesses of centralization in the Yugoslav economy. In the economic organization of postwar Yugoslavia, two different periods may be distinguished: (1) administrative, marked by strict centralization and ending in 1951; (2) the present arrangement, marked by development of the "free market" and worker self-government, which represents the laboratory conditions for testing the conclusions arrived at above. Unfortunately, no study has yet been made of the economy as a whole. See also the short work by R. Bićanić [34]. I have studied one industry (oil) in detail. I give here some data on labor productivity:

   Centralization of management began, in the main, in 1947; it reached its highpoint in 1950 and, in connection with the establishment of workers' councils, was essentially done away with from 1952 on. Against this general background, labor productivity in the petroleum industry (production and drilling) was: 1941 — 100; 1946 — 74; 1947 — 96; 1948 — 63; 1949 — 70; 1950 — 59; 1951 — 78; 1952 — 111; 1953 — 163 [35: Review 9]. Although these figures do not by any means represent the entire economy, since the oil industry is much more sensitive than other industries and the formula I constructed to measure labor productivity could not completely eliminate the effects of natural conditions, the figures still describe an impressive trend.

16. A similar idea was expressed by Clegg and Chester in discussing the future of British nationalization: "Parliament should decide which functions can and should be carried out in a wider field than individual enterprises, and should do so through a responsible regional and national authority, specifically for this function" [36: 200]. The authors emphasize that ". . . the future of nationalization depends on the discovery and use of resources which will make national ownership and national planning compatible with a detailed conduct of affairs on the spot" [36: 211].

17. For example, if a plan is drawn up for the production of 20,000 products, as happened in Soviet planning practice.

18. Our guests from recently liberated Asian-African countries often encounter great difficulties when, in their desire to get the benefit of Yugoslav experiences in planning, they interview Yugoslav economists and realize that all of it is more or less inapplicable to their countries.

19. This makes the reasoning of the protagonists of centralization naive, when they assure us that improved organization could prevent the waste of resources. The core of the matter is that centralism has a definite bureaucratic logic of its own, which is not to be "improved" in any way. Ceteris paribus, the level of efficiency of a centralized system is necessarily and everywhere lower than what is objectively possible.

20. We might take, as a good index of the degree of decentralization and de-administration, the volume of the annual issues of the Official Gazette and the number of internal instructions of the bank for the year in question.

21. Illustrative in this respect is the twenty-year history of the organization of a typically centralist branch, the oil industry. In 1945 the Petroleum Combine was set up in Zagreb, covering all the production and processing of petroleum in the country. The development of schematized state-economic centralism led in 1947 to a revamping of the Combine and to the formation of general and principal directorates of the federal and republican authorities. The directorates were eliminated in the decentralization process from 1951 to mid-1952, and market independence and competition were inaugurated. The independent firms began at once to make semilegal and legal contacts; various professional and business associations were formed, with various sections, covering the petroleum trade. This trend and tendency led, in early 1964, to the formation in Zagreb of a new Combine, which constituted about two-thirds of the branch (on the territory of the single republic), with the integrative movement continuing in the remainder of the branch. It would seem as though the circle had come around to the starting point of nineteen years earlier. But this is not the case; it is not a circle, but a spiral. The first Combine was founded by the state, even though a revolutionary one; the second Combine was formed by self-governing collectives, even though with some political assistance (although not central). The first and the last points of the spiral are separated by a period of twenty years, during which precious experience was accumulated; this not only improved the organization

119

technically but also, on the basis of definite principles, molded the consciousness of the direct producers as managers. But there are still republic frontiers that have not been overcome, an evident sign that today's integrationist movements are not complete. (After this section had already been written and published, a second Combine for petroleum was established in Voivodina as well.)

22. We owe this systematization to Comrade R. Davidović.
23. It is interesting to note the inherent inclination of administration either to desist from control or to exercise it in a strictly administrative form. This may help explain another apparent paradox, namely, that we hear at one and the same time any number of complaints of excessive decentralization and many complaints that decentralization is not carried far enough. Both are correct, and the explanation is as follows. Actually, "excessive decentralization" refers to absence of coordination that results in disorder, confusion of competence, irresponsibility, and waste. "Insufficient centralization" means the existence of unnecessary obstacles to the exercise of the right to self-government, with similar negative consequences. The procedure for obtaining loans is so complicated, niggardly, and ineffectual that it leads to serious abuses; sometimes months are needed to get approval of trifling amounts of foreign exchange, with the result that it becomes impossible to complete a many-sided operation; some economic actions depend on a number of approvals, and the application wanders from one agency to another, losing a monstrous amount of time; banks are much more administrative agencies than business organizations; etc. To that extent the demands are justified that decentralization be carried out consistently, thereby standardizing the operating conditions for economic organizations.

REFERENCES

[1] Engels' Letter to K. Schmidt, August 5, 1880, in *Selected Writings of Marx and Engels,* OGIZ, Moscow, 1948.
[2] K. Marx, "Basic Manifesto of the International Association of Workers," in *First International,* Rad, Belgrade, 1950.
[3] F. Engels, *Anti-Dühring,* Naprijed, Zagreb, 1946.
[4] Marx's Letter to Kugelmann, July 11, 1868, in *Letters to Kugelmann,* Belgrade, 1951.
[5] K. Marx, *Capital,* Vol. III, Kultura, Zagreb, 1947.
[5a] *Ibid.,* Vol. II.
[6] K. Marx, *Critique of the Gotha Program;* F. Engels, *Critique of the Draft Erfurt Program;* Kultura, Belgrade, 1959.
[7] K. Marx and F. Engels, "Economic and Philosophical Manuscripts," in *Early Works,* Kultura, Zagreb, 1953.
[8] F. Engels, "On Authority," in *Selected Works of Marx and Engels,* Vol. 1, Kultura, Zagreb, 1949.
[9] Marx's Letter to Ruge, 1843, in *Early Works,* Kultura, Zagreb, 1953.
[10] K. Marx and F. Engels, *Manifesto of the Communist Party,* Kultura, Zagreb, 1948.
[11] K. Marx, *The Civil War in France,* Kultura, Zagreb, 1947.
[12] Engels' Letter to E. Bernstein, October 25, 1881, in *Selected Writings.*
[13] Golunski-Strogovič, *Theory of State and Law,* Zagreb, 1947.
[14] K. Marx, *Mr. Vogt,* Kultura, Zagreb, 1955.
[15] K. Marx, "Critique of Adolph Wagner's Book," *Collected Works,* Vol. 15, Partizdat, Moscow, 1935.
[16] F. Engels, "Preface to Volume III of *Capital,*" in Marx's *Capital,* Vol. III, Kultura, Zagreb, 1949.
[17] A. Bebel, "Attacks on the Basic Views and Tactical Standpoints of the Party," *Marxism and Revisionism,* Naprijed, Zagreb, 1958.
[18] Letter from Marx to Engels, January 8, 1868, in K. Marx and F. Engels, *Correspondence,* Vol. IV, Kultura, Belgrade, 1960.
[19] Letter from Marx to Ruge, September 1843, *Early Works of Marx and Engels,* Kultura, Zagreb, 1953.
[20] K. Marx and F. Engels, *Works,* 2nd edition, Moscow.
[21] B. Horvat, *Note on the Rate of Growth of the Yugoslav Economy,* Papers and Monographs No. 4, JIEI, Belgrade.
[22] E. Fromm, *The Sane Society,* Rad, Belgrade, 1963.

[23] *Causes and Characteristics of Economic Trends in 1961 and 1962,* by a group of economists, Savplan, DAM-7, Belgrade, 1962.

[24] "Peaceful Transitions from Socialism to Capitalism," *Monthly Review,* March 1964, pp. 569-590.

[25] K. Marx, "Critique of Hegel's Philosophy of Right," *Early Works of Marx and Engels,* Kultura, Zagreb, 1953.

[26] F. Hayek, "The Use of Knowledge in Society," *American Economic Review,* 1945, pp. 519-530.

[27] *Joint Consultations in British Industry,* National Institute of Industrial Psychology, Staples Press, London, 1952.

[28] L. Coch and J. R. P. French, "Overcoming Resistance to Change," *Human Relations,* 1948.

[29] K. Lewin, R. Lippit, and R. K. White, "Patterns of Aggressive Behavior in Experimentally Created Social Climates," *Journal of Social Psychology,* 1939.

[30] R. Lippit and R. K. White, "An Experimental Study of Leadership and Group Life," in *Readings in Social Psychology,* edited by G. E. Swanson *et al.,* Holt, New York, 1951.

[31] K. Lewin, "Group Decision and Social Change," *ibid.*

[32] R. Bendix, *Higher Civil Servants in American Society,* University of Colorado Press, Boulder, Colo., 1949.

[33] B. Horvat, "The Organization of Enterprises for the Exploitation of Oil in Yugoslavia and Certain Other Countries," *Organization of Labor,* 1952, Nos. 11-12.

[34] R. Bićanić, "Economic Growth Under Centralized and Decentralized Planning: Yugoslavia," in *Economic Development and Cultural Change,* 1957.

[35] B. Horvat, *Economics of the Yugoslav Oil Industry,* doctoral dissertation at Economic Faculty, Zagreb, 1954.

[36] H. A. Clegg and T. E. Chester, *The Future of Nationalisation,* Blackwell, Oxford, 1953.

CHAPTER IV

Productive Labor, Social Property, and the Structure of Yugoslav Society

14. PRODUCTIVE LABOR IN SOCIALIST SOCIETY

It is commonly held that Marx defined productive labor as labor on the production of material goods. This apparently purely academic proposition has quite far-reaching consequences, one of which is that social production defines, both statistically and in conception, only the material part of production. Services are not included, which means that often no serious social accounting is made of them. In a modern economy, however, the number of those employed in the service sector increases faster than the number of those in the material production sector, so that the standard of living, economic stability, etc., depend to an almost decisive extent on what takes place in productive services. Moreover, the term "productive" has a definite emotional content. It is a good thing to be "productive" and it is embarrassing to be "nonproductive." There will even be political theories about "producers" or "direct producers," who are the bearers of the social system and for that reason are automatically progressive, in contrast to the more or less dubious "nonproducers."[1] All this indicates the great theoretical and practical significance of a correct definition of the concept of productive labor. The word "correct" should not be interpreted as meaning "true," for definitions are inherently neither true nor false, but "useful" or "adequate" with respect to a broad theoretical domain in which the concept of productive labor is to have a definite categorical function.

We may state at the outset that materiality as the criterion of productivity has no *theoretical* meaning or justification whatsoever, and that Marx did *not* reduce labor to labor in the field of material production. Not only that, but Marx characterized such a characterization as nonsense from a theoretical point of view. But let us see what is involved.

Marx on Productive Labor

Marx, thoroughgoing as he was in his theoretical thinking, did not concern himself with the unhistorical theory of productive labor *in general*. Nowhere in his voluminous work can there be found an attempt to formulate such an eternally valid theory (there are, to be sure, some general definitions, but they are very rare). He approached the theory of productive labor historically; he was interested in the problem of productive labor only in connection with the economic epoch he was studying and for which he was trying to formulate a comprehensive political economy. That epoch was the epoch of *capitalist* production. His starting point was identical with the standpoint of the typical capitalist entrepreneur. The capitalist is interested in the profitability of his business; he tries to maximize the difference between prices and costs. If this is the typical *behavior* of the typical productive subject in the capitalist system, then that must be adopted as the criterion of the productivity of labor in that system. Labor is productive when it produces surplus value.[2]

What is income from the point of view of society is *gross* income from the capitalist's point of view. What the latter regards as net income corresponds to the income of the community less wages. However, even the community's income, the gross income, "is an abstraction insofar as a society based on capitalist production takes the capitalist position and therefore considers real income only income which is dissolved in profit and rent" [3: 776].

The above two excerpts formulate the essence of Marx's problem. In what follows we discuss, in a more systematic way, some of the more important aspects of that problem. The only place where Marx treats the problem systematically is the chapter on productive labor in the first volume of *Theories of Surplus Value* (a critique of Adam Smith) and in the appendix to that volume (Marx's positive opinions). These two chapters will provide most of the citations required. Since we shall be going against the current here, a certain amount of caution will be required. To avoid the accusation of attributing our own opinions to Marx, we shall confine ourselves to brief commentaries, allowing Marx to speak for himself.

We begin with the well-known and frequently adduced statement in *Capital,* defining the labor process, independent of its historical forms, as a process between man and nature: "If we examine the whole process (of work — B.H.) from the point of view of its result, the *product,* it is plain that both the instruments and the subject of labor are means of production, and that the labor itself is productive labor" [1: 137].

To avoid misunderstandings (which, however, occur constantly), Marx immediately adds the following footnote: "This definition of *productive labor* from the standpoint of the labor process alone is by no means directly applicable to the capitalist process of production" [1: 137].

For the capitalist mode of production a different definition is required, which Marx takes over from Smith.[3] Smith, as often happened with him, really had two incompatible theories. According to the first, which Marx regarded as the correct one,[4] labor is productive when it produces capital. According to the second, the criterion consists of the production of material goods (in contrast to nonproductive labor expended on nonmaterial services). This second definition of Smith's is regarded today as the Marxist definition of the social product. It will hardly surprise any educated economist that Marx, like other economists, criticized the weaknesses of Smith's second definition.

In the system of simple commodity production, the producer exchanges his products for means of subsistence. The capitalist mode of production breaks the bond between labor and ownership of the means of production, and inserts the machinery of *capitalist* production between the exchange of labor and consumption goods. The goods produced may be the same, but the social content of production is now different.

"The result of the process of capitalist production is neither itself a product (use-value) nor goods; it is use-value that has a certain working value. Its result, its product, is the creation of surplus value for capital, and therefore the transformation of money or goods into capital.... Capital achieves this specific product of the process of capitalist production only in exchange for labor, which is therefore called productive labor" [7: 377].

The definition of productive labor follows directly:

"Productive labor, therefore — in the system of capitalist production — is labor that produces surplus value for him who

124

makes use of it, or that transforms the objective conditions of labor into capital and their owner into a capitalist. It is, consequently, labor that produces its own product as capital.

"If we speak of *productive labor,* we are speaking of specific social labor, of labor that presumes a definite relationship between the buyer and the seller of labor" [7: 373-374].

Consequently, *nonproductive* labor is defined by the same criterion as productive labor, which has no connection with nonmaterial services.

If "productive labor is determined as labor *which is directly exchanged for capital,*" it is thus "at the same time absolutely established that *nonproductive labor* is labor that is exchanged not for capital but *directly* for income . . ." [7: 244].

The same conclusion is repeated elsewhere in *Capital*:

"However much the capitalist buys with surplus value for his own consumption, it does not serve him as means of production or to produce value. In the same way, the labor he buys to satisfy his natural and social needs is not *productive labor.* Instead of using the purchase of these goods and labor to convert surplus value into capital, he, on the contrary, uses or *spends* this surplus value as income" [4: 517].

From this point of view it is obviously irrelevant whether labor results in material goods or nonmaterial services:

"It emerges from the above that productive labor first of all has no connection with the specific content of the labor or with its particular use or use-value. The same kind of labor can be either productive or nonproductive" [7: 378].

Thus, e.g., a tailor employed in a tailor shop is a productive worker. "On the other hand, a tailor's assistant (who works in my house) is not a productive worker, although his labor gives me a product, trousers, and he gets the fruit of his labor, money" [7: 379]. And what is the situation with the classic nonproductive workers, e.g., artists? Marx's answer is unequivocal: "A singer, for example, who, at her own risk, sells her singing is a nonproductive worker. But the same singer who is engaged by an entrepreneur to sing at concerts and thus earn money is a productive worker, because she produces capital" [7: 378].

Hence we conclude:

"It is characteristic of all kinds of nonproductive labor that the more I use it — like purchasing all other goods for the purpose of consumption — the more I exploit the productive worker. . . . While, on the other hand, my power to use the productive worker does not increase at all in proportion to my use of the nonproductive worker, but, on the contrary, it decreases in the same proportion" [7: 382].

Marx summed up his theory of productive labor very clearly in another passage of *Capital*. After establishing that the division of labor expands the concept of productive labor, he emphasizes that capitalist production narrows it in a specific manner:

"Capitalist production is not merely *production of goods;* it is in essence *production of surplus value*. The worker does not produce for himself but for capital. It is, therefore, no longer sufficient for him to produce. He must produce surplus value. *The productive worker is only he who produces surplus value for the capitalist, who consequently serves the self-production of capital.* If we take the liberty of choosing an example outside material production, a teacher is a productive worker when he works not only to educate children, but when he works to enrich an employer. This relationship is the same whether the capital is placed in a factory of knowledge or a factory of sausages. Consequently, the concept of the productive worker contains not only the relationship between the activity and its useful effect . . . but also the specific social relationship of production, begun in history . . ." [4: 442].

This, then, is Marx's theory of productive and nonproductive labor. But Marx goes a step further. He is now interested in establishing whether and to what extent Smith's second definition may be regarded as a first *approximation*. If this could be accomplished, his model of the capitalist system could be somewhat simplified without losing any of its essential features. He begins with a generalization of the empirical evidence of his time:

"The law of economic development is such that functions are distributed among various persons, and the craftsman or the peasant who produces his own means of production is gradually transformed into a small capitalist, who also exploits the labor of others, or loses his means of production . . . and becomes a hired worker. This is the trend of the form of society in which capitalist production predominates. In examining the essential relations of capitalist production . . . it can therefore be assumed that . . . all fields of material production — the production of material wealth — is (formally or actually) subordinate to the capitalist mode of production. This supposition, which expresses the limit, and which, therefore, increasingly approaches absolute accuracy, affects all workers employed in production of goods as hired laborers, while the means of production appear to them, in all fields, as capital. In this case it can be considered characteristic for the productive worker, that is, for the worker who produces

126

capital, that his labor produces goods, material wealth. Thus, productive labor, in addition to its *main* feature, *which has no connection with, and is completely independent from, the content of the work,* obtains *a second characteristic, different* from the first" (my emphasis — B.H.) [71: 385].

It remains to be seen whether these tendencies can be seen in the domain of "spiritual" production.

"In nonmaterial production, and when it deals exclusively with exchange, that is, when it produces goods, two things are possible:

"1. It results in goods, in use-values, which have outlines separate and independent from the producer and the consumer, which, therefore, can exist in the period between production and consumption, and which, in that period, can circulate as selling goods, such as, for example, books, pictures — in short, all artistic creations of the artist himself. *Here capitalist production is applied in only a very limited measure* (my emphasis — B.H.). If, for example, a writer for a collective work — say, an encyclopedia — uses many others as assistants . . . .

"2. Production is inseparable from the act of producing when it concerns artists, actors, teachers, doctors, priests, etc. Here, too, the capitalist form of production appears only in some fields . . . . *All these phenomena of capitalist production in these areas are so insignificant, compared with the entire production, that they can be completely ignored"* (my emphasis — B.H.) [7: 386- 387].

The following conclusion emerges. In Marx's thinking, the essential features of the capitalist mode of production can be established by analyzing the production of material goods, which in that system is for the most part organized on a capitalist basis and which constitutes the predominant portion of total production. "The kinds of labor which are not fixed in goods, by their nature, can frequently not be subject to the capitalist mode of production" [7: 279] and are not of major interest for Marx's investigation. In this sense, Marx organized his investigations in *Capital* as well, where he speaks chiefly of commodities, that is, of material products. And that is all.

The Sense of the Revision of Marx's Theory of Productive Labor

Still another interpretation is possible. Marx may have confused matters and not seen that this special theory of his contradicts his philosophical views and his general theory of the development of socioeconomic systems. That is just what is implicitly presupposed by all those authors who deduce the "Marxist" definition of the social product from Marx's philosophical materialism and his theory of the relationship between the *base* and the *superstructure*. As far as philosophical materialism is concerned, it can be said at once that materiality in the philosophical sense (except in vulgar philosophy) is not identical with tangibility, substantiality, which is precisely the criterion of the "materialist" definitions of the social product that appeal to Marx. Consequently, it is inadmissible to link Marxist philosophy with the material content of production. As for the relationship with the theory of the base and the superstructure, the best elaborated version of this doctrine I know of is from the pen of Ia. A. Kronrod, the Soviet economist; it can be judged by some illustrative quotations.

"Social production is the result of material production, the result of productive labor. Production shows the results of human labor, the aim of which is the reproduction of material conditions for the life of society, the appropriation of natural resources that satisfy human needs. But, precisely for this reason, the results of spiritual production do not create products in the economic sense, but are merely a reflection of the process of material life.

". . . confusing material and spiritual production leads to non-Marxist cancellation of the difference between the base and the superstructure, to identification of the results of material production, which creates products, with the results of spiritual production, which reflects the material process of life" [8: 9].

Marx held that the relations of people in production, economic relations, are the most important determinant of the structure of every known society. We speak of feudal, capitalist, etc., societies because of the feudal, capitalist, etc., economic relations in those societies. The ideologies or, more generally, the cultures of those societies reflect their economic bases and as such are superstructures. In every class society the culture is the culture of the ruling, i.e., the owning, class. The propertied class creates its culture either directly, "as spiritual producers," or indirectly, as purchasers. In any event, the owners and those who depend on them live off the work of the unpropertied. All that follows from this extremely simplified presentation of the materialist conception of history is the fundamental sociological distinction between the "economic sphere" and the "ideological sphere" of society. We need only glance at the preface to the *Critique of Political Economy* to see that Marx could not have identified the "mode of production of material life," i.e., the base, with the tangible material production. For him that material base of society was synonymous with the "economic structure." Distinguishing base and superstructure does not provide any criterion for distinguishing between goods and services, which is the basis of the "Marxist" definition of the social product. How are the services of the barber, nurse, and street cleaner to be classified? Should they be included in the base or the superstructure of society? Kronrod seems to be aware of the difficulty and proposes that in such cases "the concrete function of the labor must be analyzed in respect to its productivity" (p. 15), but does not give any guidance as to the way in which this is to be done.

Moreover, neither does the relationship between "material" and "spiritual" production determine the relationship between productive and nonproductive labor. We have seen that, according to Marx's definition, the mental work of the artist or writer, insofar as it is organized on a capitalist basis, is just as productive as the work of a worker, but the labor of a craftsman tailor (in the capitalist system) is nonproductive. If we do not intend to teach Marx what he *should* have thought, we have to take the definition of productiveness in the sense in which he himself used it. But from the previous quotations it is evident that Marx defined productivity in the sense of *capital accumulation,* i.e., in the sense of the social relations existing under the capitalist mode of production. This has no connection whatever with the problem of the relation between base and superstructure, or with the relation between material and nonmaterial production.

After the first inconsistency has been included, others follow. We have seen that in Marx's thinking, when "we speak of *productive labor,* we are speaking of *socially determined* labor." It follows that the *same* physical aggregates of goods and services will have *different* contents of productive labor, depending on whether the economy is capitalist or socialist. Ignoring this immediate logical consequence, the advocates of the "Marxist" definition of the social product prescribe the *same* statistical rules for calculating the social product in both economies, namely, the inclusion of material goods and the exclusion of nonmaterial services. In this connection, one refinement merits brief comment. Some authors try to develop their Marxism a step further by postulating some slightly different formula as socialism. With this we come to the next point.

From the time of Adam Smith, at the end of the eighteenth century, the distinction between productive and nonproductive labor has always had a marked class and political tone. As Marx put it, Smith in fact classified government officials, lawyers, and priests in the same category as clowns and servants. Such a procedure could not but evoke loud protests on the part of the former. The case of Malthus is typical. It was required that the above-mentioned social strata be made productive.

It might have been expected that these apologetics would reappear in the discussion on this subject in the mid-twentieth century. Kronrod is ready to supply us with the desired theory:

"On the other hand, socialism creates new productive functions. . . . The function of the socialist state and the function of the party as the guiding force of socialist society are directly productive functions, since the state and the party play an economic-organizing role, *directly* guiding and organizing the entire process of material production in socialist society" [8: 39].

For Marx, of course, the state apparatus was the prototype of social parasitism, and the thesis of the withering away of the state is well enough known not to require further proof. The quotations serve as an illustration of the fact that "Marxism" and the "Marxist theoretical inheritance" are not necessarily one and the same thing. [5]

We still have to answer the question of the origin of the "Marxist" definition of the social product, and to explain the solidarity of the two opposing camps, non-Marxist and Marxist, with respect to this problem. From among the various possible explanations, we take as the basis for ours the well-tested Marxist treatment of theory as socially conditioned.

Since the "Marxist" definitions are either arbitrary or lead to theoretically meaningless results, anti-Marxist authors can have nothing against them. The political pressure, or bias, of the last quotation from Kronrod is obvious. Identification of the product with the material product may be in part due to the influence of J. Stalin and his primitive philosophical materialism. [6] But it would seem that this identification is primarily the result of the particular economic conditions in the Soviet Union at the time when planning was instituted in that country. It seemed evident to the people who were entering on the process of rapid industrialization that the important things were steel and coal, i.e., tangible material goods, by means of which they were trying to increase the productive wealth of the country. [7] Consciously or unconsciously, labor in that field of social activity took on an aureole of special usefulness or sublimity. The suggestive Smith-Marx term of "productive labor" fitted splendidly into the emotional requirements of the situation, and the authority of Marx's name could not but reinforce the total impression. Once this process has been lived through, the postulate is evident in and of itself and there is no need for logical analysis. People simply *know* that factory workers are productive and that university professors are not, and that the latter live off the labor of the workers. The last two sentences generalize the author's personal experience.

Productive Labor Under Socialism

If we try to extend the Marxian analysis to socialist economics, we can proceed on the following basis. The Marxist approach to economic analysis means essentially the historical determination of economic categories, the assertion of their social dependence. And if we wish to include social relationships in the definition of labor productivity, then it will be clear, upon reflection, that philosophical materiality or the distinction between base and superstructure does not directly provide the criterion required and that the problem is most appropriately solved on the basis developed by Marx: by posing the question of the basic orientation of the socioeconomic system in question. The result of the process of capitalist production is capital and hence, Marx concludes, in that system only that work is productive which produces capital. This applies to both the "material" and the "spiritual" sectors of production. If, on this basis, we pose the question of what the result of socialist production is, we cannot but conclude that they are use-values. In a society in which the immediate and ultimate goals of production coincide, the function of capital as an agent for organizing production becomes superfluous and the production of profit is no longer the criterion of productiveness. In such a society, production is not organized for the sake of making a profit or accumulating capital, but for the purpose of satisfying human needs. Accordingly, any and all labor is productive that produces goods and services for the satisfaction of the needs of people, i.e., any and all labor that increases the welfare of the social community.

At the same time, the mistake should not be made of regarding all socially recognized labor as productive. Under socialism the criteria of productivity consist in the satisfaction of needs, but those needs are not abstract, national, social, historical, but quite concrete, personal, individual. The welfare of the social community is greater or smaller, depending on what happens to the welfare of each individual member of that community. Apart from the welfare of specific people, there is no other welfare. But in that context one kind of labor contributes to increasing well-being, while another kind does not change well-being but only creates the conditions for its realization and in a way represents an expenditure of production. The first kind of labor is productive,

131

the second is nonproductive. In the first kind of labor may be included labor that produces commodities, educational and scientific labor, medical and cultural labor; in the second kind: government administration, police, the armed forces, the work of politicians. It is a characteristic of socialism as a social system that it stimulates labor of the first kind and limits labor of the second kind. And from our theoretical point of view, that means stimulating productive labor and limiting nonproductive labor. In this respect the functioning of socialism is formally identical with the functioning of capitalism: both systems rely on productive labor and limit nonproductive labor. The contents of productive and nonproductive labor, however, differ considerably.

There is another mistake that should not be made. The fact that materialized and nonmaterialized labor are equally productive does not mean that there is no socioeconomic difference between them. This difference does not, of course, consist in the vulgar distinction of material goods and nonmaterial services, as in classifying the makers of boots as productive workers and barbers as nonproductive workers, a distinction made, e.g., in official Yugoslav statistics. The difference is that some goods and services are sold on the market, while others (educational, medical, and similar services) are not. The fact is that material goods dominate in the first sector, while the second consists exclusively of nonmaterial services. But these are secondary, derivative characteristics that can be used as a sort of approximation and not as a fundamental theoretical criterion of differentiation. It is interesting to note that nonmarket production (without the services of the state apparatus) in our country is already one-tenth of total production and is increasing more rapidly than production for the market.

Production for the market and production for immediate satisfaction of needs — i.e., economic and noneconomic production, to use the usual terminology — determine a definite social grouping, which will be discussed in a later chapter. Like the difference in economic organization, this makes the distinction important and of theoretical interest. At the same time, this distinction, as has been said, has absolutely no connection with asserting a criterion for the social productiveness of labor. If there were such a connection, *marketability* would then determine the *productivity of labor under socialism,* which is absurd.

We can now summarize the result of our analysis. Total socially necessary labor in a socialist society is divided into productive and nonproductive labor. The first contributes to well-being; the second serves to maintain the social framework of production.

Productive labor may take place both in the market and in the nonmarket spheres. In the first case the labor results, for the most part, in material goods; in the second case, in nonmaterial services. All these distinctions are not merely matters of abstract theory; they can be established statistically, and the results of the relevant categories of labor can be changed. [8]

15. INDIVIDUAL AND SOCIAL PROPERTY UNDER SOCIALISM

Posing the Problem

Property is one of the basic categories in analyzing social phenomena. Capitalism is said to be based on private property, [9] and socialism is based on social property. What exactly does this mean? It would be difficult to say that the problems in this field have been elucidated and solved. Nevertheless, property, perhaps even more than productive labor, is not simply an academic problem, but is involved, in a most direct way, in social organization and social practice. Vulgarization of the problem of property and naive dogmatism concerning it have led to great damage to socialist construction among us, and to an even greater extent in other socialist countries.

The socioeconomic theory of socialism began to be formed at a time when there was as yet no socialism. The basic motive that guided socialists, the theoretical and practical workers, was revolt against the social defects of the capitalist system and confidence that it was possible and necessary to construct a better social system. Because of this they were, above all, oriented toward criticism and destruction of the existing social system. Marx's *Capital* has the subtitle of "A Critique of the Political Economy of Capitalism." It is no wonder that for a long time socialism was defined negatively, as the negation and antithesis of capitalism. In capitalism the market exists anarchically; therefore, there is no market in socialism. In capitalism, economic decisions are taken by the productive units themselves, the enterprises; therefore, in socialism there can be no autonomous enterprises, but economic organizations must be subject to the central decisions of a government plan. Capitalism was based on individual initiative; therefore, individual initiative is something evil and must be replaced by social initiative, embodied in the state. Under capitalism there is private property, which is the source of crises, exploitation, etc.; therefore, socialism must do away with private

133

property and replace it with government ownership. Today we know, on the basis of practical experience, how naive and false these antinomies are. The market need not be anarchical; planning need not be administrative; individual initiative is not necessarily bad, and government initiative is not the only alternative; in addition to private and government ownership, there is a third possibility, social ownership. This last antinomy will be the subject of our next inquiry. First, however, we note that another real antinomy has developed in the meantime, the antinomy between Marx's socioeconomic theory and vulgar Marxism, which has nothing but phraseology in common with it. [10]

The dogma that there is an identity of private property and capitalism, and of government ownership and socialism, and that government ownership converts capitalism into socialism is wrong, as we now know, for three distinct reasons. First, private property exists in simple commodity production, and yet that is not capitalism; in ancient despotisms, as Marx emphasizes, there was state ownership and yet that had nothing whatever to do with socialism. In fascist countries the state totally "regulated" social and economic life, but they were still capitalist countries.

Further, we must establish the essence of capitalism. It does not consist in private ownership but, as Marx formulated so brilliantly at the very outset of his scientific and political activity, ". . . power over labor and its products." [11]

Power over labor seems to me to give the essence of capitalist private ownership better and more precisely than the usual concept of exploitation. Exploitation is an ambiguous term, literally: it has two meanings. [12] What answer shall we give to the following question: who is exploiting — a private person or a socialist enterprise — if the private person pays a worker 100,000 din. and the enterprise pays him only 80,000 din.? And what of exploitation of agricultural producers by the commune, a fact which farmer Bradić mentions? Exploitation can mean failure to make payment for work done. Such exploitation exists wherever there are monopoly situations. As a result, economic theory in the West frequently proposes to take the degree of monopoly as the only objective measure of exploitation. In that sense, because of their greatly differing operating conditions, economically privileged workers' collectives exploit others, arbitrary decisions by the state and by banks lead to exploitation, and, of course, taking advantage of or creating monopoly situations on the market means exploitation of some collectives by others. [13] This is a very serious problem, which we have hardly investigated at all. But exploitation can also signify the specific social relationship in which one class of individuals, by means of private ownership or state power, subordinates another, and larger, class economically. The latter class is that of wage workers. The former class has *power over labor.*

Evidently, that power does not consist in the replacement of private ownership by state ownership. Rather, it may even be increased, since it gives rise to *total power* of the state over labor and its products; the process of alienation may reach its absolute limit. It need not be so, but can be, and history shows that it actually does get to that point. In contrast to the vulgar Marxism embodied in the Stalinist "dialectical" reinforcement of the state, the truly Marxist judgment would be roughly as follows. Under capitalism, *power over labor* is based on (unlimited) private property in the means of production. Accordingly, the basic precondition for the construction of socialism, in which every *power over labor* will end and hence the process of dealienation will begin, consists in the liquidation of (unlimited) private property in the means of production. At the same time this is, as the mathematicians would say, only a necessary and not a sufficient condition for eliminating capitalism or for constructing socialism. In other words, the fact that private property is eliminated does not mean that socialism is being constructed or has been constructed. Something more is needed.

The third reason for the falsity of the above-mentioned identities is the following. A change in social institutions leads to metamorphosis of economic categories. Just as private ownership, under the conditions of simple commodity production, does not lead to the establishment of power over labor, although it can do so if, and to the extent that, the conditions exist for the development of capitalist commodity production, so, under the conditions of a socialist economy, private ownership need not lead to capitalist relations and can be totally integrated into the development of socialism and socialist relations. How, and under what conditions, is a question that must be investigated, and it is a question to which Yugoslav experience gives a definitive answer.

Socialist or Nonsocialist Character of
Production by the Individual Producer

We begin with a well-known practical example: the position of the craftsman in the Yugoslav economy. Starting from the dogmatic conception that individual craftsmanship (the term "individual" was used intentionally in order to avoid the negative emotional connotation of the term "private") is essentially nonsocialist, local, and not only local, agencies applied administrative measures of pressure and harassment. As a result, the number of craftsmen began to decrease. Those who left their occupations were primarily those individuals who were unwilling to endure social discrimination against their labor and the insinuations that they were speculators and antisocialist elements. There remained, in addition to the older and hence immobile craftsmen, those to whom socialism and social labels were irrelevant and who were interested only in gain, regardless of how and on what basis it was achieved. Since our economy was expanding rapidly at the same time, the demand for the services of craftsmen increased irresistibly, regardless of the social theories of our local agencies. A kind of El Dorado was set up for the speculative elements; the setup was all they could possibly desire, for an economic monopoly was given them. When this had taken place, administrative sanctions did little good. Taxes were raised beyond the real capacities of the taxed. Again the honest ones left their positions, since they could not stand the pressure; those who remained, and their numbers increased, [14] were the speculators who knew how to overcome these obstacles as well. The monopoly of the latter was reinforced still further. On this basis, our theoreticians had arrived at the point they anticipated: treating the private owner as a tax evader and speculator. This was an empirical verification of the correctness of their theory and policy, but they failed to see that their policy not only did not reduce antisocialist phenomena but increased them on a massive scale. Before the war, the craftsman was a man with a modest income, with no political ambitions, and with a certain traditional guild honesty in business; more than half of the craftsmen could not live off the earnings from their craft, and only 2% of them employed more than four assistants [17: 124-126]. In developed capitalist countries the craftsman can hardly be distinguished from the worker, the competition is keen, and the number of bankruptcies among artisans (taken in the broad sense, to include tradespeople, those engaged in services, etc.) is enormous. In Yugoslavia it was only after the war that artisans began to buy automobiles, to build villas, and to carouse in night clubs — the three earmarks of newly found wealth among those with limited means.

Twelve years ago I witnessed an unpleasant scene, in which an old electrician, presenting his bill for the work he had done, suffered a heart attack because he was told, as a matter of course, that he was a speculator and price extortionist. When he regained his composure, he got angry and rejoined: Why was he a speculator? Hadn't he done his work honestly and well? Hadn't he charged for his work strictly according to the regulated tariff? Didn't he pay taxes to the country honestly? Didn't he love his country the way every other citizen did? Why was he always greeted with insults; why was his honesty always impugned? Why wasn't he just as good and honest as any other worker or the clerks in some government office? Why did he *have* to be dishonest just because he worked for himself? It might be said of all this that one cannot generalize from a single case, that it is impossible to be sentimental about social transformations, and that this is a typical case of petty-bourgeois mentality, incapable of understanding social changes. But was petty-bourgeois psychology involved here, or a faulty theory? A non-Marxist and anti-Marxist theory, like the antinomies mentioned above? In the past twelve years, as I followed our social development, I have often thought of that old electrician with his petty-bourgeois psychology. That may have been his mentality, but its core was labor as the criterion of human worth. And that is a criterion that is socialist, beyond a doubt. After all, what is involved?

Individual Property as an Integral Category of a Socialist Socioeconomic System

Let us return to Marx's definition of capital, which provides a safe and simple guide to a decision. Does a farmer who works ten hectares with his family, or an electrician who goes around with his son repairing our home electrical systems, achieve power over others' labor? Of course not. Is there any internal economic or social logic that dictates that he may do so in the future? If the farmer or electrician works alone or with his family, there is certainly no danger of any such development. And if he works with a helper? Probably not even then. How many helpers can be tolerated? That depends on a practical evaluation, the criterion being as follows: as long as the proprietor works himself and that direct work is his basic *function,* there is no danger of capitalist development. As soon as his primary function becomes entrepreneurship, i.e., the organization of the labor of others, then even by definition he is no longer a worker but is a capitalist. Here two problems emerge that call for elucidation.

If there are cases in which private ownership does not lead to capitalist relationships, does that fact in itself suffice for private ownership to be tolerated? The answer is categorically in the negative. Capitalist relationships are not the only criterion according to which society has to be taken into account. For

137

example, we have abolished the private practice of medicine. Health care has been socialized in some socially mature capitalist countries as well. The fact is that health care is a field in which not only capitalist relationships cannot be tolerated, but commercial commodity-money relationships in general. Health, education, and culture are not commodities that can be matters of buying and selling between suppliers and purchasers; in this field, distribution is according to needs and not according to ability to pay. More precisely, it should be that way under socialism.

The second problem relates to the latent deleterious effect of private ownership arising out of the dynamics of the economy. The market leads to differentiation by way of competition; some productive units fail, while others expand. We can, without any difficulty, limit the number of assistants that the individual producer may employ, and thus we can formally make the creation of capitalist relations impossible. But when the productive unit grows to that limiting point and is capable of expanding still further, there will be a certain amount of pressure in the direction of getting around the requirements of law, and of the private proprietor turning into an entrepreneur. It is well known that such cases are constantly arising. The solution to this problem is not to be sought in exacerbating sanctions, for when a negative economic phenomenon keeps reappearing, it has a disorganizing effect, and criminal sanctions neither diminish nor avoid the harmful effects on the economic and social system. In such cases there is evidently something out of order in the system, and the remedy has to be sought in institutional changes and not in criminal law. At the same time, it does not follow that the only alternative is elimination, or at least vigorous prosecution, of private property, a conclusion that has often been drawn until the present time. The path that has to be taken, in my opinion, is the transformation into a socialist category — property based on individual labor — and the integration of the individual producers into the economic and social system as constituent and *functional* parts of that system, not leaving them as foreign bodies with serious dysfunctional effects. An indication as to how this can be accomplished is given by our practice, and I shall return to this question after dealing with another serious problem: the size of resources in private property.

In a time of automatization, the criterion of individual labor is not sufficient to make the formation of *power over labor* impossible. This power can come into being indirectly, via the market, if enough capital is owned (which we shall call resources in order to avoid an invidious connotation). Hence the criterion of labor has to be supplemented by limiting the size of production resources with private ownership. The key factor here is not that "capital bears fruit." In our country, as elsewhere, savers receive interest on their deposits in banks or cut coupons on government bonds. In that way their "capital bears fruit," but yet I do not imagine that anyone will see anything antisocialist in it. Some save, and others consume beyond their incomes (by means of consumer credit), the latter paying a premium to the former in the form of interest — not directly, of course, but through the banking mechanism; and economic equilibrium is established in the sphere of consumption. [15] In fact, the fundamental meaning of interest-bearing savings is precisely accumulation for the purpose of consumption. Saving for the purpose of productive investments is another matter. A shipper who systematically puts his savings into the purchase of new trucks, which he rents out, or a farmer who does the same with newly purchased land or tractors does not employ labor power directly, but still practices *power over labor,* indirectly, via the market. How far and in what way the possession of means of production has to be limited is a question of practical evaluation. It may be decided that no one may own more than one or two houses (besides his own) and rent them out; it may be decided that owners of tractors or automobiles may only work with them themselves and may not hire them out.

We thus come to the conclusion that individual ownership of means of production, with which the owner himself works, is not only compatible with socialism but is an integral category of the socialist mode of economy. Socialism is a socioeconomic system based on personal productive labor. Since everything that contributes to the affirmation of personal labor as the criterion of social value is a socialist factor, everything that leads to the control or degradation of individual labor initiative represents an antisocialist factor. In this sense, individual property in the means of production represents a socialist category insofar as it satisfies the following three conditions: (1) if the owner continues to be primarily a worker and does not become primarily an entrepreneur, i.e., provided the employment of others' labor power is adequately confined; (2) if the amount of productive resources is adequately limited; and (3) if money-making, commercially oriented activity does not appear in fields that, because of their social function, must be divorced from direct relationships of purchase and sale, as is the case with education or medical care.

139

Collective Property and Social Property

Socialism aims at high development of the economy and hence cannot be based on individual ownership of means of production subject to the three limitations mentioned above. Socialism is obviously based on social ownership, and individual ownership plays a peripheral role. But a peripheral role is not the same thing as an insignificant role. When all is said and done, half of our active population consists of individual owners, and the conditions under which these producers are inserted into the process of socialist construction are of great importance. Limitations by criminal law, when they clash with economic processes, cause great economic harm and serious social deformations. The former are well known. The thing then is that the economic process should channel itself *economically* in the desired direction, namely, in the direction of socialist construction. We noted earlier that successful productive units will try to break down or get around the limits set them. As long as we remained at that point, individual ownership would remain a foreign body in socialist construction, something that on a petty-bourgeois basis constantly gave rise to capitalist tendencies. If we were to reinforce sanctions, we would repeat the story of the artisanry. It is evident, therefore, that the only correct path consists in making the transition through the set limitations, in making a single continuous evolution from individual to social ownership, from small artisan workshops to modern factories. Let us look at this problem in a single illustrative instance.

A young skilled worker (farmer, trucker, tavern-keeper, etc.) has inherited his workplace (farm, truck, bar, etc.) from his father. The young fellow is capable and enterprising; he has expanded his business and hired a helper. At this point he works out a practical little idea that he patents (the idea may consist in the use of a new system, in an original way of organizing transport, in good organization of tourist propaganda, although this kind of idea cannot be patented). Our craftsman is able to find a buyer for his patent (let us say it is a lock to protect automobiles from theft) and draws royalties. But he is not inclined to live the life of a rentier; he wants to produce his product and develop it further. And here the danger of coming into conflict with the law arises. A second (and much more common) possibility is that our craftsman cannot sell his patent. We know that inventors among us have enormous difficulty in finding takers for their inventions. Many of these discoveries remain unused, to the great harm of the economy. Now what should be done in these two cases?

Obviously, institutional possibilities must be created for our producer to bring out the industrial potential as far as possible. Since this is largely based on individual ownership, the transition must be prepared to the subsequent category of ownership. [16] But even before this can be done, it is possible and even necessary to introduce elements of self-government.

This next category is collective ownership; we call this form of organization a cooperative [*zadruga*]. We have production cooperatives. Some of these cooperatives involve up to several hundred people. From the standpoint of the problem we are concerned with here, this is economic nonsense. But in practice it has a meaning, at least in those cases in which they form such associations. Until now, cooperatives have had certain privileges as compared with enterprises. For this reason some technologically less advanced producers, some kinds of manufacture, have organized in the form of large cooperatives. In such cases the cooperative does not present the appearance of collective ownership, but the legal form of primitively organized production. This probably represents an anachronism, and it may be predicted that such associations will not persist. [17] It may be expected that cooperatives, like one-man workshops, will be limited as to the number of people engaged and the amount of resources they use. Just what those limits should be is a practical matter. The criterion could be based on the principle that a cooperative should in essence be a transitional form between the individual craftsman and the fully developed enterprise. Given this criterion, the transition would have to be prepared for in good time, psychologically and organizationally.

Agriculture is a special case. Cooperation there has proved to be one of the most efficacious transitions to higher forms of ownership. At the same time, it is not clear why farmers' working cooperatives have been neglected, and their number is decreasing. In some countries, cooperatives have developed very well for some reasons that have not worked with us. General agricultural cooperatives give the impression that they are local monopolies, artificially set up by administrative measures, rather than a natural intermediate in the social organization of agricultural production. To the extent that this is correct, it is economic loss.

Finally, when production has outgrown the sphere of the cooperative, the cooperative is converted, by a definite step, into a self-governing enterprise with modern productive organization and equipment. Further development is via cooperation and integration, with restrictions to prevent monopoly.

If he is hard-working and capable, our artisan will begin his working career as the owner of a one-man shop and end it as the manager of a large modern factory. During the phases of his development, he will regard himself, and act, as a socialist laborer. Not for an instant will his ethics as a producer conflict with socialist ethics. From the first day he will be stimulated to develop production and to achieve social and material appreciation for the results obtained. Property will never appear to him as the goal (his goal is the effectiveness of labor), but as a means, as the correct form of organization of production in a definite stage of development or in definite functional situations. [18] And in this sense all three forms of ownership form a single, labor-conditioned, socialist ownership. Naturally, only a small number of enterprises will travel the road that has been depicted. Competition will do away with some of them at the outset; some will prove to be excellent organizers of work on the level of five employees, but very poor organizers on the level of 100 or more. Nevertheless, on the one hand, those who succeed will produce what would otherwise be lost to society, and, on the other, the firmness and consistency of system will contribute to the general cohesion of our socialist society. The importance of this last result for the further development of democratization and humanization of social relationships can hardly be exaggerated.

Conclusion

All three forms of ownership have a single characteristic in common that has not yet been discussed. It distinguishes socialist property from capitalist property, in economics and in principle. This is the principle that the means of production, no matter by whom they are managed or how they were acquired, are basically social. Therefore, anyone who withdraws a productive capacity from the potential general social fund of resources has to pay a definite price for the privilege of having that capacity redound to his benefit and no one else's. That price is interest, and it has to be paid on resources used, whether by a craftsman, an association, or an enterprise. Social ownership of the means of production means, among other things, that socialist society allocates the available productive forces in such a way as to achieve maximum productive effect. In this sense, uniform interest is one of the means of allocation. Another is rent. All producers have to pay a marginal interest and rent; this merely equalizes the demand for means of production with the supply, which in principle indicates optimal distribution. Those producers who are unable to pay the marginal interest and rent cannot get economic permission to make use of the social fund of means of production, since withdrawal from the fund would deprive another producer of the possibility of employing those means more efficiently and thus better meeting social demands. The fact that the purchase of such means of production is financed from "own" income, whether individual, cooperative, or from the enterprise, and not from credit, does not alter the situation in any way. Insisting on "own" means in that sense signifies operating with a nonsocialist category.

Frequent mention has been made recently of the need to do away with interest on basic resources, since it is said to discourage the introduction of new techniques. Such a thesis is faulty in both theory and practice. If the interest is set properly, in line with the principles that have been stated, it cannot discourage the introduction of new techniques if those techniques mean *an actual rise in the social profitability* in the given situation. But not everything that is new is necessarily most profitable, or at least not in every situation. If we come across some evident anomalies, the fault cannot be attributed to interest, but to other means that are poorly defined: imposed prices, excessive installment payments, inadequate amortization, or something else. Doing away with interest would mean introducing elements of private property into our system. It would mean that the enterprise can do what it pleases with "its" resources: invest in projects of substandard profitability, fail to use available capacity, etc. Such a posture for the productive process seems to me totally unacceptable in a socialist society.

In practical application, of course, various adaptations of the principles stated will be required. There will be withdrawals and exemptions called for by the technological, organizational, and other characteristics of the productive process. We cannot go into them here. However, there is one theoretically and practically important conclusion that must be drawn. Interest and rent represent not only means of allocation, [19] but also means of *economic expropriation* and, in that sense, are essential to the operation of social ownership. Workers' collectives may appropriate only that part of revenue from production that is *above the minimum social profitability* of the means employed, to the extent that that part is the product of their work, and not due merely to the fact that they have the resources at their disposal. Something of the kind already exists in our practice, although very inconsistently and not thought through theoretically. Interest is charged on basic resources. And land prices, because of the charging of rent, are considerably lower than before the war, reflecting the process of economic expropriation.

143

On this basis we have concluded our analysis — in a circle that seems paradoxical at first sight. We began by arguing that under certain conditions individual property likewise has a socialist character, and that therefore individual production should be encouraged just as much as cooperative or enterprise production. We concluded by observing that socialism implies social ownership, and that social ownership presupposes *economic* expropriation of all *concrete* owners of means of production. The paradox is only apparent, of course. The latter is the condition of the former. It is at the same time the analytical statement of the content of the category of social property.

It is of interest to note that nothing essentially novel has been uncovered in this discussion. All the phenomena we have dealt with already exist in our economy. At the same time, as Hadži Vasilev remarks: "When we turn the bases of analysis of a society upside down, we have to pay for it in theory and practice. And we are paying . . . by making it possible for us, in the sphere of essential relations, to take certain decisions by the unconscious force of objective laws, and thereby give those decisions the imprint of empiricism and improvisation rather than conscious socialist practice" [18]. The attempt has been made, in this direction, to interpret the already known phenomena within the framework of a single consistent Marxist-based theoretical approach. This is not a matter of recommending a pragmatic approach to the problem, as in the following way of thinking. Because of the unevenness of social and economic development in every social system, there are survivals remaining from previous systems, remnants of feudalism in capitalism, remnants of capitalism in socialism. The individual peasant, innkeeper, peddler, and craftsman, like the individual lawyer, artist, etc., are remnants of this kind among us. But the activity of these people is useful as a supplement to *social* production and they are therefore to be *tolerated.* In point of fact, these working people (and they constitute half the active population of our country) are, or at least should be, just as much builders of socialism as those in factories and offices, and as such should be not tolerated but integrated into our social system. In this respect our system of self-government makes it easier to consider and solve the problem. Self-government means that the direct producers themselves organize their work and autonomously distribute the income from their labor. This principle applies to collectives numbering thousands of workers, but it also applies, and most directly, to the individual producer. However, it is not only that individual producer that is involved. Along with him, we have inherited from capitalism the cooperative and the state enterprise. Are they to be tolerated? Obviously, none of these three types of productive organization is to be tolerated as a relic of the past; they have to be *transformed* and directly included in a single socialist organization of production.

At the same time, the fact is that the problem of ownership, especially individual ownership, is looked on as a delicate topic that it is not politically opportune to discuss at any length. The cause of this opportunism is, as far as I can see, not only that no adequate theory has been devised, but that in practice there are aberrations, fluctuations, misunderstandings, and serious political and material losses. Characteristic in this regard was the reaction to the 1953 regulation, providing that groups of citizens might also establish enterprises. "The liveliest and most typical reactions," Milentije Popović wrote on this point [19: 67-69], "came from reactionaries on the one hand, . . . and from Communists on the other, even from people in positions of leadership in districts and cities. . . . The reactionaries applauded the decree, some Communists were firmly opposed to it. . . . In fact, those Communists viewed the famous 'citizens' group' also as a group of capitalists — to them it meant a possibility of a revival and rehabilitation of capitalism. . . . We must make it clear that the 'citizens' group' was a group of working people, not of capitalists." Today, the "citizens' groups" would not cause any excitement, even though, unfortunately, the decree in question did not lead to any significant new initiatives, because in past years administrative initiative was regarded as something more deeply socialistic. But even today the discussions concerning farm tractors [20] and individual taverns arouse suspicions that an overt or covert tendency toward the restoration of capitalism is involved. Hence the great personal risk, which others will not understand and will attack, for anyone who takes up this theme. And hence the regular avoidance of that theme.

16. VERTICAL STRUCTURE OF YUGOSLAV SOCIETY: STRATIFICATION

A number of strata and groups can be discerned in our country, with differences, tensions, and conflicts of interest among them as the result of real or imagined opposing interests or simply as the result of various factors arising out of group psychology. Thus, we can distinguish among farmers, farm workers, workers, and tradesmen. Then there are skilled and unskilled workers; the latter are to a great extent included among the farm workers. Within the economic organization there are groupings of workers, subordinate employees, and responsible officials. In educational, scientific, and cultural institutions, collectives consist of creative workers and professional, administrative, and adjunct personnel. Differences exist between physical and intellectual work, between town and country. There are relationships of subordination between chief and underling in the time-hallowed hierarchical structure of the government administration. State officials (especially if they are not merely hierarchically delimited "bearers of rank" but bearers of power as well) are contrasted with groups outside the government sphere. As in every country, there are also various interest groups.[21] There are also purely psychological antitheses. The aggressive and dynamic businessman differs from the critical, contemplative, and systematic scholar, who in turn is unlike the optimistic, improvising, and compromise-oriented politician. All these differences give rise to social tensions, but they represent structural cross sections at very different levels and of very different importance. It will be necessary, therefore, to introduce some system into our investigation.

Social Stratification in Yugoslavia

Social differentiation, and hence structuring, may be horizontal or vertical. By definition, horizontal differentiation postulates differences among groups, and those differences may (and in fact do) lead to conflicts of interest. But these conflicts are not antagonistic. Antagonistic differences are characteristic of a vertically differentiated society, and vertical differentiation is inherent in any class society.

Horizontal groupings are arrived at because of differences in social role, as the result of the division of labor. Vertical groupings are arrived at by virtue of differences in the *status* of the various social groups.[22] As with Stoetzel [23: 363], we may also define the status of a person as the sum of the behavior that he may rightly expect from other persons, and we may define his role as the actions that other persons may rightly expect from him. On this basis the sum total of all the statuses and roles of a society would make up the social system. In this section we shall consider status, or vertical social differentiation. In other words, we shall examine how groups differ by virtue of occupying different positions in the social *hierarchy*, how those positions are interrelated as *higher and lower*, with the result that groups represent strata, and social differentiation appears as a process of

146

differentiation.

Strata are never distinguished by only a single characteristic. On the other hand, the individual characteristics that enter into the determination of strata are not absolutely correlated with one another and hence do not define the stratum with complete precision. In view of this, we believe that strata may be approximately, determined on the basis of (a) differences in social repute, prestige, which in turn is mostly the result of the two following characteristics: (b) financial status [23] and (c) social power, which is shown by the possible and actual making of important social decisions. [24] Unfortunately, since empirical work in this field is rare and often unrepresentative, we shall be compelled, in analyzing the stratification of Yugoslav society, to rely on experience, intuition, analogy, and general ideas. These heterogeneous and scientifically rather unimpressive bases may, for the time being, outline the following hierarchy of social groups.

1. Government political figures, economic and noneconomic leaders. The members of this group make the most important social decisions, have the highest incomes as a group, and for both reasons have the highest prestige as a group.

2. Intellectual workers in economic, noneconomic, and government administrations. This group by and large coincides with the group of university-trained graduates. But there are exceptions. For example, teachers would probably have to be included as well. And on the other hand, not all graduates of university *education* are necessarily *educated* people, i.e., intellectuals. In the framework of their position in the social division of labor, the intelligentsia falls into three fairly well-differentiated subgroups: the technological-economic intellectuals ("technocrats"); the upper administrative echelons ("bureaucrats"); and the intelligentsia in the narrow or classical sense (humanist intelligentsia).

3. The (routine) office workers correspond to what are called "white-collar workers" in Western societies. This stratum constitutes our "middle class" and sometimes gives a particular imprint to social occurrences (see the analysis, in Section 19, of the genesis of the bureaucratic mentality in the party). Office workers are divided into three strata: those with secondary education, with lower education, and adjunct personnel.

4. Workers as a stratum are pretty clearly differentiated into three or even four substrata: (a) highly skilled; (b) skilled; (c) semiskilled; and (d) unskilled, including the transitional category of farmer-workers. There are significant social differences between

the first two and the second pair of categories.[25]

5. Artisans represent a residual category; in addition to artisans, in the strict sense of the term (owners of shops for material production and services), the classification should include all other private persons engaged in economic activities (except in agriculture). It is characteristic for this group that it has the lowest percentage of self-renewal: only 9.2% of the children of artisans remain in that social group (compared to 21% for unskilled workers, 32% for office workers, and 64% for peasants). The largest proportion of sons of artisans become skilled and highly skilled workers (26%). It emerges that in today's social situation the artisan stratum is subject to constant dissolution and does not show any tendency to persist.[26]

6. Peasants, who today are differentiated by regions and not by substrata, as they were at one time.

The above list calls for some comment. The strata are presented in sequence, from highest to lowest. The sequence is unreliable only for the artisans, for whom there is considerable difference in ranking based on social consideration and income; their social status is low, just below that of the peasant, while their income is relatively high. When this social group is better integrated into Yugoslav society, its status will probably coincide with that of skilled and highly skilled workers, who occupy the largest share of all groups in the formation of artisan cadres, both within and between generations. An indication in that direction is given by empirical studies, which show that highly skilled and skilled workers regard artisans as the closest social group.[27]

An empirical test of the vertical stratification of Yugoslav society emerges from the above-mentioned study of Vojin Milić [16: 213]. [28] We can assume that lower intergeneration mobility will correspond to higher social status in a stratum, i.e., that their children will prefer to stay in the social group of their parents more than when the status of the group is low. If stratification is very significant, the differences between the lowest and the highest strata will be very great. We now consider three series of Milić indices of association (the ratio of observed and theoretical frequencies corresponding to complete mobility). Indices higher than unity indicate that social origin facilitates entry into a category, and vice versa for indices greater than unity. The first series shows the extent to which children remain in the social category of their parents above the degree corresponding to complete mobility: peasants, 1.30; unskilled and semiskilled workers, 2.23; skilled and highly skilled workers, 2.32; routine office workers, 4.03; and professional and managerial cadres, 8.82.

The second series indicates upward mobility, i.e., the chances that persons from lower social strata have of reaching the professional and managerial group: for persons of peasant origin, 0.45; of worker origin, 0.84-1.07; families of white-collar workers, 4.01; and families of professionals and managers, 8.82. Hence, workers' children have only one-ninth the chance, and peasants' children one-twentieth the chance, of getting into the leadership category of professionals and managers than children born to families of the latter group. Downward mobility, as we can illustrate from the third series in Milić's tables of indices of association, encounters even greater obstacles, as might be expected. The flow of persons from the highest social group to other groups has the following indices: to white-collar workers, 4.93; to workers, 0.45-0.22; and to peasants, 0.13. Compared to the chances of remaining in their own social group, the highest one, these persons are twenty times less likely to become workers and seventy times less likely to become peasants.

It must be remembered that the scale of stratification is not discontinuous; there are no gaps between the strata and they interpenetrate; the upper portions of lower strata overlap the lower portions of upper strata. Highly skilled workers rise far above the lower limit of the stratum of white-collar workers; the highest intellectual cadres rise to the first ranks of the managerial stratum. This "overlapping," this blurred differentiation, and continuity are of great importance for the consequences of stratification, as will be discussed later. It is only if we imagine each stratum to have a center of gravity that it is possible to form a discontinuous hierarchical classification into six centers of gravity, as was done.

It will be seen that with the exception of the first stratum, stratification is a function of education. The higher the education, the higher the social status. Higher education makes the type of work more intellectual; only manual occupations are left for the semiliterate. This is the basis of the frequent observation that manual labor is lower per se, and that an intellectual social status is higher. Actually, the status of physical and intellectual workers is derived from their educational status, and in itself does not contain any hierarchical differentiation. In other words, there is nothing inherently inferior about physical labor. There is no physical labor as strenuous as top-flight sport, and no physical labor as dirty as war; yet both are ranked very high on the scale of social values. Participants in volunteer youth labor projects evaluate outstanding achievements in these projects at least as high as brilliant results at school. The fact is that there has never yet been a society with sufficient economic resources to render an essentially equal education possible for everyone. On the one hand, education is requisite for the performance of complex social tasks [29] and, on the other, it obviously affords tangible advantages to its possessors in the daily struggle for a place in society. Therefore, the strata to whom education is accessible, who have a *monopoly on education,* occupy a higher position in the social hierarchy in their societies. We may add here that in situations in which wealth begins to lose its significance for vertical differentiation, as is characteristic of present-day society, education becomes the key factor in social stratification. [30]

If we try to define the above-mentioned strata quantitatively, we come to the classical pyramid of 1961. [31]

			Thousand	In %
Managerial cadres			60	0.7
Intellectual workers			170	2.1
Functionaries:	secondary training	343		
	primary training	410		
	adjuncts	82		
			835	10.1
Workers:	highly skilled	163		
	skilled	843		
	semiskilled	426		
	unskilled	1,032		
			2,464	30.0
Artisans			292	3.5
Peasants			4,408	53.6
Total active population			8,229	100.0

Since statistical studies in this field have not been completed and the available statistical data are partial and random, a desirable comparison of the changes in social structure according to periods is not yet possible. It can only be stated that over the six-year period of 1957-1963, for which data are available, the number of workers rose by 58%. [32] If this rate continues in the future, workers will make up half the active population of Yugoslavia by 1970.

On the basis of the meager scattered data, we may conclude that our society is more open than any other society at a similar stage of economic development: the mobility between its various strata is greater. This is particularly true of the highest stratum, [33] and is obviously the direct result of the revolution. However, general social mobility and, hence, openness have not permanently attained the degree of social mobility of the most developed industrial countries. According to the figures of Milić, the degrees of openness are, in percent of theoretically possible mobility: France, 49%; Switzerland, 51%; West Germany, 60-63%; Yugoslavia, 65%; Sweden, 66%; and the USA, 68% [16: 226].

At the same time, we should not be deceived by the persistence of the social pyramid or by today's mobility. They reflect a momentary situation, which will change as a function of the rate of economic development. In particular, we can with certainty predict a change in the pyramidal structure.

In the first place, the base — the peasantry — is changing very rapidly. Also, along with numerical changes, the peasantry is being transformed into groups that are very different sociologically — farmers and workers. In addition, after migration from the villages slows down, there will be an absolute decrease in the number of unskilled workers. The number of skilled workers, lower functionaries, and intellectuals will increase both absolutely and relatively. This will gradually change the pyramidal structure into a spheroidal one, with the extremes not emphasized and the basic mass of society concentrated around the equator. Education eliminates the stratum without any skills. The lowest stratum, the peasantry, will be transformed and will decline as a function of economic development. The highest, or governing, stratum will, if present social trends continue, dissolve in the institutions of self-government and gradually turn into a professional group of administrators. In that society the distribution of education might to a great extent coincide with the natural distribution of intelligence, and property differences would be trifling. [34]

The question now arises: what are the relationships of social stratification and classes in our country?

Social Classes

"Class" is one of those concepts that are much used but not precisely defined. Almost every author has his own definition. We must therefore begin by arriving at a suitable definition for our analysis.

It should first be noted that the term "class" is used in at least two widely differing senses. Marx's dictum that all previous history has been the history of class struggles is an instance of its employment in the sense of an essentially bivalent social structure, in which the struggle of two antagonistic classes (or class groupings) is the motive force of history. These two classes are the class of the propertied and the class of the nonpropertied. In another sense, "class" is used to denote differences with respect to estate and caste. The latter are "closed," while a "class" is an "open" group determined by exclusively economic factors, i.e., by private property. In that sense, classes exist only in capitalist society. In what follows, the concept of class will be used in either sense, without explicit specification, since it will be obvious from the context what is involved.

The question now arises: what about classes after capitalism? If property is the key criterion for defining classes, the answer was very simple at one time, and for many sociologists it still is today. As long as there exist three kinds of property — private, cooperative, and state — there will be three class groupings. In subsequent development the first two kinds of property will be eliminated and, with it, class society, since state ownership provides the basis for the formation of a single class, which thus becomes identical with society. Today, on the basis of historical experience, we know how naive and incorrect that conception is. If we use the concept of class in the first sense, then class polarization is possible on the basis of state ownership as well (the class of [indirect] owners is called the bureaucracy), as on the basis of the previous kinds of property. And Marx spoke of the étatist societies of the ancient Orient as class societies. On this basis, property and class society are Siamese twins, and fit together well theoretically.

Difficulties arise with social property, and they are not only sociological difficulties. Jurists too have great trouble in defining social property. We encounter the idea that social property is a *contradictio in adjecto.* A society comprises all the members of the society, and property can only be defined in relation to those excluded from it. Social property might be defined as national property — to be sure, in relation to other national economies; but this is not operationally applicable in the domain of our analysis. Hence, it is probably most suitable to consider *social* property as the *abolition* of property. Now, our theory can also include this case; a society whose productive organization is based on social property is a classless society.

We might also insert an element of evolution into our theoretical approach. In precapitalist societies the strata are more and more open (castes — estates — classes), and private property becomes more and more the dominant principle of organization of

152

social production. This development reaches its culmination in capitalism, in which classes appear in the second sense, after which those classes undergo further transformations. In postcapitalist bureaucratic structures we can speak of quasiclasses. [35]

As we know, property relations play the key role in Marx's definition of class. At the beginning of the chapter on classes in Volume 3 of *Capital,* he wrote: "Owners of naked labor power, owners of capital and landowners, to whom rent, profit and ground rent are a specific source of income, that is to say, hired laborers, capitalists, and landowners, are the three great classes of modern society based on the capitalist mode of production" [3: 816]. This gives a succinct picture of the relatively simple structure of English society of the last century. Thereafter matters became much more complicated and we therefore require a reworking of the definition of class. One of the most complete is Lenin's well-known definition [31: 162]. He gives four attributes of a class: (1) classes are groups that differ in their position in a historically determined system of social production, i.e., they are themselves historically determined; (2) they differ in their relation to the means of production (property criterion); (3) they differ in their role in the social organization of labor; and (4) they differ in the ways of acquisition and in the size of their share in the wealth of society. To these should be added two more: (5) on the basis of 1 to 4, classes differ in their social influence and, particularly, in their position in the system of political power; and (6) "classes in themselves" become "classes for themselves" when they develop a consciousness of their class interests and their historical identity, which enables classes to perform their social role.

After the definition has been established, we still have to define the basic factor that converts a social group into a class with the above-mentioned attributes. We believe that this factor consists in *monopoly in making important social decisions.* What are to be regarded as important decisions in a given society can be determined empirically. Social importance depends on what the members of the concrete society think of it, as well as on the essential existential importance of the decision. In view of the latter factor, we can go a step further. Just as human work activity is the essence of his existence *as human,* so *monopoly of the conditions of labor* is the necessary and sufficient condition for class differentiation. [36] It follows directly that a bureaucratized Stalinist society is a class society with a classical two-class structure. However, the identification is not always so simple.

It will be necessary, therefore, to do as the mathematicians do, to work out an operational test for determining the cases in which the condition of monopolization of important social decisions is satisfied. This test consists of two requirements. First, a prestige differentiation must exist in the given society. This means that the upper stratum (or strata) has (or have) what is generally regarded as very desirable (wealth, education, political power, etc.) in considerably greater measure than the lower stratum (strata). For the status of the upper stratum to be conserved and perpetuated, there must be some barrier that prevents the members of the lower stratum from penetrating the reservation of the upper stratum and taking part in its advantages. This gives rise to a tendency for institutional checking of social mobility, and consciousness of contrary interests develops (since the quantity of the things desired is limited). Second, not every prestige differentiation is necessarily of a class nature. Talented artists always enjoy greater social respect than those without talent. That has no connection with class contradictions, since no artist can guarantee that his son will also be a talented artist. For a prestige difference to have the above-mentioned consequences, it must be based on *inherited* and not *achieved status.* [37] Hence, the second fundamental condition for class differentiation is the existence of a sufficiently high correlation between family connections and social status. But the problem of inheritance calls for brief supplementary analysis.

First of all, we consider the developmental aspect of the inheritance of social status. In feudalism, for example, political or social status was directly inherited, and this was expressed in membership in a relatively closed order of society and in inheritance of titles of nobility. In capitalism, only wealth is directly inherited, but that is quite sufficient to create class barriers. In a certain postcapitalist bureaucratic system, neither political position nor capital is inherited, indicating further weakening of class barriers. But it would be a mistake to regard them as insignificant.

Let us make a definition. The direct inheritance of property is not in and of itself sufficient to insure the perpetuation between generations of bourgeois families. Cases are familiar in which capital piled up in one generation is lost in the following one, leading inevitably to loss of bourgeois status. For that status to be maintained, the capital has to be invested productively, according to all the rules of the capitalist order. In that process it is irrelevant whether the investment is made in a factory, in stocks or personal education or, as occurs most often, in some combination of these. Something similar occurs in a bureaucratic system as well. Functionaries — economic, political, governmental — cannot transmit their functions to their children by inheritance. But they can recommend their offspring to their friends, who are also functionaries, when the time comes for them to find a place in society. Insofar as a centralist cadre policy is in force, which may be taken to be the rule, we obtain the phenomenon we could describe as quasi-inheritance. That does not signify, of course, that certain bureaucratic positions are absolutely guaranteed. As in the case of their capitalist colleagues, they have to satisfy certain prerequisites of the system. They must have certain minimum qualifications for execution of the functions in question, and they must be fitted to the rules of the bureaucratic code. But both of these are to a great extent guaranteed by their home training. Even when there is no abuse of "connections" at all (which is, of course, an academic supposition), the offspring are formed in the spirit of the milieu in which their parents move, and even for that reason alone (they are reliable, positive, communicative, cooperative, etc.) they are more acceptable than other candidates. This gives the young bureaucrat, at the very beginning, a definite advantage over his competitors from other social strata, as is the case with a young entrepreneur starting with his father's capital; each of the two inherits a kind of capital. This class differentiation is all the stronger, the greater the privileges of the bureaucracy (and hence the desirability of remaining in that milieu are greater), the lower the educational level of the population, the less democratic the political system, and the lower the economic development of the country. If the capitalist shares in the distribution of surplus value in proportion to his capital, the bureaucrat shares in proportion to his status in the power hierarchy.

In this way we have defined the criteria for asserting the existence or nonexistence of class differentiation in Yugoslavia. The stratification structure spoken of earlier is in no way specific to Yugoslavia and in no way prejudges the answer to the question. Development may proceed from the same initial structure in the direction of forming classes and in the direction of overcoming class residues. The direction the development will take depends exclusively on whether the social system produces cohesive forces that will cement the various strata, or whether it produces forces that will dissipate them.

But before proceeding to a definitive evaluation of our situation, a warning must be given against another frequent error. From the functional differences of organizational and executive work, and from the fact that *today* and *among us* the former ranks higher than the latter, the conclusion is drawn that there is an *inherent* hierarchical quality in the two kinds of work, and a

155

consequent tendency for society to be differentiated into leaders and the led. This tendency does in fact exist, but the division of labor is not necessarily hierarchical. Organizational work merely calls for specific qualifications and specific abilities, as does any other kind of work. In milieus with a developed scientific tradition, deans of faculties, university presidents, and directors of institutes are not better scholars, but better organizers or people with social connections. They are far from having the greatest social prestige; in fact, it would seem to be held that a scientific worker, even if he is a good organizer, should not waste his time in "administration," for which less capable people can be used. Likewise, there are countries with old and well-developed democratic traditions in which generals, functionaries, and ministers have very modest prestige and incomes. And finally, to put it quite plainly, the paid manager of an estate, even if he is an organizer, is certainly not above the owner of the estate. The contradiction between organizational and executive work is itself a historical contradiction, like many others we have encountered, and is determined by the social system. The fact is that, in certain historical societies, organizational work provides the opportunity of accumulating social power (and the larger the organization that is being managed, the more power), and this becomes the basis for prestige differentiation. In such situations, organizers set up a monopoly of government; more precisely, it is possession of that monopoly that gets them to "specialize" in organizing, and executive labor, which is deprived of any power of decision as to working conditions, appears as wage labor.

A precise answer to the question of the extent to which the various strata of Yugoslav society are compact or disintegrated can only be given by empirical studies. Here we confine ourselves to the statement of certain processes. Thus, for example, a centralistically conducted cadre policy leads to creation of a first stratum and to reinforcement of class elements. Positions of leadership are arrived at by political criteria, [38] which means that the candidate meets the requirements of the establishment. Since in this way the existence of individuals is linked to fitting into the hierarchical structure, they try to fit, and they arrive at equalization of stations, conceptions, conduct — and interests. The first stratum becomes internally homogeneous and externally different from the other strata. [39] One of the empirical indications of the formation of a first stratum consisted in the familiar tendency to take on more than one function; still another is the tendency to live in separate districts of the city.

On the other hand, the institution of self-government

constantly makes innumerable vertical cuts in the stratified structure, connecting previously opened local managerial summits with the executive base in ascending lines of self-governing decisions, by means of which the strata are disintegrated horizontally and integrated vertically in the work collective. The weaker the intensity of stratification in the initial phase (which the revolution took care of in our case) and the lower the degree of interference from outside, the more successfully these integrative mechanisms function.

The conclusions are fairly obvious. Social openness (intergeneration mobility) guaranteed by equalized educational opportunities; self-governing integration; and political democracy — together they destroy stratification, eliminate class residues, and prepare the way for a classless society.

17. HORIZONTAL STRUCTURE OF YUGOSLAV SOCIETY: QUASIPROFESSIONAL GROUPS

It has already been emphasized that self-government makes vertical cuts in the social pyramid and leads to integration of the individual strata. On the other hand, the functional division of labor in societal life leads to the formation of groups distinguished by their functions and not by their position in the social hierarchy. These groups may, and in fact always do, have different interests, but those interests are by their nature nonantagonistic, nonpolarized. Critics of the Marxist thesis of the possibility and necessity of development of the classless society had emphasized that in any existing society there must be social, and hence class, differentiation. But this is a *non sequitur*. There must be some differentiation in any developed society, if for no other reason than the division of labor. But only a vertical status differentiation, stratification, represents a class differentiation. Horizontal differentiation into quasiprofessional groups is characteristic of a new, classless society.

In the horizontal structure of Yugoslav society we can distinguish the following four groups: peasants; other producers for the market; workers in nonmarket occupations; and those in the state apparatus. Of these four groups, the peasantry is a group that has a place in both horizontal and vertical structures. The formation of that group is historically conditioned, and today it is undergoing greater qualitative and quantitative transformations than any other group. We begin our analysis with a consideration of the social position of the peasantry in Yugoslavia.

157

The Peasantry

Peasants still constitute about half the population of our country. But this fact need not alarm us too much, since it is the statistical aspect of the problem. An intensive exodus of the active population from the village and from agriculture, at a rate of about 2% per annum, is under way. Twenty years ago three-fourths of all Yugoslavs were peasants; during the life of this generation the proportion of the peasantry will drop by some 15%, as is the case in other developed countries.

The peasants doubtless constitute the most conservative social group in our country. It should be noted at the outset, however, that their conservatism is not due to the fact that they are small holders, as is generally thought, but to other causes. Actually, the popular notion that the peasant, fully and rationally motivated, holds on to the land fanatically, has a fanatical belief in property, and anarchistically resists progress — that belief confuses cause and effect and is in flagrant contradiction with the facts. An inquiry conducted in Croatian village schools showed that *not 1%* of the 8th grade enrollment of 1963/1964 wanted to remain on their parents' farms [59: 74]. The reasons for the peculiarities of peasant social behavior may, I suppose, be reduced to the following four points:

1. *Cultural backwardness, lack of education, even illiteracy.*[40] The historically conditioned ideological heritage of primitive and conservative beliefs, traditions, and notions, of patriarchalism and other encumbrances, has been conserved to a certain extent to this very day. The reason for the negative inheritance of the past being stronger among peasants than among other groups and for its tighter hold is to be found in the following three characteristics of their present situation.

2. *Existential tie to the soil.* In a situation where there is not an unbounded possibility of productive employment outside of agriculture, and where, within agriculture, surplus labor power constitutes up to one-third of the active population [60: 106], possession of one's own land, the struggle for the land, and economic independence represent a rational way of insuring the peasant's own existence.

3. *One-dimensional social mobility* outward is linked with the preceding point. In a factory, people from the village and from the city mix. There is a lively exchange of ideas and experiences, making it impossible to retain petrified views and positions, hindering manifestations of cultural limitation. People come from the village but do not move back; a person remains a peasant

but does not become one. Furthermore, the mass exodus from the villages rapidly alters the age structure in the direction of the older generations, which are more conservative by nature.

4. *Economic backwardness and communication-isolation of villages.* Labor productivity is considerably lower in villages than in nonagricultural occupations.[41] In 1960, 46% of our peasant fields were still harvested with the sickle, and an additional 38% with the scythe. Because of the well-known "differences between village and city," the village has lagged in general social development and hence appears as a sort of social ballast.

But the village situation is changing rapidly in all four aspects. And in this connection "there is no doubt whatever that the peasant himself will change as socialist development insures him more stable and profitable sources of income, a higher standard of living, a more cultural life" (Kardelj [61: 180]). The decisive impetus toward social transformation was given by the people's liberation war, in which the peasantry took part in full force. Today education is much more available to the villager than ever before, although it must be said that much more could have been done in this domain. The productivity of agricultural labor is rising more rapidly than the productivity of labor in industry, in Yugoslavia as in other countries. Differences in the standard of living between the countryside and the city are diminishing. Large-scale farming is introducing into traditional production methods not only elements of modern technology but also a new organization of work and echoes of the social processes that are taking place in the city. Various forms of cooperation between the peasant and large farms make the social effect of the modernly organized sector of agriculture greater than the percentage of area or production covered by that sector.

Here we must return to the problem of personal (private) property as an automatic criterion for being progressive. The peasant is not reactionary because he is a small holder. We noted earlier that this "reactionary" peasant won the war of people's liberation and the social revolution, not only in our country but also in Algiers, Vietnam, and elsewhere. It would seem that a general confusion exists between the effects of private property under capitalism and the effects that can be expected under our institutional system. Under capitalism, the peasantry is constantly subject to stratification. A few peasants get rich and become landowners, who exploit the labor power of others. A certain number of peasants get poorer, lose their land, and are proletarianized. Most peasants continue to defend themselves against being proletarianized and hope to make their way into the

159

class of agricultural capitalists.

Nothing of the kind is taking place in Yugoslavia. The agrarian maximum makes it impossible to act in the direction of exploiting the labor of others. Leaving the farm does not mean proletarianization. In fact, conditions have been created under which personal possession of land has become a legal fiction, and the essential social position of the individual producer is not different from that of an associated producer. For example, the first statement can be seen from the ordinance on the agrotechnical minimum. Further, if it is necessary to expropriate rent on land, that can be done by a tax on cadastral income. If private means of production have to be treated as social capital, interest on the basic resources or on the operating fund can likewise be approximated by a definite tax. Individual and associated producers sell and buy land and basic resources in the same manner. The second statement is based on the fact that in Yugoslavia the worker is both *producer and manager*. If this holds true for the associated producer, it is equally valid for the individual producer.

In connection with the problem under discussion (and this applies as well to the problem of the individual producer in other sectors of production), it is of interest to note that our consciousness has arrived at a kind of mystique of the collective. Collectively organized production is automatically progressive and socialist, and individually organized production is "petty-bourgeois" and nonsocialist. This prejudice, which has hardened into a tight dogma, has its roots in the social experience of the capitalist system, and is transferred uncritically to the new institutional bases. Indeed, the revolution does not depend on the small *owner* but on the nonpropertied; and it is much easier to organize collectives and to set them in motion to destroy the social system than it is for individuals to do so.

It is also of interest to note that individual producers, and hence peasants too, are an element openly opposed to a Stalinist system of socialism. Such a system aims at total control of the personal labor of the individual, and this aim is most effectively attained by liquidating all independence and including every individual in a definite hierarchical organization, a bureaucratic structure.

Finally, peasant groups have to be given at least one social plus, along with their various minuses. Our associationist society is bipolar; one part of social activity proceeds at work and is oriented toward work, the other part takes place at the place of residence and is oriented toward the satisfaction of other human needs. In the first case, working bodies are involved; in the second,

160

communal bodies. As an individual producer, and to the extent that he is only an individual producer, the peasant is disqualified for working collectives. But that is not all there is to socialism. There are indications that peasants are more active in communal organizations than members of other social groups.[42]

We may conclude that the individual peasant is also a potential socialist producer. The fact that he is not one is actually conditioned by the four factors noted. But economic development automatically transforms the village in the direction of increasingly greater identification with socialist goals. Paraphrasing the well-known dictum of Lenin, we could say that socialism, based on worker self-government, constantly creates socialist tendencies even in those sectors that formerly were nonsocialist.

Nonpeasant Producers for the Market (the Working Class)

"The working class" is one of the political terms we use the most, but it cannot be said that the term is precisely defined. Even the Program of the League of Yugoslav Communists fails to state what is meant by the working class, of which it speaks at length. Sometimes workers are identified with manual laborers [38: 41]. This identification is vague and, to a great extent, meaningless, for typists are also manual workers, and so are peasants; as far as the quantity of manual operations is concerned, surgeons and pianists do not differ from workers in the optical or electronic industries; moreover, technological progress is constantly eliminating manual work — but not workers, to the same extent. Further, a simple division into manual and intellectual workers leads to obvious nonsense. It turns out that a skilled mechanic who diagnoses what is wrong with our car is a manual worker, while the porter of a government institution is an intellectual worker! The division into intellectual and routine workers makes more sense, with the latter divided into manual and nonmanual workers. Even here caution is required. From the Marxist point of view, the *physical* properties of a phenomenon have little relevance for *social* analysis. The key factors for analysis are social relations, a point that is often overlooked. In line with what Gramsci says about intellectuals and proletarians, "the most widespread methodological error consists in seeking the criteria of differentiation only in the nature of intellectual development and not in the entire system in which they (and hence the groups embodying them) were in the general complex of social relationships. In fact, the worker or proletarian, for example, is not characterized by his manual or instrumental work, but rather by that work under given conditions and social

161

relationships . . ." [39:312].

We often come across a definition of the working class as comprising producers who work with social means of production. [43]

It is typical, first of all, that this definition excludes workers of the private sector, i.e., just those who are closest to the classical concept of the working class. Evidently, it is implicitly presupposed and intuitively felt that today's working class differs considerably from that of former times. Further consideration of this definition depends on the meaning of the word "producer." The commonsense interpretation is simple: a producer is a workingman who produces something, something tangible. Are workers in transport also producers? Most people will probably agree that they are. And salespeople in shops? Here opinions will differ. [44] Then what are bank and insurance employees? Here, I suppose, a majority will agree that they are neither workers (and that is why we call them employees) nor producers. However, are not banks *traders* in money, so that what applies to the salesgirl also applies to the bank clerk? And further, where do nurses fit, for example? In the "middle class," along with teachers, bookkeepers, and other workers in white coats and white collars? What exactly does that mean in our social framework? Obviously, our traditional set of categories is no longer very useful. Here I should like to warn against the previously elaborated and very widespread theory of production, according to which only work in what is called material production is productive, and all other work is nonproductive. For this purpose transport and trade are included in material production, and our statistics even add the hotel and restaurant industry. In that case salespeople, waiters, and chambermaids would therefore be included in the working class. To my mind, they should be so included, but not because of this theory of productive labor. The differentiation of productivity (a socioeconomic phenomenon) on the basis of materiality (a physical phenomenon) is theoretically meaningless. Marx emphasized very clearly that the same physical work may be economically either productive or nonproductive. The next question relates to the place of work in a given branch of production. A man working at a machine in a factory is undoubtedly a worker. But does his foreman also belong to the working class? Here opinions will differ. [45] Even more so, an employee in the commercial sector is obviously not a worker. On the other hand, what essential difference (if any) is there between an unskilled worker in a government monopoly and an assistant clerk?

Here again we recognize an uncritical transfer of capitalist social relations. If the production of a factory has to be decreased, the worker at the machine will be discharged — not the foreman and the clerk, because they represent fixed charges, overhead. Therefore, workers at machines, "in direct production," must organize in unions, and their interests come to differ from those of the overhead personnel, whose interests are identified with those of the employer. At the same time, a capitalist factory is hierarchically organized, with the workers as the "base" and the employers, controllers, and other management personnel as "superstructure." The employer is thus vitally interested in having his management personnel identify with his interests.

In a Yugoslav factory all these differences become void, to a great extent. The employees do not identify with the employer since there is no employer, and the workers do not organize in a union to defend their special class interests. There are all sorts of contradictions in a Yugoslav factory, to be sure, but they are of a different nature. They are contradictions within a collective which, with reference to the outside world, does not appear as a conglomeration of contradictory and polarized interests, but rather as a social whole, as a *collective* entering into interactions with *other collectives.*

Empirical studies of Yugoslav factories have only been begun, so that any generalizations will have to be formed and taken with a great deal of caution. One possible generalization relates to internal groupings in an enterprise. If the members of a collective are grouped on the basis of the influence they have on the work and the decisions of the workers' council, three groupings appear, with a clearly hierarchical differentiation:[46] (1) managers of firms and economic entities, and experts; (2) foremen, employees, and skilled workers; (3) semiskilled and unskilled workers. What is significant in this grouping is that foremen, employees, and skilled workers have equal influence, which means that the classical gap in the capitalist factory has been eliminated.[47] It is equally significant that workers are not at all a homogeneous group; it is sharply differentiated on a qualification basis. This result is in full agreement with the results of the previously cited empirical study, which showed that the lowest two categories of workers were not content with their position as workers (about 5 times more unskilled workers were discontented than highly skilled ones). It is also in accord with the fact that minor absences from work, of which the administration of enterprises gets notice, are mostly from semiskilled and unskilled workers [42: 202]. Finally, it would seem that we can conclude that grouping in Yugoslav factories is almost exclusively based on skill and education. Education is of primary importance in the prevalence of group tensions and social stratification.

In the organizational structure of Yugoslav economic organizations, one function has always been a stumbling block: the function of manager. It is one that is inherently contradictory. When the process of eliminating administrative management of the economy was begun, the manager was installed as curator of society's interest in the enterprise, and hence installed from outside. This police function stayed with the manager in the later stage of full development of self-government. But by now pressures have appeared in the direction of defending the rights of the collective to self-government, and the solution found has been increased limitation of the *operative* jurisdiction of the manager. Thus, the hybrid role of the manager, attempting to use two divergent systems, administrative and self-governing, has the result, first, that operative efficiency is considerably lessened, and second, that the manager becomes a foreign element in the collective. In most cases the manager is imposed[48] on a collective from without, fundamentally on the basis of what are called political criteria. Both factors lead to faulty selection, and people with decidedly low professional qualifications retain positions of this kind. Data on the amazingly low educational level of some managerial cadres are too well known to require citation. In order to maintain themselves, such managers tie up with political elements outside the enterprise and set up cliques of people of the same sort inside the enterprise. "Sociological studies," Veljko Rus states in his lucid report, "show that groups with low education are less inclined to cooperate with other groups of workers, less inclined to critical communication, less interested in exact information, less ready to correct faulty orders by higher agencies, and much more aware of hierarchical differences" [33: 1086]. Clique formation is a source of the conflicts that fill our newspapers.[49] On the other hand, it is precisely for these reasons, paradoxical as it may seem at first glance, that positions as managers sometimes remain unfilled for a long time. Qualified candidates are either unacceptable to the various unofficial groups or are unwilling to expose themselves to being mistreated by those groups.

Thus, the tensions and contradictions in Yugoslav enterprises have fairly clear sources. Those sources have little in common with the social situation in capitalist enterprises, and the tendency of development is obviously in the direction of eliminating them.

I think we can say that for all the incompleteness of the system as it now exists, and the deformations that occasionally appear, after ten years of workers' self-government, during which hundreds of thousands of employees have gone through the school of self-government, the goals that were set have begun to be realized. The formerly heterogeneous, even antagonistic elements have merged or are merging into a single collective. *Diversity of interests within the collective are of secondary importance as compared to the unity of interests vis-à-vis the outside world.*

If this analysis is correct, it leads to extremely important consequences. The classical concept of the working class has lost its social content. To a certain extent this is evident. The working class was always the class of wage workers. As wage labor disappears as a social category, the working class will cease to exist. [50]

What is left are working people, the working folk or workers, as a synonym for the active population. [51]

It emerges, in short, that in our social situation the working class is transformed, incorporating other groups (office workers and professionals) with whom they work in the process of production into a single quasiprofessional social group, which we could call producers producing for the market. [52] Those producers are vitally interested in maintaining and further developing their autonomy, and in eliminating contradictions within their collectives. In this sense, their interests are identical with the interests of developing and affirming socialist classless society. And because they control the productive resources of society, they represent the principal motive force of socialist development.

Workers in Nonmarket Occupations (the Intelligentsia)

In a technical sense, the intelligentsia should comprise engineers working in factories, jurists in government departments, professors of philosophy, and scientists. In a socioeconomic sense their position is very different, and they must be grouped apart. Here, we shall designate as the intelligentsia highly educated working people in the fields of health, education, science, and culture.

It should be said at once that this differentiation is most unorthodox. As a rule, the intelligentsia is subdivided into two groups, creative and reproductive workers or, as the American philosopher Hodges calls them [45: 428], intellectuals and professionals. In the first group come scientists, artists, philosophers, and all those who create culture, for whom ideas and culture are ends, not means. The second group comprises engineers, physicians, journalists, and all practitioners whose job it is to apply and diffuse culture. In this sense D. Pejović finds that

165

there is an "immeasurable distance between the activity of, say, a philosopher or an author from any engineer or physician" [36: 267]. It is not my intention to contest the validity of these distinctions or their relevance to an analysis, for example, of the formation of the culture of a given society. At the same time, such a classification would be quite arbitrary, and hence inapplicable, in analyzing the socioeconomic position of the various groups in Yugoslav society. Perhaps, in some sense, the activity of a philosopher is really immeasurably different from that of a physician. With reference to the socioeconomic conditioning of the existence of the people in question in our society, their activities are of the same kind.

Ever since it appeared for the first time in Russia in the latter half of the nineteenth century, the term "intelligentsia" has always had a slightly subversive aura.

I think we may say frankly that communist parties have traditionally been distrustful of the intelligentsia, and that traces of that attitude still remain among us.[53] The reasons for it are probably stated most explicitly by Lenin:[54]

"No one can deny that the *intelligentsia,* as a *particular stratum* of modern capitalist society, is marked generally by *individualism* and incapacity for discipline and organization; in this it differs, among other ways, and in a negative sense, from the proletariat; this is also one of the explanations of intellectual sluggishness and inconstancy so often felt by the proletariat; and this characteristic of the intelligentsia is inseparable from the daily conditions of its life and work, which in very many ways are close to the conditions of *petty-bourgeois existence* (individual work or work in very small collectives) [46: 378-379].

Rosa Luxemburg reacted to this evaluation of the intelligentsia, and it will undoubtedly be of historical and theoretical interest to cite her criticism, even at the cost of prolonging citations:[55]

"According to Lenin, this aversion to submitting to the absolute power of the Central Committee is found in the intellectual, who has remained an individualist and is inclined to anarchy, even when he has adopted socialism, while the true and genuine proletarian draws from his class instinct a kind of pleasure in surrendering to a power that rules and combines an unremitting discipline with its rigor . . . .

"We begin by noting that exaltation of the innate inclinations with which proletarians are endowed with respect to socialist organization, and mistrust of the intellectuals, are not in essence an expression of the 'revolutionary Marxist' way of thinking; on the contrary, it can easily be shown that these arguments border

166

on opportunism . . . .

"No doubt it cannot be denied that in most socialist parties of Western Europe there are links between opportunism and the intellectuals, as there are between opportunism and decentralizing tendencies.

"But there is nothing so contrary to Marxism, to its historical dialectical method of thought, as the separation of phenomena from the *historical background* out of which they arose, and their formulation into theoretical patterns of absolute and general significance.

"Reasoning abstractly, one can only recognize that 'the intellectual,' as a social being who came from the bourgeoisie and is alien to the proletariat, may approach socialism not basically but against his class consciousness. That renders him more liable to opportunistic fluctuations than the proletarian, who finds a very reliable revolutionary support in his class instinct. . . ."

Autonomistic and decentralistic tendencies "are therefore to be explained, not as Lenin does, by the unbalanced nature of the 'intellectual,' but by the needs of the bourgeois parliamentary politician, not by the psychology of the "intellectual,' but by opportunistic policies. . . .

"If we took Lenin's position as a basis, and were afraid of any intellectuals' influence in the labor movement, the greatest danger to the Russian Socialist Party would be the organizational plans proposed by Lenin. Nothing would more certainly subject the labor movement, still so young, to an intellectual elite, hungry for power, as this bureaucratic armor, motivating it and converting it into an automate ruled by the 'committee.'

"And conversely, there is no more effective guarantee against opportunistic intrigues and personal ambitions than the independent revolutionary activity of the proletariat, by means of which it comes to the conception of political activity."

The polemic between Lenin and Rosa Luxemburg was conducted in 1904, long before any workers' party had firmly attained power. In a situation of that kind, "decentralist tendencies" could be objectively dangerous to the struggle, especially the illegal one, which called for a firm and centralized organization. As a result, Lenin, regardless of the correctness or incorrectness of his argument, could voice a certain mistrust of the intelligentsia. In Yugoslavia, however, a quarter-century has passed since the outbreak of the successful socialist revolution. In this situation "decentralist tendencies" are not only not undesirable, but in fact represent the fundamental line of further development, the most effective "guarantee against opportunistic intrigues and personal ambitions." This last statement by Rosa Luxemburg, in the context of contemporary political events and the Fourth Plenum, has a prophetic ring.[56]

The intelligentsia, in the narrow sense of the word as defined above, is oriented toward a special field of human activity. Producers for the market turn out external elements for human welfare or, rather, they create the material base of that welfare; the intelligentsia is aimed directly at man, its activity is directly humanist. This holds true for the health workers who take care of preserving man's physical life; for the workers in education whose task it is to develop man's intellect; for cultural workers, artists, and philosophers who discover the meaning of life and form the values of their era. And even scientific workers, whose discoveries are used by the economy or the army, go beyond the utilitarian character of their patents by insisting that, above all, they are discovering and asserting scientific *truth*. Although it would probably be wrong to say that the intelligentsia *represents*[57] the conscience and the consciousness of their era, there is little doubt that by their activity they express, explain, and form the conscience and the consciousness of their era.

That expression and explication may be accurate or distorted, useful or dangerous, for ruling circles and ruling classes. Consequently, regimes pay close attention to the activity of the intelligentsia, and attempts are not wanting to control them in one respect or the other. What is the situation among us in this respect?

I think the following three factors may be noted:

1. The large majority of today's intelligentsia, more than three-fourths,[58] were formed after the war, i.e., against the background of socialist construction.

2. Since higher education is free and, at least in principle, available to all, intellectual cadres are recruited from all social strata; hence we may speak of a *people's* intelligentsia.

3. The intelligentsia took a very active part in the prewar revolutionary movement[59] and in the battle for national liberation and postwar construction, so that many prewar cadres not only identified with socialism but represent the most active factors of socialist development.

We may draw the conclusion that the Yugoslav intelligentsia has a very broad social base and is now one of the mainstays of the system. There may be isolated abuses, it is true, as is the case with factories as well, but deviations en masse are quite impossible.

We could now take a step forward in the analysis similar to the one in considering the position of producers for the market. Just as all who work in factories identify with the interests of the worker, so do those who work in institutions identify with the interests of the intelligentsia. In hospitals and schools, groups work that are professionally and otherwise heterogeneous. But under conditions of self-government, those groups still represent individual working collectives. For this reason it is probably better and more suitable today to speak of the intelligentsia as workers in nonmarket occupations.

The term "nonmarket" should be made clear at the outset. Although, in principle, hospitals, schools, theaters, museums, etc., may sell their services on the market, they do this only exceptionally in any civilized country. Health, education, learning, and culture are too important for the life of the society to be left to the automatic action of the market. Further, it is much harder to measure production in these activities than in the market sector, and often it is impossible in principle. What is the value of saving a human life, or of Einstein's theory of relativity?

What has been said does not signify that no economic considerations are possible or required. A certain monetary evaluation of the effect is both possible and necessary, since the conditions are thereby created for the financial independence of nonmarket activities, and hence of their operational autonomy. A university or scientific institute, which "lives off the state budget" exclusively, must inevitably end up in a situation where the desires and interests of the controller of the budget, and not scientific truth, are the criteria of its work.

At the same time, no matter how the financing of nonmarket activities is organized, it can never be reduced to the supply and demand mechanism of atomistic subjects on the market. Definite social decisions are necessary, which are only the financial expression of some sort of tax or subsidy (for social insurance, for schools, etc.). Since any such tax has to be collected in the market sector, a certain conflict of interest arises between workers in market and nonmarket activities. In such contradictions the latter, as recipients, are in an unfavorable position. Consequently, personal incomes in the nonmarket sector show a chronic, and sometimes a critical, tendency to lag behind incomes in the market sector. This violation of the principle "to each according to his labor" is the source of political discontent and a certain hypercritical attitude.

On the other hand, it is important to see that *historically, self-government first arose in the nonmarket sector.* Even in the Middle Ages the universities had already won their autonomy, and have kept it down to the present, developing their self-governing organization and resisting the attacks of the state bureaucracy.[60] The humanist character of nonmarket activities makes those engaged in them highly sensitive to class and social differences, so that they spontaneously resist bureaucratic pressures and equally spontaneously undermine hierarchical social structures. The high education of the workers in these activities operates in the same direction. If socialism should mean a society without classes, socially organized as a community of associated individuals, then the intelligentsia and all workers in nonmarket activities represent, to the highest possible extent, an active social force in socialist construction. This is easily understandable. Education, culture, and humanist activities and orientations have always characterized advanced systems and movements.

The State Apparatus (the Bureaucracy)

The danger of bureaucracy manifests itself in all large social organizations, in large enterprises, in unions and parties, and in the state apparatus. Irrespective of the unity of the interests of the workers' collective, therefore, it would be both naive and dangerous to neglect the analysis of and the struggle against bureaucratic tendencies. Furthermore, sectoral bureaucracies have definite common interests and show tendencies toward forming a cartel with the state bureaucracy. This is the situation in which modern societies find themselves, as expressed in this eloquent parable by Maurice Duverger:

"Instead of a single tyrant and his few adjutants, we have a multiplicity of petty tyrants. Each of them has his sphere of action. But the pressure of all of them paralyzes, more or less, people's freedom of movement; people are a good deal like Gulliver, when the Lilliputians tied him down with thousands of threads, each of which was insignificant, but all together were overpowering.

"Modern government tends to be more than just the group of chiefs, authorities, administrators, who individually abuse their power. It has become an enormous machine, whose overall functioning goes beyond the activity of each of its chiefs. Its mere mechanism is oppressive, apart from the intentions of the people that make it up. We call this phenomenon "bureaucracy." It does not confine itself to government, i.e., to power over nations; it spreads to all the domains of power in large modern communities: to giant firms, political parties, mass organizations, etc. Even if abstractly, mechanically, without passion, without physical violence, the oppression that emanates from the bureaucracy is in no way less than what arises from the power hunger of the chiefs.

"This is probably one of the basic factors of antagonism in highly developed societies. As we approach the level of abundance, class struggles and rivalry between citizens lessen (subject to the reservations that we have presented). On the other hand, the conflicts between the authorities and the citizenry are sharpened" [53: 172].

Although individual propositions of Duverger's may be disputed or criticized, they undoubtedly form a realistically drawn picture, on the whole. If we except the Pharaohs or the Chinese administration, which were quite specific at that, bureaucracy as a mass social phenomenon is something entirely new. It is a child of our century. But the most complex of bureaucracies, and the most dangerous, is the state bureaucracy. It differs from others in one essential property: it relies on physical force.[61] It is for this reason that I set the state apparatus apart as a special social group. In the state apparatus I include the government administration, the judiciary, the police, armed forces, and professional politicians.

In developed countries the key positions in the apparatus of the state are as a rule held by highly educated people, i.e., the intelligentsia in the technical sense. In our country this is not altogether the case, but insofar as there are deviations, they obviously broaden rather then narrow the social base from which government officials are recruited. This too is one of the results of our revolution. By virtue of their origin and previous activities, government officials, like market and nonmarket workers, constitute progressive elements. But in *contradistinction to the latter, who are permanently revolutionized by their social situation, officials in the government, as wielders of power and living in strictly hierarchical social structures, are exposed to fearful conservative and antisocialist pressures* relating to the situation that is conditioned by tendencies to deformations in consciousness, to deformations in behavior, and to the well-known bureaucratic phenomena of which the antisocialist activity of the police group around Ranković is only the most flagrant example.

Consequently, it is no wonder that the establishment of self-government in government agencies came latest, that self-government develops most slowly there, and that the formation of a unified collective is most difficult. Obviously, the integration into a single collective of the minister and his staff, of the general and his soldiers in the ranks, of the chief of some division of the state and his employees, is much more difficult than similar processes in a factory or scientific institution.

Of all the social groups we have considered, the state apparatus is numerically the smallest. But because of the fact that it is the group that holds power in its hands (even though under some control), the social effects of its behavior far exceed the size of its numbers. I shall not discuss here whether and to what extent "power corrupts just as money does."[62] But some observations may be not uninteresting.

M. Duverger says that we have inherited from the theologians of the Middle Ages a classification of such basic human impulses as the sexual impulse, the desire for learning, and the desire for domination. The last-named, *concupiscentia dominandi,* concerns us particularly. Hobbes asserts that hunger for power is a "general inclination of all men" [54: 83]. He explains it by the fact that people have the same drive toward riches, and since wealth is insufficient to go around, conflict arises, in which he who has more power gets more. In modern psychoanalysis, Adler regards the drive toward assertion as one of the two key conceptions of his individual psychology. It is a drive arising out of the child's feeling of inferiority toward adults, and it "drives children to set themselves goals that would make them dominant over those around them" [55: 55]. According to Adler, the drive to power has an exclusively rational character, namely, to prevent the dangers that come from inferiority. However, Fromm [56: 135-168] warns of the irrational elements in the nonphysiological drive which, according to him, represents only one pole of a single symbiotic relationship, the other pole of which is yearning for submission. When, with the development of capitalism, the individual was torn from his social ties, he was not only liberated from his former bonds but also felt himself isolated, unsupported, helpless, petty, and full of anxieties. Overcoming the intolerable anxiety and isolation, and returning to certainty, can be made possible by restoring the symbiotic relationship with other individuals by means of domination or by means of one's own subordination, depending on the situation. We could also add the empirical fact that, in both animal and human communities, individuals appear who dominate and wage unremitting warfare for the sake of that dominant position.

The foregoing is like bits in an incomplete mosaic, enabling us to form a picture of the total. I see that picture somewhat as follows. In historical societies the existence of each individual is threatened, and he wages a perpetual battle for survival.[63] In that battle, force — power — may play the key role. The more powerful the individual, the greater his share in the limited riches of society, and the more assured his existence and that of his offspring. Those who are not in a position themselves to insure domination over others find it advantageous, to the degree of their weakness, to put themselves under someone more powerful and together to plunder the weak. In this way the drives to domination and subordination are complements of the single drive to insure existence. This drive is then reinforced by irrational components, as Fromm emphasized, arising out of the psychological inability to endure the isolation that is reached in today's class society. In this way the social situation forms a definite type of behavior that is so intensive as to resemble a physiological drive, and represents one of those "survivals of capitalism in people's consciousness" of which there is so much talk. It may be added that particular personal characteristics may favor the assumption of a state of domination or subordination, as the case may be, and that particular social structures may favor or hamper the development of such relations.

Evidently, then, either because of personal predispositions or because of social conditioning, a certain number of individuals have a very active drive to dominate. This drive may be satisfied in sports, in public activities, or at the place of work, in the form of being the first or the best. Success is rewarded with social prestige or material benefits. In these cases, personal and social interests coincide for the most part. It is true that success may also be attained by fraud, but there is little chance that this will be lasting. When power is involved, the situation is very different. There is always the possibility of abuses, which sanctions and controls are not effective or thorough enough to prevent, with the result that the freedom of others is fettered, while private ideas, wishes, and interests are imposed with definite — sometimes violent — forms of exploitation of individuals and groups. Historical examples are too well known to require iteration.

If our analysis is accurate, then (unlike collectives in market and nonmarket activities) the state apparatus cannot be regarded as an autochthonous socialist force. On the contrary, we may expect that strong conservative and bureaucratic tendencies will appear in that social group. As has been said, it is not a matter of the good or evil intentions of the individuals who perform government functions. The Marxist position, "which regards the development of economic social formations as a natural-historical process, is less able than any other to shift off to the individual the responsibility for conditions that are socially created" [4: liii]. Therefore society, by means of effective control, must provide assurances against disagreeable shocks. And that is what our society does: rotation, deprofessionalization of politicians, spreading of power (communal arrangement and other forms of decentralization), strengthening of control over representative agencies, and total liquidation of such organizations as the political police. But there still remains much to be done, particularly in forming a responsible, democratically trained and active public opinion, which is the most effective instrument for preventing abuses of power. It would be naive, of course, to expect that the elements of power in the state could be quickly, or easily, or totally eliminated or rendered harmless. That is why we speak of the withering away of the state as a long and painful process. But there is no doubt that to the extent that the state apparatus loses the attributes of power and is transformed into an expert servant of society, that social group will be transformed, from a potentially conservative and antisocialist one, into a vehicle of social progress.

Conclusion

If we consider the process of social production from the economic standpoint (i.e., how the demands of the members of that society are met, how their economic welfare is raised), we readily see that market and nonmarket activities make positive contributions toward that goal, while the work of government administration is necessary, to be sure, yet does not add to anyone's well-being, and has the character of a social expenditure. Obviously, the less government administration there is, the more resources are left to satisfy the material and nonmaterial needs of the members of society. This brings out still another aspect of the special position of the state apparatus in the process of social production, which was discussed in connection with setting up the theory of productive labor.

Further, we separated out of the group of producers (market and nonmarket) the peasants, who are different, mainly because of their historical heritage.

We saw that there are weighty reasons why market and nonmarket producers cannot be treated as a single social group. Their material interests may even conflict. At the same time, these two groups are natural counterpoises. The producers for the market may exert a positive influence in correcting unrealistic programs and conceptions on the part of their humanistic colleagues, who are sometimes inclined to idealize things and to make proposals that are incompatible with the material possibilities of the country. On the other hand, workers in the nonmarket sectors are both interested in and capable of supplying a social criticism of deformations that manifest themselves as consequences of commodity-money relations (bureaucratic and monopolistic tendencies, uncontrolled race for profits, petty-bourgeois mentality, etc.).

Thus, our investigation has led us to the conclusion that there are, or are emerging, four social groups in Yugoslavia at the present stage of development. Two of these groups (the nonpeasant producers in market and nonmarket activities) are instruments of socialist development. One of these groups (the peasants) are by heritage a conservative element. It is the largest group numerically, but its social influence is small; in addition, as the result of economic development, a very intensive process of social transformation is taking place within the group. The last group (the government apparatus) is likewise a conservative element, although of a different type. We may not expect that economic development will automatically transform it in the socialist sense; here effective social control is required.

In this investigation I have tried to state how the various groups of society developed out of preceding classical forms of classes and strata. I believe it is evident that those classes and strata have not disappeared, that in varying degrees they blend with and attach themselves to the new forms, and that as a whole our society has for a long time been undergoing an intensive process of social transformation and restructuring. But the evolutionary connections are visible. The final picture is most unorthodox. Neither differences in income level, nor differences between mental and physical labor (with the only exception of the difference between city and country), and hence, and even more so, differences in property or inherited status, which are the traditional sources of the division of society into classes and strata — none of these are essentially operative in the structuring of today's Yugoslav society. And this should not surprise us. Group loyalties are determined by position in the process of social production. By means of the institution of self-government, that production is immediately socialized, eliminating the basis for the formation of classes and creating the preconditions for their withering away, where they exist. In the place of classes, various kinds of professional groups are beginning to form. Nor is it accidental that this new social structure is reflected to a definite extent in the structure of the Federal Assembly, the highest political body of the country, where there are four different chambers (political-economic, education and culture, health and social welfare, and administrative).[64]

Finally, our results can be quantified. The structure of the active population, arranged in the above-mentioned groups, would appear as follows, in census years:[65]

175

| | (thousands) | | | |
| | 1953 | | 1961 | |
	No.	%	No.	%
Peasants	5,003	67.8	4,408	55.4
Other market producers	1,943	26.2	2,887	36.3
Nonmarket producers	224	3.0	408	5.1
Government apparatus	220	3.0	257	3.2
Active population	7,390	100.0	7,960	100.0

It will be seen that the structure is changing very rapidly, and in the direction of a decrease in the proportion of market producers and an increase in the proportion of nonmarket producers. The number of peasants is decreasing absolutely, but the government apparatus remains in a state of expansion. All these tendencies (with the exception of the last) are familiar from the development of other countries as well, but these processes were formerly much slower. If the present rate of economic development (and thereby of social transformation) also continued over the next eight years, at the end of this decade, workers in the economic sector would be the dominant group and would comprise over half the active population, the proportion of nonmarket producers would increase by one-tenth (almost doubling in absolute number), and the proportion of peasants in the population would drop below 40%.

In the further course of socialist construction in our country, we may expect, in addition to the falling off of the peasantry and the transformation of the state apparatus, an increased social homogeneity within the various groups. Three important factors operate in that direction. One is the systematic decrease in the spread of personal incomes. This phenomenon is observed in all the countries for which data exist, and particularly in countries that abandon the capitalist mode of production [57: 162-169]. The second factor is the gradual equalization of standards of education and culture. The third factor consists in the integrative effects of social self-government. In this way a classless society is being constructed in Yugoslavia.

FOOTNOTES

1. Thus e.g., the Federal Conference of the Socialist Alliance of the Working People of Yugoslavia, in its document dated May 27, 1967, found it necessary to call for an ideological-political struggle for the formation of a self-government consciousness in the character of education, science, and culture: "This will combat the idea that activities living off surplus labor are parasitic, without distinguishing that part of social reproduction without which there can be no rapid advance of productivity and

without which it is impossible to meet the needs of the working man" [1: 13].

2. This proposition does not characterize only the capitalists of Marx's time; identical ideas appear among contemporary — let us say, American — capitalists: "Government is powerless to create anything in the sense in which business produces wealth and individuals produce ideas [and] inventions . . ." (Sutton *et al., The American Business Creed,* p. 195, cited by Galbraith [2: 184]).

3. Accordingly, it appears that not only must Marx be defended against Soviet economists, but Smith too needs protection from some of his Western colleagues. An excellent defense was presented by A.W. Lewis. In two of his articles he deals with the basic classical approach [5: 6], interpreting Smith on the same basis that Marx does (although, as far as I know, he is not familiar with Marx's interpretation), as can be seen from the following excerpts: "As Smith put it, there are two elements in productive labor. First, his product is composed of wages goods (goods that are part of the worker's consumption — B.H.) and excludes services. Second, productive labor produces a profit above wages and therefore has a greater average product than nonproductive labor. This distinction is made and used only for the purpose of analyzing the accumulation of capital." Note: "Strictly speaking, Smith's definition differentiates between goods and services. But our modern distinction between wages goods and other production appears to be precisely what he was aiming at and which best agrees with his analysis." "Neoclassical economists attacked this distinction from the standpoint of the theory of values, but since this was not thought of in that context, the attack is irrelevant." And finally: "Classical economists approached the analysis of accumulation through consumption of wages goods. They divided consumers into three classes: (1) the capitalist and landowner; (2) producers of services and luxury goods; and (3) producers of wages goods. In a broad sense, the consumption of non-wages goods was part of the capitalists' and landowners' consumption since they considered that class (2) supports class (1) for entertainment, etc., from the profits wrung from class (3). Thus, when they spoke of the savings of capitalists, they sometimes thought of a reduction of their personal consumption of wages goods, but more often they thought of less personal service, thereby reducing the number supported in class (2)" [7: 239].

4. "Let us consider the first, correct definition. Productive labor, in the sense of capitalist production, is hired labor, which in exchange for part of the capital not only reproduces this part of the capital . . . but also produces a surplus value for the capitalist . . . Only the part of hired labor that produces capital is productive" [7: 239].

5. The somewhat more cautiously formulated statement of Notkin is still another example of the same doctrine [9: 83b]. It should be added that Soviet statisticians do not follow the advice of their economist colleauges and do *not* count government and party services as additions to the social product.

6. Thus, Kronrod reinforces his position by citing these philosophical reflections by Stalin: "For people to be able to live, they need food, clothing, shoes, houses, heating, etc.; in order for these material goods to exist, they have to be produced" [8: 3].

7. Kronrod writes: "The great tasks posed for our country by the new five-year plan call for increasing still further the part of labor devoted to the sphere of material production . . ." [8: 39-40].

8. Actually, this has already been done at the Yugoslav Institute for Economic Research. See B. Horvat [10].

9. But property under capitalism is undergoing a certain metamorphosis and limitation of property rights, an impersonalization and disintegration. On this see the intelligent and succinct text of M. Pečujlić [11: 37-47].

10. We can add to vulgar Marxism vulgar socialism in general. Thus, vulgar socialists would not permit even individual ownership of consumption goods; owning an automobile or a house was regarded, and sometimes is still regarded, as an expression of bourgeois appetites; and it was demanded, and is still demanded, that consumption goods be owned in common and that the individual's life be completely regimented. It is not hard to discover the essence of all such theories: their petty-bourgeois mentality. As usual, Marx had something to say about this phenomenon. He calls it *primitive* communism, which, as "the first positive abolition of private ownership . . . is only, therefore, a *manifest form* of the vileness of private ownership, which wants to establish itself as a positive community." In one remarkable passage Marx writes: *"Communism* is . . . primarily *general* private ownership . . . Direct physical possession is to him the one aim of life and existence; the laborer's work is not abolished but is extended to all men . . . That communism

177

— since it negates man's *personality* — is only the consequential expression of private ownership, which itself is that negation. General *envy,* which is constituted as force, is merely a concealed form in which greed is established and satisfied, only in another way. The meaning of all private ownership as such is directed, *at least,* against *richer* private ownership as envy and a desire for equalization . . . The primitive communist is merely a completion of that envy and desire for equalization in regard to the *demonstrated* minimum . . . The fact that the abolition of private ownership has little to do with actual appropriation is proved by the abstract negation of the whole cultivated and civilized world, the return of the *unnatural poor* and unnecessary simplicity of man, who has not only not overcome private ownership, he hasn't even achieved it" [12: 225-226].

11. K. Marx, *Economic and Philosophical Manuscripts, 1844* [12: 167].

12. The two meanings of the concept of exploitation have also been discussed by R. Lukič, although his analysis is somewhat different. See "Exploitation as an Element of Social Classes" [13: 369-373].

13. In my article "Division Between Collectives According to Labor" [14], I have shown how the popular slogan that individual incomes in enterprises should rise in proportion to the increase in labor productivity negates distribution according to labor and thus leads to exploitation.

14. It is a characteristic feature that artisans are the social group that is the least self-reproducing: only 9.2% of the children of artisans remain artisans themselves. Also characteristic is the intrageneration mobility of persons active in 1939 and 1960: less than a third of today's artisans were artisans before the war, half of them were recruited from among prewar workers, and 7% from among prewar peasants (V. Milič).

15. The theory of this problem is dealt with in detail in my book *Ekonomska teorija planske privrede* (The Economic Theory of a Planned Economy) [15: 65-91].

16. In connection with this transition, a news item from *Borba,* October 1966, is instructive. We cite it in full: "The municipal council in Sombor recently handed down an unusual decision in the case of artisan Ana Kreko, a weaver from Bezdan, under which there will be applied in the shop the principles of employment and self-government that are valid for artisan shops with social ownership. Specifically: the decision stresses that self-government by the workers who are members of the working organization will be introduced in the workshop in question. Further, there is to be free entry into the workers' organization and free exit from it, on the basis of a decision by the members of the collective, each member having equal rights and obligations. Most important, decisions as to distribution of the income and the means for individual income are to be taken by all the members of the workers' cooperative. This step was decided on, as Ana Kreko states, 'in order to take full advantage of the possibilities for operation and expansion of the material basis of the workshop.'"

17. In general, the domain of "the artisanry" has not had any functional significance in our economic classification for a long time, and causes unnecessary difficulties for economic analysis and economic policy and planning. Cooperatives of artisans, which produce as any enterprise does, should be included in the economic branch and grouping into which their production fits. However, every attempt at such a reform has been vigorously opposed by artisan chambers of commerce and by other agencies representing artisans. One artisan official gave me this explanation: Economically, that would be correct, but then the artisanry would be reduced to the level of the private craftsman, and artisan officials don't want to be considered as representing a private owner.

18. At the present level of socioeconomic development, small-scale trade, small-scale hotel and restaurant business, miscellaneous services, etc., are much more efficiently conducted by individual initiative than by cumbersome enterprises.

19. In tax terminology, they can appear in the unpretentious forms of capital tax and land tax.

20. Ten years ago this was the dominant conception, as is shown by the following statement from Kardelj's book on farm policy: "Another indispensable administrative measure is the prohibition of the purchase of basic means for large-scale production, such as tractors and similar machinery. These means . . . can only serve to render services to others or for various nonagricultural activities. In other words, those resources (since they were in private hands for the most part) could be a source of reinforcing capitalist tendencies on the farm. In any event, tolerating such a state of affairs could only favor antisocialist tendencies on the land and create obstacles to the realization of our socialist farm policy" [61: 310-311].

21. Cf. J. Djordjević [20: 264 - 266].
22. Cf. M. Popović [21: 34] and V. Milić [22: 3 - 38].
23. A study made by P. Novosel on 350 urban and rural subjects showed a correlation of 0.8-0.9 between the rank of individuals in social prestige and the income it was felt they should receive. It is interesting that all the subjects, regardless of their socioeconomic status (with the exception of one peasant), gave approximately the same rank listing (correlation coefficient: 0.91) [24: 622-623].
24. A similarly three-dimensional determination of social stratification, inspired by Weber, is given by K. Mayer [25: 330-331]. Weber defines power as the ability to control the behavior of others; Mayer defines it as the control that certain groups are in a position to exert on the opportunities of others.
25. Typical in this respect are the results of an inquiry by A. Todorović, who questioned 5,012 workers. He received the following answers to the question, "Are you content to be a worker?":

% in given category

	very well satisfied	dissatisfied
Highly skilled	41.2	5.4
Skilled	22.5	11.4
Semi-skilled	19.4	17.9
Unskilled	15.8	24.0

About half the highly skilled workers are very well satisfied with their status; a quarter of the unskilled workers are dissatisfied in the main or altogether (the others said: "satisfied by and large," "all the same to me") [26: 165]. Further, in 1960 the first two groups took part in workers' councils to twice the extent of their proportion among workers, while the second pair of groups participated to only half the extent of their proportion among workers (SZS, *Bilten 230*, p.9). An IDN inquiry brings out the fact that in no case were less than half the members of the workers' council highly skilled workers, while for semiskilled and unskilled workers the figure was nine-tenths. Again, about half the unskilled and semiskilled workers owned land, as against 29-38% for the other two categories [27: 9-10, 42].
26. See [16: 202, 206]. The data relate to the AZS definition of artisan.
27. At the same time, semiskilled and unskilled workers regard peasants as closest to them, which is reasonable in view of the fact that two-thirds of them come from peasant families. See M. Ilić [28: 82, 286].
28. Additional information is given by an inquiry by IDN, according to which 80% of industrial workers are satisfied to belong to the working class, 70% believe that workers are valued and respected among us, and 95% believe that the working class rules; nevertheless, 85% want their children to be office workers [27: 43].
29. Education likewise makes the relationship of the individual to Yugoslav society positive. In studying the degree of social integration of the various categories of worker (combating inadequecies in commune and enterprise, participation in worker and social self-government, political membership, satisfaction with status), M. Ilić finds that " . . . the level of qualification of the worker is directly proportional to his degree of integration" (*op. cit.,* p. 93).
30. In this context, what happens in our higher education — namely, the insistence, on pseudodemocratic grounds, that everyone who wishes to should be admitted, regardless of his working and intellectual qualities, with a simultaneous decrease in the number of scholarships — leads to petrifaction of the hierarchical structure. The criterion for admission to the university becomes the property (and educational) status of the parents. To some extent these negative aspects counteract the increase in the number of cities with higher educational institutions.
31. One of the criteria that can be used to determine the number of *managerial* persons is personal income of over 70,000 din. per month in 1963, which includes about 2.5% of all employed persons in the social sector (*Indeks,* November 1966, p. 46). Breaking this down into individual categories in terms of mean incomes, in thousands of dinars, we have: managers of industrial and construction enterprises, 77 and 75; heads and assistant heads of cities, districts, and communes, 76 and 62; government administration functionaries, 76; federal and republic secretaries, 92 and 90; chief justices and district attorneys, 72 and 83; managers of chambers of commerce, 77; and managers of commercial agencies and insurance companies, 80 and 66. The incomes of university professors and teachers were 76,000 and 35,000 dinars,

respectively (SZS, *Bilten 400*, pp. 20-51). In 1961, the SZS registered 93,366 persons as managerial personnel in the following categories: (1) permanent members of representative bodies, 2,110; (2) government administration functionaries, 2,270; (3) supervisors and inspectors of government administration, 12,672; (4) heads of institutions, 10,800; (5) assistants to heads of institutions and supervisors, 13,269; (6) managers of business firms, 27,175; (7) technical directors, 8,942; (8) commercial and financial directors, 2,648; (9) others, 13,480 (*Bilten 312*, p. 89). This spread is evidently too broad. If we subtract categories 3, 5, 7, and 8, we have a total of 55,835 persons left. If we take into account in all the categories only those with secondary, college, and university education, there remain 61,012 persons. On the basis of these considerations, the number of managerial cadres comes to 60,000. It is of interest to note that the educational level of managerial personnel is rising rapidly. According to an SZS survey in 1953, of a total of 51,911 persons, 9% had university training and 21% had secondary education; in 1961, of 93,366 persons, the relative figures were 39% and 36% (*Bilten 73*, p. 10). Of the managerial cadres, 29,000 were "recruited" from the ranks of the intelligentsia and 31,000 from functionaries with secondary education, so that these two categories should be diminished by these numbers. Intellectual workers are persons with college and university training, and their number is drawn from the same source as the number of officials and workers (*Bilten 312*, p. 88). *Artisans* are a residual category: the figures given show 152,000 private productive and service artisans and 139,000 private persons employed in other economic fields, especially in trade and in the restaurant business (*Bilten 312*, p. 23). *Peasants* are those engaged in agriculture who are neither workers nor functionaries (*Bilten 312*, pp. 22, 23).

32. *Jugoslavija 1945-1964*, p. 60.

33. This thesis is convincingly supported by the data of Milić on the social origin of government employees (in %) [16: 209] :

	Father's Occupation			
	Agricultural		Manual	Nonmanual
Assistants and those with primary education	55.1	84.2	29.1	15.8
Employees with secondary and college education	31.9	64.9	33.0	35.1
Employees with university education	27.2	48.9	21.7	51.1
Managerial cadres (SZS definition)	36.7	61.6	24.9	38.4

It will be seen that, as we come to higher positions in social stratification, there is a clear and regular decline in the share of manual labor groups as compared with workers of nonmanual origin (mainly functionaries). The rule does not prevail for the managerial cadres. But it must be kept in mind that the degree of self-renewal among managerial cadres is one of the highest (36.2%) and that, as in other societies, there will be a strong tendency for that rate to rise, the further we go from the time of the revolution.

34. The conversion of the pyramidal into a spheroid structure is an empirical fact today in the industrially most developed countries. This stems from the change in the overall distribution of the national income, from the rise in the general level of education, and from the diminution of income differentials. The last factor is impressively illustrated by R. Supek's data concerning the real income of a French state councilor and an American skilled worker. At the beginning of this century the income of the councilor was five times as great. Thereafter it decreased and workers' income increased, so that in the middle of this century an American skilled worker earns more than a French state councilor [29: 111].

35. I borrow this term from M. Pečujlić, who holds — quite correctly, it seems to me — that bureaucracy should not be identified with class because, although it has the monopoly of governing, it possesses it not on the basis of its own right of ownership, but on the basis of a delegation of right. "Actually, the separation of property from

government is the historical basis of the formation of the bureaucracy and its differentiation from class" [30: 14].

36. This is the conclusion of M. Pećujlić as well: "If this activity is the basis of people's existence, then power (monopoly) over the conditions of labor is the factor that must determine the position in production relations" [30: 8].

37. Cf. also "ascribed status" and "achieved status" in R. Linton ("Status and Role" [32: 202-203]).

38. S. Mozina reports on an inquiry in which potential candidates for the position of manager were asked what the criteria were that decided on preference for their choice as directors; four-fifths declared that the criteria were political, and only one-tenth regarded the criteria as professional [33: 359].

39. 1. Empirical studies on the local level show that managerial cadres choose their friends from the same stratum (in three- quarters of cases), while lower functionaries choose among their friends someone from higher strata. "In this connection," Z. Mlinar concludes, "it is an obvious characteristic that those who already hold the highest position in a given community cannot make contacts on a stratum higher up in the vertical scale of the community's structure. Therefore he makes relatively higher intracategorial friendships with his equals, and thereby produces a relatively *closed* structure in the community" [34: 934]. V. Rus' investigations lead him to a similar conclusion: "Legalization of arbitrariness, respect for an isolationist policy, and the inefficacy of public control, even of criminal actions of managerial personnel (in 1965, managerial positions in our republic were held by 1,500 persons who had been convicted of abuse of their official positions) — all this leads us to the presumption that individual 'meritocratic' groups imperceptibly lead to a more or less homogeneous social stratum, which by now already has considerable social power, since even the courts cannot master it" [35: 1094]. By "meritocracy" Rus means "gradual formation of a managerial summit that controls social-political organizations." V. Vlahović emphasizes the fetishization of statements by people in high managerial positions and adds: "We speak of the fetishization of functions, which leads us to look less at what people are worth and know . . . and more at what function they hold. On the basis of function we form our relations to people" [58: 729]. The comments of Mlinar, Rus, and Vlahović reflect the phenomenon of the bureaucratic alienation of man, of which M. Marković aptly says:" . . . in choosing those whom they wish to have close relations with, the primary factor will not be who the other person *is* but *what function he has*. A function will be friendly with a function, not a man with a man" [36: 57].

40. In 1961, 4.5% of the workers and employees and 29% of the rest of the population over the age of 15 were illiterate. The latter figure may be taken as representative of the illiteracy of the peasantry (reconstructed from *Statisticki bilten 312,,* p. 210; *Jugoslavija 1945-1964,* pp. 44-45). Thus, about one-third of the peasants are illiterate.

41. In 1955, for a million dinars of market value, 10 work-years were required in agriculture, but only 3 work-years in industry. [cf. B. Horvat, 37: 519]. Something less than 4 million Yugoslav peasants provide a population of 20 million with food, as compared with 7 million American farmers who feed 200 million — i.e., Yugoslav agriculture is one-sixth as productive as American; industry is twice as productive, relatively (data from S. Stajić).

42. An empirical study in the Kraljevo district leads K. Kilibarda to the conclusion that peasants submit more proposals relating to the community and are better informed on these matters than industrial workers. Kilibarda explains this greater social commitment by the following factors: (1) the worker can have his interests served through his worker organization better than the peasant can at work; (2) very frequently, the problems that one village wants to have solved essentially affect another village or villages, and often affect the district as an association of villages; (3) in the winter, peasants have relatively more time to get acquainted, to discuss and criticize, and to call for and make proposals for solving the problems of their community than industrial workers; (4) workers influence their community agencies indirectly, through their worker organizations, while farmers can do this only directly; (5) farmers are more independent than workers. "The private farmer on his farm often feels less dependent on community agencies . . . than the worker does with respect to the leaders of the worker organization. The former does not have to fear being discharged, or other reprisals on the part of the wielder of social power, who may see its interests threatened; (6) peasants seem to know the people and the problems in community agencies better than workers do. This is a result of the greater communication in connection with various questions for which a worker does not have to go to the local authorities" [62: 46].

43. This definition also appears in the League Program, pp. 118 and 125.
44. Marx includes sales assistants in wage workers [3: 255].
45. E.g., M. Pećujlić classifies foremen with technicians in a transitional category [27: 38].
46. In a study by J. Županov and A. S. Tannenbaum [40: 121], questions were put to workers (89% were members of the League of Communists) of the two-year courses at the Workers' University of Zagreb. The influence was rated from 1 (= none) to 5 (= very high). The grouping is mine.

Managers of firms	4.7	Highly skilled	2.5
Experts	4.1	Skilled	2.2
Managers of economic enterprises	3.4	Semiskilled	1.6
Foremen	2.7	Unskilled	1.5
Employees	2.7		

47. An interesting bit of information (which calls for further analysis) is that skilled workers and employees with secondary education are numerically dominant in governing bodies. These two categories appear in governing bodies to a greater proportion than their proportion in the working force. Employees with university education, semiskilled workers, employees with lower education, and unskilled workers (in that order) are less than proportionately represented [41: 222, 225].
48. In an empirical study in a large collective, K. Kilibarda finds that about 60% feel they cannot essentially influence the choice of a manager, and that about four-fifths of League of Communists members and nonmembers want to have a direct and strong influence on the choice of a manager [62: 119-120].
49. Analyzing the 1965 volume of *Delavska politika*, V. Rus [35: 1082] concludes: "As a rule, the agents of arbitrariness are the manager and other leaders in the workers' organization . . . the victims of arbitrariness in smaller workers' organizations are most frequently skilled workers and, in larger enterprises, professionals . . . . Incidentally, the violent, arbitrary, and illegal cadre 'policy' of leaders toward skilled workers and technicians points up the professional inferiority of the hegemonic groups in workers' organizations."
50. It is worth noting that in one Stalinist system the working class still retains its social content.
51. A similar conclusion is reached by H. Hadžiomerović (*Pregled*, 1964, No. 6, pp. 599-600). This is intuitively felt by our political workers as well, who practically never speak of the "working class" except in the customary phrase "the working class and all working people." Likewise, differing from previous statutes, the Statute of the League enacted in 1958 begins with the words: "The League of Communists of Yugoslavia is the organized political power of the *working class and working people* of Yugoslavia" (my emphasis – B.H.). The Statute of 1964 begins with the identical formulation. Thus the concept of the working class is extended to cover the entire active population, with the possible exception of the peasant and the craftsman: "Thus, social labor today comprises, and links in the same labor process, people from unskilled workers to those who work in institutes, hospitals, education, administrative agencies, etc. Because of these considerations, the concept of the working class is changing, taking on a broader meaning. In essence this concept comprises all working people who take part in the social labor process and in socialist economic relations. All have the same goals; greater productivity, development of productive forces, increased production distribution according to work, and ever greater development of society as the community of producers" (E. Kardelj, [43: 77]). This conception is close to but not identical with Marx's extended conception of the productive worker as a consequence of the cooperative nature of labor [4: 441].
52. M. Pećujlić reasons in the same way: "The far-reaching changes that are beginning in the nature of the social division of labor, in production relations themselves, lead to the dissolution of all old relations and strata. The inherited differences between strata . . . are beginning to disappear. . . . The gap, the social distance, is diminishing between the formerly sharply polarized, separate, and hierarchically arranged social strata. There is coming into being a closer connection, an interpenetration, an *integration of the working class in the old meaning of the word,* particularly of *its most developed sectors,* with the strata of the technical intelligentsia. They are beginning to act in similar ways. And the development of modern technology is also working in the same direction . . . But the social conditions under which producers work, the labor situation in which they are, are already acting directly in the same direction. . . . the trend to wipe out the

distinction between administrative and executive mental and physical labor (by means of self-government) are leading to the establishment of a *modern class of physical and mental producers under conditions of self-government and self-distribution*. This is what is beginning to characterize today's working class under the conditions of self-government . . ." [44: 28-29]. It is not clear why Pećujlić calls this new quasiprofessional group a "class," when that contradicts his own theory of the class [30] and when the meaning of socialism consists in the abolition and not the formation of classes. I have the impression that Pećujlić is aware of this, and that the reasons for the terminology are practical-political rather then scientific.

53. This is expressed, although in a mild form, in the relevant formulations in the *Program of the League of Communists* (cf. p. 145).

54. As Lj. Tadić remarks [36: 279], Lenin took his thesis as to the intelligentsia from Kautsky. But long before the formation of communist parties we find anti-intellectualism in the labor movement among the anarchists. Typical in this respect is the criticism Bakunin aimed at scholars: "By his very nature the man of learning is inclined to every kind of mental and moral perversion, and his greatest offense is that he overrates his knowledge, his own intelligence, and despises anyone who is not learned. Give him the power to rule and he will be the harshest of tyrants, for the scholar's arrogance is repulsive and distorted and limits freedom more than any other kind of arrogance . . . [47: 119].

55. "On the Organization of Russian Social Democracy"; we cite from [48: 183-187].

56. In addition to the historical instances that Lenin and Rosa Luxemburg dealt with, it is worthwhile considering some present-day historical examples. Anti-intellectual feelings are characteristic of today's bourgeois parties and milieus. In America intellectuals are called eggheads; in England, Gaitskell, the former Labour Party leader, would take off his jacket and tie at meetings, to show that he was not an inveterate intellectual, as he was accused of being. To a great extent these are petty-bourgeois antagonisms, but there are substantial differences as well. If one of the criteria of the progressive nature of a social group in America today is its attitude toward the war in Vietnam, then the "eggheads" are the only progressive group. The working class takes a passive attitude and occasionally participates in anticommunist demonstrations. The big bourgeoisie is openly aggressive. This situation is not unexpected. In its day the McCarthy terror was also aimed primarily at the American intelligentsia. An interesting analysis of the roots of anti-intellectualism is given by E. Fischer, the Austrian Communist, in his article "The Intellectuals and Power": . . . the 'egghead' is bitterly accused of being an 'unsettling factor,' of lacking political consciousness,' of not being 'linked to the people,' of being unreliable, unstable, inconstant; . . . His learning does not respect tactical considerations, the reliability of the faithful party man, the indestructible devotion of the ordinary man." Anti-intellectualism is not aimed at the specialist who obeys orders, but at "the intellectual who poses questions and brings taboos under discussion." At the same time, Fischer says, "the preference of a considerable number of intellectuals, in conjunction with their masters, makes it easier for anti-intellectualism, in times of crisis, to evoke aversion to the intellectual among the people, among the members of a party or organization." Seen in historical perspective, it is characteristic that "even in the last thirty years of the last century, when the notion of 'intellectuals' first appeared, it was not so much a synonym for 'mental workers' as it was a mocking collective name given to those who defended Dreyfus, sympathized with the proletariat, stood for modern art. Anti-intellectualism was blended with antirationalism, anti-Marxism, anti-Semitism, with every kind of reactionary movement and ideology. In the Nazi jargon the intellectual was defined as 'the beast of intelligence.' In most countries, anti-intellectualism was spread in order to take an aggressive attitude at any moment of crisis; it even infected, sometimes more and sometimes less, the labor movement and the countries engaged in constructing socialism" [49: 1029-1035].

57. "Their job [the intelligentsia's] is to be the conscience and the consciousness of their era . . , ." (D. Pejovic [50: 261]. W. Mills, the well-known American sociologist and unsparing critic of his society, observes:
". . . a type of social man, the intellectual has no particular political direction, but the work of each man of knowledge has a completely specific kind of political importance: his politics are primarily the politics of truth, because it is his duty to maintain an adequate definition of reality. . . . The intellectual should be the moral conscience of his society, at least in so far as the value of truth is concerned, because that *is*, in the final analysis, his politics" [51: 31].

58. According to the 1948 census, there were in that year a total of 79,000 persons with university or college diplomas. In the 1945-1965 period, 222,000 students obtained diplomas from universities and colleges. In the meantime a certain number of older intellectuals died (*SGJ 1955*, p. 59; *Jugoslavija 1945-1964*, p. 303, *SGJ 1965*, p. 500).

59. It is not without interest to note that the intelligentsia is playing a similár revolutionary role in contemporary undeveloped countries. In this connection T.B. Bottomore, the English sociologist, observes: "In almost all Asian and African countries the intellectuals have played outstanding parts in the struggles against colonial rule. University students have often been the shock troops of the independence movement, and those who were studying abroad formed or helped form new national parties" [52: 109].

60. In this context, recent university resistance to the dictatorship in Argentina is only a natural expression of a secular trend. One should interpret student movements in a number of European and American countries in the same sense.

61. Some authors maintain that possession of power is the fundamental characteristic of the bureaucracy, and that therefore it can only be governmental. In that case, the business bureaucracy is called technocracy (cf. J. Djordjević [47: xv-xxviii]).

62. The French have a characteristic saying which, so far as their experience in the matter goes, figures as a popular proverb: *homme élu, homme foutu* (a man elected is a man done for).

63. It is worth noting that the notorious conception of the "struggle for existence" arose first not in the natural but in the social sciences. Biologist Darwin borrowed it from his countryman, economist Malthus.

64. However, in the light of the above analysis, I see no justification for the existence of an administrative house.

65. The data are only approximately correct because of the inadequate subdivision and mere inaccuracy of our demographic statistics. Thus, in one publication (SZS, *Bilten 312*, pp. 22, 23) military personnel is included in the group of "government and courts" for 1953, but is not stated for 1961. This suggests that the state apparatus has diminished, whereas in fact it has increased. The number of peasants is obtained by subtracting the number of workers and employees from the total active agricultural population *(ibid.)*. "Other market producers" is a residual category. The number of nonmarket workers, (cultural-educational, scientific, and health-social activities) is increased for 1953 by 28,000 persons employed in mass organizations, professional associations, the liberal professions, and religious organizations (SZS, *Bilten 73*, p. 9), while for 1961 the number added is 53,000, an approximation for the same category, obtained by including persons from "other activities" without counting employees in economic associations (6,559) and military personnel, the number of whom, although data are insufficient, we presume not to be greater than in 1953 *(Bilten 73*, p. 9; *Bilten 312*, pp. 22, 23, 169). For 1953, the government apparatus is taken from the SZS, but for 1961 it is augmented by military personnel (75,000, according to the situation of 1953, *Bilten 73*, p.9). Not counting the armed forces, whose cadre makeup is conditioned by the international situation, the apparatus of the state grew as follows over the eight-year period (*Bilten 73*, p. 9; *Bilten 312*, p. 169):

	1953	1961	Index
Federal agencies	4,443	17,191	388
Republic agencies	9,661	24,772	256
Other agencies and courts	130,859	139,910	107
Totals:	144,963	181,873	125

Inactive persons and persons of unknown occupation are subtracted from the active population (*Bilten 312*, pp. 22 and 23).

REFERENCES

[1] *Socio-Political Trends and Actions of the Socialist League After the Sixth Congress*, Federal Conference of the Socialist Alliance of the Working People of Yugoslavia, *Borba*, Belgrade, 1967.

[2] J. K. Galbraith, *The Affluent Society*, Houghton Mifflin, Boston, 1958.

[3] K. Marx, *Capital*, Vol. III, Kultura, Zagreb, 1948.

[4] *Ibid.*, Vol. I, Kultura, Zagreb, 1947.
[5] W. A. Lewis, "Economic Development with Unlimited Supplies of Labour," *Manchester School*, 1954.
[6] W. A. Lewis, "Unlimited Supply: Further Notes," *Manchester School*, 1958.
[7] K. Marx, *Theory of Surplus Values*, Vol. I, Kultura, Belgrade, 1953.
[8] Ia. A. Kronrod, *Basic Questions of Marxist-Leninist Teaching on Productive Labor in Capitalism and Socialism*, Naprijed, Zagreb, 1948; translation of work published in *Izvestiia Akademii Nauk SSSR*, 1947, No. 1.
[9] A. I. Notkin, *Essay on the Theory of Socialist Production*, OGIZ, Moscow, 1948.
[10] B. Horvat, "An Integrated System of Social Accounts for an Economy of the Yugoslav Type," report to Conference of International Association for Research in Income and Wealth, Maynooth, Ireland, 1967; *Review of Income and Wealth*, 1968.
[11] M. Pećujlić, *Classes and Contemporary Society*, Contemporary Administration, Belgrade, 1967.
[12] K. Marx and F. Engels, *Early Works*, Kultura, Zagreb, 1953.
[13] R. Lukić, "Exploitation as an Element of Social Classes," *Socialism*, 1966, No. 3.
[14] B. Horvat, "Distribution According to Work Among Collectives," *Naša stvarnost* [Our Reality], 1962, No. 2.
[15] B. Horvat, *Economic Theory of a Planned Economy*, Kultura, Belgrade, 1961.
[16] V. Milić, "Review of Social Mobility in Yugoslavia," *Statistical Review*, 1960, No. 3-4.
[17] K. Mičić; "Professional Morals of Craftsmen-Small Owners," *Sociologija* [Sociology], 1965, No. 3.
[18] M. Hadži Vasilev, "Phenomenon of Private Ownership in Socialism," *Komunist*, May 5, 1966.
[19] M. Popović, *Socio-Economic System*, Kultura, Belgrade, 1964.
[20] J. Djordjević, *Socialism and Democracy*, Contemporary Administration, Belgrade, 1962.
[21] M. Popović, "A Theoretical-Hypothetical Frame for the Study of the Stratification Structure of Socialist Society," *Sociologija*, 1966, No. 1-2.
[22] V. Milić, "A Conceptual-Hypothetical Frame for the Study of Social Structure," *Sociologija*, 1960, No. 2.
[23] J. Stoetzel, "Psychology of Interpersonnel Relations," in *Sociologija*, Vol. II, ed. G. Gurvitch, Naprijed, Zagreb, 1966.
[24] P. Novesel, "Social Stratification and Income Norms," *Naša teme* [Our Themes], 1966, No. 3.
[25] K. Mayer, "The Theory of Social Classes," in *Reader in Bureaucracy*, by R. K. Merton *et al.*, Free Press, Glencoe, 1952.
[26] A. Todorivić, "Social Consciousness of Workers and Class Stratification," *Sociologija*, 1965, No. 3.
[27] M. Pećujlic, *Changes in the Social Structure of Yugoslavia*, VSPN, Belgrade, 1963.
[28] *Social Structure and Mobility of the Working Class of Yugoslavia*, edited by M. Ilić, IDN, Belgrade, 1963.
[29] R. Supek, *Sociology*, Školska knjiga [Schoolbooks], Zagreb, 1963.
[30] M. Pecujlić, "Theoretical Frame for the Study of Class Changes in Socialism," *Sociologija*, 1966, No. 1-2.
[31] V. I. Lenin, "Great Initiative," *Selected Works*, Vols. II-III, Kultura, Zagreb, 1950.
[32] T. Parsons *et al.*, *Theories of Society*, Vol. I, Free Press, Glencoe, 1962.
[33] S. Možina, "Participation of Leader and Expert Cadres in Workers' Self-Management," *Gledišta* [Views], 1966, No. 3.
[34] Z. Mlinar, "Some Structural Aspects of Authority in Local Communities," *Gledišta*, 1966, No. 6-7.
[35] V. Rus, "Cliques in Working Organizations," *Gledista*, 1966, No. 8-9.
[36] *The Meaning and Perspective of Socialism* (collection of papers at Second Session of Korčula Summer School, 1964), Praxis, Zagreb, 1965.
[37] B. Horvat, "Working Value of Production in Yugoslav Agriculture and Industry," *Ekonomist*, 1961, No. 4.
[38] *Social-Political System of Socialist Countries*, Institute for Study of the Workers' Movement, Belgrade, 1964.
[39] A. Gramsci, *Selected Works*, Kultura, Belgrade, 1959.
[40] J. Županov and A. S. Tannenbaum, "Distribution of Influence in Some Yugoslav Industrial Organizations as Seen by Members of Those Organizations," *Ekonomski pregled* [Economic Review], 1966, No. 2-3.

[41] Ž. Tomić, "Structure of Workers' Councils," in *Social Self-Management in Yugoslavia*, Yugoslav Sociology Association, Belgrade, 1966.

[42] B. Kavčić, "On Protest Work Suspension," *Gledišta*, 1966, No. 2.

[43] E. Kardelj, "New Constitution of the SFRY [Socialist Federal Republic of Yugoslavia]," in *Draft Constitution of the SFRY*, Komunist, Belgrade, 1962.

[44] M. Pećujlić, "Class and Political Avant-Garde in the Contemporary Struggle for Socialism," in *Current Problems of Reorganization and Further Development of the LCY* [League of Communists of Yugoslavia], VSPN, Belgrade, 1967.

[45] D. C. Hodges, "Anti-Intellectualism in a Society of Eggheads," *American Journal of Economics and Sociology*, 1966, No. 4.

[46] V. I. Lenin, "One Step Forward, Two Steps Backward," *Selected Works*, II/2, Belgrade, 1950.

[47] *Bureaucracy and Technocracy*, Book I, edited by V. Stanovčić and A. Stojanović, Sedma sila, Belgrade, 1966.

[48] Lj. Tadić and T. Indjić, *Party of the Proletariat*, Sedma sila, Belgrade, 1966.

[49] E. Fischer, "Intellectuals and Authority," *Naše teme*, 1966, No. 10.

[50] D. Pejović, *Against the Current*, Mladost, Zagreb, 1965.

[51] W. Mills, *Knowledge and Power*, V. Karadžić, Belgrade, 1967.

[52] *Bureaucracy and Technocracy*, Book II, edited by V. Stanovčić and A. Stojanović, Sedma sila, Belgrade, 1966.

[53] M. Duverger, *Introduction to Politics*, Savremena administracija, Belgrade, 1966.

[54] T. Hobbes, *Leviathan*, Kultura, Belgrade, 1961.

[55] A. Adler, *Knowledge of Man*, Kosmos, Belgrade, 1958.

[56] E. Fromm, *Flight from Freedom*, Nolit, Belgrade, 1964.

[57] B. Horvat, *Economic Theory of a Planned Economy*, Kultura, Belgrade, 1961.

[58] *League of Communists of Yugoslavia in Conditions of Self-Management*, collection of texts edited by M. Nikolić, Kultura, Belgrade, 1967.

[59] S. Šuvar, "Basic Characteristics and Conditions of the Process of Socialization of Land in Yugoslavia," *Sociology of the Village*, 1966, No. 11-12.

[60] I. Klauzer, "Surplus Labor Force in Yugoslav Agriculture," *Sociology of the Village*, 1965, No. 7-8.

[61] E. Kardelj, *Problems of Socialist Policy in the Village*, Kultura, Belgrade, 1959.

[62] K. Kilibarda, *Self-Management and the League of Communists*, Sociological Institute, Belgrade, 1966.

[63] M. Djurić, *The Sociology of Max Weber*, Matica Hrvatska, Zagreb, 1964.

CHAPTER V

Conversion of the Party into a League of Political Activists

As Marxists, we can expect that the establishment of worker self-government should lead to considerable changes in productive relations, and that these changes in turn should condition and produce equally major changes in the political superstructure. The question of a thoroughgoing coordination of the political system was only a question of time. That coordination, of course, has been in progress for a long time, so that the preconditions have been created for a radical reform.

Further, just as the introduction of worker self-government had been greeted with skepticism and with criticism that it was an impractical and utopian undertaking, similar manifestations of distrust were shown in connection with the impending political reform. In the Social Democratic West it was said that worker self-government had failed wherever it had been tried, that it destroys necessary labor discipline, and that it slows down economic development because workers would use up all their income instead of putting some aside as accumulation. Out of the Cominform East came the condemnation that worker self-government weakens the dictatorship of the proletariat and stands in contradiction to the integrated planning of socialist economy. [1] Today it is said that society has never been organized without political parties, that the absence of one or more strong, well-organized political parties could not but lead to chaos in social life, that the withering away of the state and of parties is a utopia and means mortal danger to socialist construction.

These criticisms may be more characteristic of the foreign scene than our social picture. More characteristic of the latter may be a certain confusion, due to the fact that there is no clearly elaborated theory (except for some statements of principle) to serve as a basis. In any event, the need for an elaborated theory of the party at today's stage cannot be disputed.[2]

18. POLITICAL PARTIES

Rise of Political Parties

As is usual, a *historical* approach to our problem will be useful. Political parties have not always existed, and it is reasonable to expect that they will have their end just as they have had their beginning. The fact is that we have become so accustomed to the existence of political parties in today's world that we do not even reflect that parties (apart from some rudimentary beginnings) only appeared on the stage of history during the last century, parallel to the rise of a new social class, the bourgeoisie, which organized its parties in the struggle for power and for the defeat of feudalism. A certain policy of democratization was also in keeping with the interests of the bourgeoisie, and the right to vote was extended, although with various restrictions, such as literacy and property qualifications. Under the pressure of workers' organizations, unions, and parties, which (with insignificant exceptions) appeared in European countries only in the second half of the last century, universal suffrage was gradually won. However, women won the right to vote only here and there before World War I, and in one civilized country in the heart of Europe, women still do not have that right. We are so accustomed to the existence of universal suffrage, as we are to parties, that we tend to forget how relatively late they appeared and how slowly they developed. This relatively slow development made possible the democratization of political life in the countries of Western Europe without major social convulsions. Certain traditions, customs, and habits grew up that made possible the resolution of political disputes without dangerous or excessively brutal social conflicts. Our lands are belated in this respect. It is hardly over a century that serfdom was done away with (and not in all regions at that), and national union was obtained less than fifty years ago. There has not been time for a democratic tradition to develop nor (as Veljko Vlahović would say[3]) for citizens, by participating in political life, to develop the culture of democracy. The general lack of economic development and the lack of education among the broad masses have limited and restricted the process even more. These facts must be taken into account.

Furthermore, not only were political parties late in appearing, but in the interim they went through a definite process of evolution. The first parties developed out of election committees, which were organized at each election for the purpose of supporting candidates and organizing the campaigns. "Modern parties arose when these election committees associated on national scales, when they became permanent instead of dissolving after the election, and when they were organically linked to parliamentary groups" [2: 90]. Around the election committees were gathered the socially prominent and wealthy citizens, who were able to finance election campaigns and whose social status gave them some influence over local voters. All the conservative, liberal, and radical parties of Europe have maintained this traditional patrician basis down to the present.

In the second half of the last century, the labor movement introduced an important innovation in political organization by founding *mass* workers' parties. The traditional patrician parties, M. Duverger writes (calling them "cadre" parties), "corresponded to the era of conflict between the aristocracy and the bourgeoisie: these two classes were few in numbers and could be perfectly represented by their prominent spokesmen. The limited scope of the parties expressed the limited nature of the political domain and gave its hallmark to the democracy from which the majority of the people were practically excluded. The mass parties, on the other hand, corresponded to an expansion of democracy, which became available to virtually all the population: it could exercise its rights only when it was not confined to vote once every four or five years, but could really and continually take part in the administration of the state" [2: 34]. The workers' parties, whose model was the German Social Democratic Party (in whose formation Marx and Engels took part), worked to politically activate an ever-increasing number of the working class, and by political and theoretical work in the sections educated the members for political battles. To be effective, those parties had to be firmly organized, which was not the case with the traditional bourgeois parties. Hence centralism. But at the same time those parties fought for socialism and had to foster democracy, which was manifested in broad exchange of views and in election of their leaders by secret vote. Hence democracy, as was emphasized in the names of the parties. Thus, before the term came into use, the workers' parties applied democratic centralism as their principle of organization. To quote M. Duverger again [2: 34], "No other type of party carried democratization as far as the socialist parties." But on the very next page the same author notes that internal democracy is very limited, that the leaders are recruited mainly by co-optation, that their election is actually only ratification, and that the professionals can manipulate the elections as they please. This opinion is interesting in that we can discern in it many of our present problems, and the question naturally arises: if that is the highest stage of intraparty democracy, what is the situation with democracy in other parties?

Conditions of illegal struggle by the working class led, at the beginning of this century, to the formation of still another type of labor party. This is Lenin's cadre party, later to be called communist parties. A communist party is characterized by extreme centralism, strict discipline, and directives proceeding from the top down.

Both types of workers' party insisted on the *struggle for winning political power.* It is from this that their organizational forms obtain their functionality. Our problem, however, lies in the construction of the party *after* power has been won and *after* the creation of the preconditions for the construction of socialism, and thus in the formation of a party (with reference to political organization) that is to construct that socialism most directly. In other words, we know what workers' parties look like and how they function when their function is the conquest of power. We likewise know what parties look like that have to retain power. But history has not yet showed us how parties should look that set themselves the task of doing away with power.

Multiparty and One-Party Systems

The fundamental justification of multiparty systems is the assertion that they insure political freedom. Political freedom is, naturally, something that is of value in and of itself. But a more pragmatic explanation is also possible. A certain minimum of political freedom is necessary to insure the stability of a social system. An autocratic regime is sitting on a volcano, and is therefore short-lived as a rule. Multiparty systems show their vitality by "natural selection," since they make it possible temporarily to attenuate high tensions.

A political party is founded not to insure freedoms in general, but its freedoms, i.e., to attain power. In order to attain power, a party has to be well organized; it must have its professional apparatus, material resources, etc. In this way a bureaucratic structure is formed, with oligarchical characteristics. This phenomenon was observed half a century ago by R. Michels and formulated in his well-known "iron law of oligarchy." Because of the division of labor in large organizations and the psychological need of members of large organizations for direction and leadership, Michels holds, the individuals who are in positions of leadership are not, and in the nature of things cannot be, controlled by those in lower positions. The leaders are restricted only in the sense in which sculptors are limited: by the nature of the materials they work with [3]. Speaking of the relatively democratic Labour Party, R. McKenzie, the well-known British political scientist, concludes: ". . . the annual Party conference has the right to be consulted, the right to encourage, the right to warn. But this does not mean that members of a mass organization in the British parliamentary system have the right to control or direct their parliamentary leaders" [4: 583].

Oligarchy within the parties leads to oligopoly in the political life of the country as a whole. In the most stable Western democracies the number of parties has been reduced to two, which monopolize the entire political life of the country. Despite the existence of political freedoms, it is practically impossible to organize a new party and almost impossible for independents to compete successfully in elections, and representatives elected by a given party risk their political careers if they show any tendency to be independent. The party oligarchies then tie up with other oligarchies in society, and the political rights of the individual citizen do not in fact give him any influence on the functioning of the machinery of the modern state. In the Western countries this effect is compounded by the effect of private capital. The information media are available to all, in principle, and free from government control, but are not free from the control of money. But the information media clearly form opinion in the modern state. An instructive instance of the inability of the citizen to resist the modern Leviathan, even when it is on the brink of disaster, is the failure of all the actions of progressive intellectuals in the United States to force (or convince?!) the government to stop the war in Vietnam.

As for the one-party system, it can be said in general that it has all the negative characteristics of multiparty systems without their positive characteristics.

Temporarily, however, the one-party system can be the most effective method for bringing about the transition from capitalism to socialism. To be sure, socialism can also be constructed with a multiparty system, but in that case conservative resistance comes into play. Socialism implies the withering away of the state, the diffusion of power, the destruction of bureaucratic structures, and direct democracy. The existence of many parties implies the existence of party machinery, the struggle for power, and indirect democracy. Accordingly, the multiparty system, which served as an instrument in accelerating the development of capitalism, can prove to be a stumbling block in the construction of socialism. It can, but need not.

In our concrete historical situation, there are certain facts that are relevant, over and above these general considerations. Let us suppose that a course has been set toward the formation of a plurality of parties. Then, judging from the events of the last few years, the single communist movement would probably split into a conservative and a progressive wing. Further, in view of the numbers of the peasantry and the prior traditions of peasant parties, a peasant party would in all likelihood also appear. That party would in the nature of things be conservative. Further, the long-standing and substantial differences in development of the various regions would be a natural basis for the formation of political parties with differing interests. After all, Yugoslavia is a country with many nationalities, in which national antagonisms have not yet subsided, and with considerable national cultural differences.[4] All these could be bases for party formation. And if two or more bases coincided, the parties could by the nature of things develop into harshly hostile groupings. Thus, for instance, peasants are most numerous in the economically undeveloped republics, and the most developed republics contain a minority of the population. Under these conditions a multiparty system would in all probability arouse serious nationalistic conflicts, which incidentally were apparent before the war. Socialism and economic development would fade into the background, the international prestige of Yugoslavia would sink to the prewar Balkan level, and instead of creating democratization we would have a fierce struggle for power.

For these reasons a multiparty system is obviously not the desirable alternative. Neither is a one-party system. What is left is a nonparty system. This would have to retain the positive aspects of the multiparty system and avoid the negative aspects. How can this be done?

19. THE REVOLUTIONARY PARTY AND THE GENESIS OF BUREAUCRATIC MENTALITY

Before we try to answer the question that has just been raised,

192

we must analyze some processes within the party after it has won power. We must explain how the Brioni Plenum of the Central Committee of the League of Communists in 1966 was arrived at, and what essential problems have to be solved by the projected reform of the party organization.

The Revolutionary Party and the Party in Power

To meet its objectives, a political organization has to change with the social conditions under which it operates. This applies particularly in a society in which the changes have been as intensive as in our society. It is almost universally agreed today that a gap had arisen between the proclaimed and the actual role of the League of Communists, that the League, as a political organization, was not adequate to the demands of the time.[5] As a result, party forums decided to reorganize the League. In order for the reorganization to succeed, it was necessary to establish: (a) how the League of Communists should act, what social functions it should perform; and (b) how and why the present situation, which was evaluated as unsatisfactory, had been arrived at. The first task relates to defining the socially requisite operation, with which we shall deal in the next chapter. The second relates to discovering the internal processes out of which the recognized phenomena sprang. In fact, this is the precondition to successful solution of the first problem. In the analysis that follows, I shall start from the hypothesis that development of the bureaucratic mentality is the basic source of the operational inefficiency, ideological inadequacy, and a certain estrangement of the LCY as a political organization from the fundamental currents of our actuality, always keeping in mind that it was the LCY that initiated and to a great extent organized those currents. By mentality I mean conceptions, beliefs, behavior. Mentality is only in part a function of organization; to a greater extent it is determined by the general social situation. Consequently, a narrowly conceived reorganization of the LCY (and we have already had reorganizations) would not be much help. If the hypothesis set up is correct, then our analysis leads to finding the genesis of the bureaucratic mentality. Recognition of the genesis should make it possible to overcome that mentality, and that, it seems to me, is the fundamental task of the LCY reorganization.

The prewar communist party in Yugoslavia, as in most other countries, had to operate in deep illegality. Those conditions of struggle called for a very specific organization, whose basic characteristics are: strict centralization, firm discipline, complete unity of action and ideology, and a monolithic quality. Positions of leadership entailed not advantages but responsibilities and great personal risks; hence, the hierarchy that resulted from the centralization did not lead to bureaucratization.[6] The discipline was the precondition for survival and so was not a barracks discipline but the discipline of conscious and entire personalities; it was discipline and not obedience. Experience showed that factions destroyed the tissue of the party like cancer; hence, completely monolithic quality was a precondition of success. The objectives were relatively clearly defined, the enemy was known, the alternatives were evident. Therefore, unity in ideology and action was compatible with democracy, which was essentially present, if not always formally. Differences of opinion and individual preferences paled into insignificance in comparison with the magnitude of the goal, on which there was complete agreement. In this way, unity was neither imposed nor formal; it arose from the existential conditions of the political organization of that time. That organization either was united and attained the desired goals, or it was not united and was hopelessly lost. The moral qualities of the members of the organization — courage, frankness, principle, comradeliness — were likewise existentially conditioned. The organizational principles of the communist party and the conditions of its struggle nurtured heroes.

This picture of the Communist Party of Yugoslavia may seem somewhat idealized; nonetheless, I imagine it is accurate; after all, the facts involved are historically verifiable. But in this case it is well known that today's League of Communists differs from its predecessor in many respects.[7] And here the ethical question is often asked: What has become of the heroes of those days? How is it that our present political organization does not train personalities with the same moral qualities? Why do Communists unanimously adopt conclusions they are not in agreement with and by which they do not live? Why do Communists not oppose conceptions that they know to be bad, even if that would interfere a little with their advancement? What has happened to our comradeship, when we do not react to injustices that are evident? Once we were ready to do battle for our convictions, and today we keep our convictions carefully to ourselves. Where have principle and courage gone to?[8] The answers given to these questions stress that heroes are made in war, not in peace; that the generation that made the revolution is now much older and hence more cautious, more conservative; that people cannot be expected to be ascetics, and that it is normal for people to want to enjoy the fruits of their struggles, to seek the reward for their services.

Further, a party in power attracts careerists, and commodity-money relations and fetishization of the standard of living undermine morality. Probably all these answers have some part of the truth. But it would be defeatism to take such answers as *explanations,* because they do not indicate how the existing situation can be overcome.

Road to Bureaucratization

All phenomena have their history of development, including those we are concerned with here. One event was most important in this respect: the Cominform attack in 1948. We have pointed out how this event accelerated the maturation of the social and political awareness of Yugoslav Communists, and that a process of fundamental importance was soon initiated: the process of decentralization and self-government. But 1948 also initiated a parallel process, which has not yet undergone analysis and which (unlike the progressive nature of the first process on the general economic and social plane) represents a regress on the moral plane. In short, that year the police entered the party for the first time, and Communists began to doubt Communists. This event alone shows that the party was not ideologically prepared for all the complexities of peacetime construction from a position of power. Courage and trust in authority led a certain number astray, and the monolithic ideology of discipline put the majority of the others in a psychologically contradictory situation, in which one party, at that time the minority, stood in opposition to all the other parties, at that time the majority. In time these situations were overcome, but the party organization has not yet recovered from the consequences of the ethical shock. In this respect, 1948 represents a marked breach of continuity between the earlier and the later parties. The collectives were transformed into aggregates of private individuals, frankness and openness gave way to reserve and calculation, egoistic opportunism took the place of comradeship, principle was replaced by conformity, courage by careerism.[9] And the police, once inside the party, never left on its own initiative. Even more, there was no serious opposition to this practice. Government and party agencies were quite pleased to obtain "reliable" information about everyone and everything without effort or responsibility, and awareness of the consequences of such opportunism was not sufficiently developed. Communists became, as it were, collaborationists, not against the foreign enemy and internal diversionists, which is a matter of patriotism, but in the matter of informing on their own comrades.

Along with the official party organization, which to all appearances functioned as before, an unofficial police organization was formed; it usurped the right to evaluate, without appeal, the patriotism and political reliability of every citizen, including Communists. Naturally, police control kept expanding until it succeeded in taking full cover — to use its technical term — and after it was found that listening devices had been placed with the most prominent persons in our public life, this malignant tumor on the body of society was surgically removed at the Brioni Plenum.

Although the police violation of party ethics explains many deformations in our social and political life, it does not explain everything. Moreover, it calls for an explanation in itself. The Cominform attack was the occasion, and probably hastened the process. But other countries had no such occasion, yet similar processes began to develop there, and with much graver consequences. Then what is the matter?

The centralized and hierarchical organization of communist parties is a potentially bureaucratic structure. Under the conditions of illegal struggle and the war of national liberation, that organization was functional and, for reasons we have given, did not behave bureaucratically. But when the party had come to power, the possibility of realizing those potentialities arose. In the first place, the first years of construction witnessed a centralization in which the party and government hierarchies merged.[10] Further, the new social system required that the leading positions in the state and the economy be filled by politically reliable people — that is, the leading cadres were chosen by political and not by professional criteria. Discipline was needed for the apparatus to function properly. However, it was no longer revolutionary discipline, of course, but bureaucratic discipline — in other words, obedience.[11]

In radical social changes, such as the revolutionary replacement of one social system by another, it is crucially important to insure a certain order in the development of the life of society. The fundamental mechanisms for maintaining social order — traditions, institutions, customs, mentality — are dysfunctional (insofar as they arise out of the old system) or nonexistent (insofar as the new system goes). The only available temporary substitute is conformity to the decisions of the revolutionary governing bodies. This is, incidentally, another aspect of the familiar thesis of the necessity of the dictatorship of the proletariat. Conformity then becomes very desirable politically; political criteria generally dominate social values. At the same time, conformity as a quid pro

196

quo mechanism may easily change from being *a temporary means* (and historically has often done so in fact) to being *a permanent aim,* so that the dictatorship of the proletariat turns into dictatorship over the proletariat and revolutionary spirit turns into opportunism.

In the course of these processes, the meaning of political criteria likewise goes through phases of development.

At the outset, the political criterion means choosing cadres who are dedicated to the revolution, that is, choosing people on whom higher agencies can rely and who are obedient, so that the apparatus can count on them. It is important to note that a centralized cadre policy generally, and especially so in politics, lowers the quality of cadres on every level. Not the best are chosen, but mediocrities. [12] The leader can have full confidence only in someone who is less competent than himself. [13] Naturally, this sort of cadre policy defends itself by referring to the requirements of "state security." [14] In the course of time new cadres appear, who form a system and who objectively meet not only political but also professional criteria; they are thus competitors of the earlier leading cadres. The latter, in order to maintain themselves, enter into various clique arrangements and make connections with the leaderships of sociopolitical organizations. [15] Clique politics produces lack of principle and inevitably leads to serious social excesses. [16]

Finally, in order to insure even further the obedience of the lower strata, in order that the hierarchical apparatus may be able to function without any hindrance, its authority has to be fortified. The leading cadres are made prominent, put on pedestals, described in superlatives; their figures gradually take on unreal dimensions. Giving the names of individual functionaries to cooperatives, streets, and cities is only one of the more violent manifestations of this process (which, incidentally, was noted some years ago and corrective measures were taken). "For years," states K. Crvenkovski, "individuals among us raised themselves to the heights just by means of this irrational authority. In other words, power on one side and fear on the other. And if we carry the analysis further, it means reinforcement of the bureaucratic mentality, a characteristic of the psychology of the rank and file of the League of Communists" [10: 132]. The speeches of people from the Central Committee leadership are fetishized, "as if we were the only people in the whole society who could think" (V. Vlahović [24: 729]. There are two measures, two criteria, in the League of Communists: one for those below and one for those on top (Tito [24: 133]).

In contrast to the war and the illegal struggle, peacetime life does *not* present only two clearly differentiated alternatives with equally clear consequences. The alternatives are numerous, diversified, nuanced, and the consequences do not have evident, or at least not obvious, ethical content. With the number of alternatives and the number of conflict situations, the individual now plays a larger number of different parts in society, which are not necessarily in harmony with one another [6: 15-16]. In war, a man is either a patriot or a traitor, i.e., he is on one of two clearly demarcated sides. In peace, imperceptible degrees of transition are possible, from a high degree of moral integrity to amorality and immorality, and people have time to make psychological adaptations and to retain an honorable aspect. Further, war is an exceptional, transitory condition; peace lasts all one's life. A person is not inclined to be always risking his future; he will usually think: If I fall out of favor with the higher-ups, if I get the reputation of an unreliable man, if they put something down about me somewhere in some record, I can ruin my career. And since there are so many good things in life, why should a man be willfully careless? But all these are only external circumstances, which are not decisive. What is crucial for the behavior of the individual are social values. In this respect the bureaucratic system spontaneously presents obedience as the basic virtue, and attacks on the hierarchy as the most serious sin.[17] Once this has entered into the consciousness of people, failure to conform to the system of values seems like Don Quixotism. A man goes to the barricades because he has his friends' support there, social acceptance. A man does not criticize his superior, does not come out in public with ideas that are not official, does not oppose decisions that he does not intend to carry out, is no more conscientious than is absolutely necessary, or is nonconscientious to the extent that is useful to him, does not react to falsehood, does not combat injustice,[18] and does not feel it necessary to do battle for his beliefs, because if he did, he would not get public support, would be regarded as an eccentric and hard to get along with, and often as an undesirable element. Insofar as Communists are concerned, they would be regarded as antiparty elements. Bureaucratic systems have their own unyielding logic; goodwill is of no avail. "The party organized the state, and the state governmentalized the party," E. Redžić commented in an article [13: 190]. In this situation "the field of action was broadened for the most conservative forces in the party and society" (V. Vlahović [24: 730].

198

Social Structure of LCY

To get a better idea of the above-mentioned processes of the formation of the bureaucratic mentality, it would be necessary to make a closer inquiry into the strata that are bearers of that mentality. In other words, inquiry would have to be made into the social structure of the membership of the LCY. Unfortunately, party statistics are very deficient,[19] and previous investigations in this field have simply not been completed (or at least have not been available to the scientific community), so that our analysis will be fragmentary.

At the beginning of 1967 the League of Communists numbered over a million — that is, it constituted one-eleventh of the adult population of the country. This is an enormous potential force. The number of members rose most rapidly in the period after the war to 1952 (from 258,000 in 1946 to 773,000 in 1952) and then rose rapidly again in the 1956-1960 period (from 649,000 to 1,006,000) — in the period, that is, of the second five-year plan, when the most rapid postwar rate of economic growth had been attained, with relatively greatest social, political, and economic stability. The 1952-1956 period saw the reformation of agricultural cooperatives, the abandonment of perspective planning, and the conversion of the Communist Party of Yugoslavia into the League of Yugoslav Communists; the number of members dropped from 773,000 to 649,000. From 1961 on, a period with well-known economic and political problems, the number of members stagnated. The following data sum up the development of the party in the postrevolutionary era:

Social Composition of League of Communists

	1946		1952		1966	
	Thousands	%	Thousands	%	Thousands	%
Workers	71	27.6	249	32.2	355	33.9
Peasants	130	50.4	331	42.8	77	7.4
Other jobs (employees)	27	10.3	146	18.9	408	39.1
Students, military, pensioners, others	30	11.7	47	6.1	206	19.6
Total	258	100.0	773	100.0	1,046	100.0

199

If career military men and a part of the pensioners are included in the "employees" category, then at the beginning of 1967 about half of all members were employees. It would follow from this that the League of Communists was primarily an employees' rather than a workers' organization. And since, because of the conditions of the social situation, the mentality of the employee is in general closer to the bureaucratic mentality than to that of the worker, the hypothesis might be stated that the bureaucratic process in the LCY, in the state, and in society corresponded to a change in the social structure of the LCY, in the direction of employee domination, which in turn would favor further bureaucratization. Because of the total absence of empirical studies, we cannot definitively accept or reject this hypothesis. We can, however, look into it a little further. To this end we shall try to squeeze a maximum of information out of the published statistical data. We can apply the following seven criteria to test the correctness of the impression as to the employee character of the LCY: (1) the absolute and relative number of employees; (2) the relative increase in the number of employees; (3) the social structure of the membership in the most developed republic as an indication of the inherent tendencies of future development in the country as a whole; (4) the percentage of LCY members in individual categories of those employed; (5) the acceptance and exclusion of members; (6) the abandonment of the LCY; and (7) the social structure of the party leadership. After that, we must inquire into the structure of the employees themselves. Finally, the peasant problem calls for special consideration.

The first criterion has already been considered. As for the second, it will be seen from the table that in the course of the two decades after the revolution, the number of workers in the LCY increased by a factor of 5, while the number of employees increased by a factor of 15, or *three times as fast*. The entire period is not homogeneous in this respect; two periods must be distinguished: the CPY up to 1952 and the LCY from 1953 to 1966. It should also be kept in mind that, from 1953 on, a different method of social classification was used.[20] In the first period the number of workers rose by 3.5 times and the number of employees by 5.4 times, or 1.5 times faster; in the second period the number of employees rose only 1.1 times faster.[21] The rapid increase in employees as compared to workers in the first postrevolutionary period is logical and to be expected: it was the time of setting up the new apparatus of power and the new administration. However, a similar tendency, although weaker, occurred later as well. At the same time it should be noted that for a long time the employee position was strengthened on account of the absolute and relative decrease in the number of peasants along with a gradual reinforcement of the workers' position. From 1961 on, however, when it reached a maximum of 37%, the proportion of workers has steadily decreased.

If we may take it that Slovenia, which today is approximately twice as developed as the average of Yugoslavia, represents the entire country in the near future, then the evolution of the social structure of the membership of the League of Communists of Slovenia may give certain indications as to future changes in the social structure of the LCY, if there are no essential changes in the social situation. In 1946, workers constituted 43% of all members of the CP of Slovenia, and by 1948 the percentage reached its maximum, 57%. Thereafter the proportion of workers dropped steadily, and was 33% in 1966. The proportion of employees (without career military and pensioners), however, increased from 8% in 1946 to 48% at the end of the period.

Different social strata and different job categories expand (or contract) at different rates in the course of economic development. This makes it impossible to directly compare the growth of individual social categories of members, since that increase would have to be related to the changes in the number employed. In 1966, the following proportions of all employed were members of the League of Communists of Yugoslavia:

Employees with college education	58.7%
Employees with university education	43.8%
Employees with secondary education	39.3%
Employees with primary education	37.0%
Highly skilled workers	34.8%
Skilled workers	20.6%
Semiskilled workers	12.0%
Unskilled workers	5.0%
Average	21.5%

What is most striking about these figures (and this is probably the most precise indication that all the published statistics can give us) is that *all* categories of *employees are above* the average and *all* categories of *workers are below* the average, that even *among employees with primary education there are more members of the LCY than among highly skilled workers.* Because of the avant-garde role of the LCY in society, it would be natural to expect that the level of its members' qualification would be considerably above the social average. For this reason, and because of the rise in the general educational level of the population, a rise may be expected in the proportion of highly skilled categories. In fact, in the last eight years, for which there are data, the proportion of highly skilled workers in the group of worker members of the LCY doubled, the proportion of skilled workers was unchanged, and the proportion of semiskilled and unskilled workers decreased. In the employees group, only the proportion of those with primary education decreased, while all the other categories rose. But employees as a group expanded faster than workers as a group. And yet it might have been expected that by this year the League would have relatively more highly skilled workers than employees with primary education. But as matters stand up to the present, it would seem we could conclude that there is more affinity for the party among routine employees than among workers, and that the party showed more affinity[22] for routine employees than it did for workers. As to why exactly employees with college (not, e.g., university) education were definitely at the head of the list — this raises an interesting question, which calls for further investigation.

As regards the admission and exclusion of members during the last decade, for which comparable figures have been published, the following fluctuations are found: the proportion of workers among new members fell; among those excluded, it rose;[23] the proportion of employees among new admissions rose sharply (from 18.9% in 1958 to 29.3% in 1965); among expulsions it was stationary (19% to 20%). The fluctuations of admissions and exclusions are doubly inverse: within each group, and for one group as compared to the other. Further, from the fact that workers are admitted in about the same percentage as employees, but are expelled at two and a half times the rate, the conclusion may be drawn that workers are less linked to today's LCY than employees, that from the point of view of party practice as it exists they are an unstable element. Such a conclusion is supported by the data on voluntary resignations from the organization. In 1966, 7,640 members resigned from the LCY; 53.6% (in 1965, 61.4%) were workers.

We must now consider the social structure of the party leadership. In 1963 workers and peasants made up 20% of the membership of communal committees, and 13% of the membership of district committees, of the LCY [24: 693]. No data have been published for the higher echelons, but evidently the percentage must be still lower.

We get the following picture. Workers form a minority in the

League of Communists and, in particular, a small minority in the leadership of the League. Employees dominate the organization, and especially its leadership. All the known tendencies of development point to continuance of this state of affairs. If we add to this the fact that relations in the League were "hierarchical and semimilitary" (M. Todorović), it becomes clear how dangerous the pressures toward bureaucratization were in the League of Communists of Yugoslavia.

After the workers and employees, the peasants also have to be looked into. It is well known that the peasants put their backs into the war of national liberation and into the revolution. That made it natural for peasants to constitute half of all party members immediately after the war. If we wanted to give labels to the changes in the social structure of the party, we could say that this was the peasant phase, while the period after 1952 was the employee phase. As the proportion of the peasantry in the population decreases, and the more rapidly the economy develops, it should be expected that the proportion of peasants in the party membership should diminish. What is characteristic of this evolution is not that there was a percent decrease, but that there was a *severe absolute decrease* in the number of peasant Communists. In the first years after the war, the number of peasants in the party rose as a result of collectivization, which those activists were supposed to advance. When the collectivization policy turned out to be faulty, the cooperatives were reformed in 1952.[24] In connection with this, during the same year, 39,500 peasants were expelled from the party (as against 25,400 and 19,600 in the previous two years), and only 8,200 peasants were admitted (as against 54,000 and 63,400 in the previous two years). Thus, the number of peasants (except for a small increase in 1957-1959) fell steadily, and in 1966 was half of what it was at the beginning of the postrevolutionary era. In comparison to the total number of active persons, peasants are represented in the LCY one-half as well as unskilled workers and one-fifteenth as well as employees with primary education. Obviously, what was involved was a sectarian attitude toward the peasants, arising out of dogmatic ideas as to the social being of the peasant. [25] These conceptions cannot imagine the *individual* peasant as a *socialist* builder. The only thing they can think of as socialist is groups of producers included in a hierarchical complex covering the entire state and subject to direct administration and command. Anything that was not under such "social," that is, bureaucratic, control was nonsocialist. And so, when administratively formed collectivization was abandoned, it was held that the socialist transformation of the village had been put off for some future date, and the individual peasant was left by and large to himself. By 1966 the number of peasants in village party organizations fell to a third of the membership. The party points that were left in the villages were the government agencies and administrations of general agricultural cooperatives, which are given a commercial monopoly. The political task of this apparatus of functionaries consisted in controlling undependable individuals, and in some places that task was understood to include restriction of the economic activity of the peasant. Once again we note the opposition of the functionary to the producers, and this time in a very explicit form. Bureaucratic tendencies in the party now became even more powerful. We know what political and economic problems were caused by that policy toward the village and the peasants.[26]

Another factor to be considered is the age structure. As things stand, the party is old, especially its leadership. The number of its members less than 25 years old fell from 40% in 1950 to 12% in 1966. Over the same years, the number of members over 40 rose from 10% to 30%. In sixteen years, we see, the twenties and the forties have changed places. Aging is a natural process, of course, and cannot be avoided, but it has major negative consequences. Older people are more conservative, and since their development took place at a time when there was more state control and less self-government, they exhibit a tendency to retain the structure of state control. This is the origin of the fact that the aging of the party also furthers the growth of bureaucratic tendencies.

Our analysis now needs to be made more precise in one important aspect, namely, the category that up to now we have provisionally called "employees." In a capitalist or state-capitalist (Stalinist) system, employees are in the main an apparatus of power and government. Accordingly, we would not be making a major analytical error, most likely, if we contrasted them as a group to the workers and peasants. In a society that is developing self-government, the picture changes: *important differences arise within the employee group.* More and more employees begin to break away from their former master (the private owner or the state) and begin to develop social loyalty, which we studied thoroughly above, loyalty to the other groups with which, by the objective functioning of the self-governing organization of work, they are in the same or a similar existential situation. And it is just in this sense that it can be said *that the institution of self-government has essentially diminished bureaucratic pressures in the League and made it possible, despite all opposition, to go*

204

ahead with the reorganization of the LCY. In this context it would seem that we could invert the above-quoted dictum of Redžić to read: the party established self-government, and self-government provided for the renaissance of the party.

Carrying our analysis further, we shall group the members of the LCY into quasiprofessional groups (see Section 17), i.e., look into the horizontal "social" structure of the membership. A determination of the horizontal structure of the active population and party membership in 1961 (there are no party statistics for 1953, so that no determination is possible) yields the following picture.

Active Population and Membership of the LCY by Quasiprofessional Groups, 1961

	Active population (thousands)	LCY members	% members, ref. to active population (%)
Peasants	4,408	99	2.2
Other market workers	2,887	560	19.5
Nonmarket workers	408	105	25.8
State apparatus	257	155	60.4
Totals	7,960	919	11.5

Note: "Market workers' include workers and employees in material activities, and in communal and financial activities. "Nonmarket" workers include persons engaged in cultural-educational and public health activities, and in agencies of sociopolitical organizations. In "state apparatus" are included government administration, law, and career military.

Party membership is by far most frequent in the state apparatus, all but nonexistent among peasants, with market and nonmarket workers somewhere in between. These facts reflect the crucial trend of the party to control the agencies of power. As has been noted, such a trend is natural in the period immediately following the revolution, when the construction of the new social order has to be insured against all eventualities. In the course of time, however, that trend begins to give a very specific, bureaucratic imprint to the entire party organization, and the hierarchical mentality of the agencies of power (with cadres whose qualifications are considerably above the average) begins to impose itself on the party organization with a force out of all proportion to the physical proportion of the employees of the state administration in the total activity of the population.

In this context it would be very important to establish the extent to which the party organization has penetrated the various strata of society. There are no precise data, but on the basis of the statistics given above, it would seem possible to give an approximate reconstruction. Giving the strata from highest to lowest, then the membership of the various strata of society in the LCY is:

Leadership cadres (over)	60%
Intellectual workers (approx.)	50%
Routine employees (approx.)	40%
Highly skilled and skilled workers (approx.)	25%
Semiskilled and unskilled workers (approx.)	7%
Peasants (approx.)	2%

This means, as might be expected, that the highest party cadres are recruited from the highest social strata. This is characteristic of a party in power. By comprising the higher social strata to a much greater extent than the lower, a party in power insures its power, as well as its political control. But thereby it also operates in the direction of conserving stratification, conserving the state; it contributes to the politicalization and bureaucratization of its own membership and of society as a whole. To the extent that these processes develop, the party changes from an avant-garde organization to an elitist one. This makes it crucially important that the LCY should contain, in addition to employees, a sufficient number of workers and peasants.

The foregoing observations would have to be amended by a dynamic analysis, i.e., by ascertaining the tendencies toward changes in the horizontal and vertical structure. Because of the absence of party statistics, it is not possible to go prior to 1958, even for the horizontal structure.

Structure and Membership of LCY by Quasiprofessional Groups, 1958 and 1966

	1958	1966	Increase (+) Decrease(−) (%)
	(thousands)		
Peasants	122	77	−37
Other market workers	401	539	+35
Nonmarket workers	67	129	+93
State apparatus	148	154	+ 4
Totals	738	899	+22

In the last eight years there has been a drastic decrease in the number of peasant Communists, as we found previously. As the result of the decrease in the number of workers from 1961 on, the last five years have brought about a decrease in the number of

206

Communists in the nonagricultural economy as well. The conclusion is justified that economic instability and uncertainty as to the practical-political orientation of the LCY in the last five years found expression in the loss of party influence among market workers. But the most interesting information in the table relates to the stagnation of the state apparatus and to the extremely rapid growth of the number of Communists in the nonmarket category. The first is evidently the result of a purposeful restriction of the expansion of the state apparatus, and is a very positive phenomenon. The sources of the latter phenomenon are not as obvious. A possible presumption is that the development of self-government (which reached nonmarket workers only in the last decade and with a considerable lag as compared to the market sector) and the general democratization of social and political life favored the expansion of the LCY in the nonmarket sector.

Rapid expansion of the number of Communists in the nonmarket sector as compared to the state apparatus might have evoked certain tensions between these two quasiprofessional groups. At first glance these tensions might appear to be a kind of struggle for power, but actually what is involved is the clash of two differing mentalities and struggle for public opinion in the party on the part of two groups with equally high qualifications. Further economic development will most likely lead to a weakening of the influence of the state apparatus, since the nonmarket sector must expand faster than the state apparatus. Once the economy stabilizes and returns to a high rate of growth, the number of Communists in market activities will begin to rise, thereby diminishing still further the influence of the apparatus. And the constant rise in the qualification of economic cadres operates in the same direction. Probably, the period 1960-1966 may be regarded as a transition period, during which the party oriented toward power and, under the strong influence of its own power apparatus, began to convert itself into an organization of political activists, oriented toward becoming a *social* avant-garde, toward keeping its distance from power and substituting self-governing structures for power. And it is just because it is a transition period, in which the old structures are no longer functional and the new ones are not yet erected, that we have begun so painfully to feel the burden of the dysfunctionality of the bureaucratic mentality.

Significance of the Institution of Self-Government
and Democratization of the LCY

If it is correct that the bureaucratic mentality has begun to check the activity of the League of Communists as the social avant-garde, the question arises: where did the League find the strength to cope successfully with conservatism and, in particular, to settle accounts with the main source of bureaucratism, the political police? One possible explanation is that there were always enough personalities among Communists who were sufficiently autonomous to be able to overcome the deformation of the system. I have no way of evaluating the extent to which this explanation is correct, nor how such a thesis could be scientifically corroborated. But this question is possible: why were there not enough such persons in other parties, not even in parties that had made social revolutions? One seeking the answer to this question might well orient himself not toward personalities but toward the institutions that condition social processes and situations. In that case, it is evident that *self-government* is the foundation of the vitality of the Yugoslav social system.

Self-government is the direct opposite of the hierarchical nature of the bureaucratic system. The parallel existence of these two opposing systems of societal organization led, as we know, to many confusions, misunderstandings, contradictions, and disputes. At the same time the development of self-government put ever-increasing pressure on the bureaucratic structure, and the possibility of its forcing itself on society became smaller and smaller. Bringing the bureaucratic processes under control was made possible by two factors: consolidation of the Yugoslav social system on a basis of self-government, and establishment of the possibility of continual comparison of self-governing and bureaucratic activities. In this way political stability, social pressure, and known alternatives made it possible to gain the victory over the conservative forces.

This provided, at the same time, a way out of the situation and a guide to further action. If something happened in the past only because there were certain personalities, then in the future something else may happen if there are different personalities. If desirable social trends depend only on "good leaders," then the training of those good leaders, if they are not already there, represents an insoluble task — as the French Encyclopedists discovered. But if an institution spontaneously produces the desired effects, then the whole business is reduced to the development of that institution.

Until the present, self-government has been primarily oriented toward working organizations. On higher levels the party and state apparatus intervened. That phase of our development is evidently over. The necessary experience has been gained and a definite self-government consciousness has been formed. In the next phase, self-government has to be carried over to the total community. In this process the League of Communists will be in a position to lead only if every member of the League will be in a position to come to his own conclusions quite independently and to act on the basis of personal responsibility and personal commitment not on the basis of directives from above. The precondition for this is the democratization of the League of Communists, and "what is basic for the democratization of the League is the liquidation of its hierarchical, semimilitary relations" (M. Todorivić [24: 679]). That means that the League must transform itself from an organization with centralized initiative into an organization with decentralized initiative, from an organization where the leadership exclusively controls the membership into an organization in which the members also have the possibility of controlling the agencies of leadership and where, in the decision process, communications and directives circulate both up and down. "The present role of the League," say the conclusions of the Sixth Plenum of the LCY Central Committee, "is to be understood as increasing democratization of its internal relationships, which presupposes above all the openness of the League of Communists to all creative and progressive social initiatives . . ." [24: 20]. The ideas of "must" and "require" are not moral or abstractly political postulates, but express the need of coordination with the indispensable social processes by means of which the League intends to maintain the role of a social avant-garde. Only democratization and openness are reliable guarantees against putschist groupings in the future and the only effective means for replacing the "appearance of dogmatic unity" by genuine "unity in views and action" (Sixth Plenum). In all this there will probably be relatively few mere organizational changes. Organizational frameworks are relatively narrow, and the same organizational forms can serve very different purposes. What it is essential to change, or what "must" be changed, is not the organization in the narrow sense of the term but the general approach to the solution of social problems. Naturally, this cannot be accomplished overnight. [27] But precisely for this reason it is of the utmost importance to affirm developmental tendencies and to reveal the roots of the phenomena.

20. FUNCTION AND ORGANIZATION OF LEAGUE OF YUGOSLAV COMMUNISTS

The entire preceding analysis was required in order to establish what functions the political organization should perform in the current state of our social and economic development. Political scientists distinguish two forms of political organizations: parties, which aim at achieving or participating in power; and pressure groups, which put pressure on those who have power in order to further their own interests. Parties are the product of capitalism; pressure groups have existed under all systems.

The political organization that our historical situation requires is clearly no longer a party. However, it cannot be a pressure group either, because its purpose is not to influence those who have power, and in particular not to further partial interests; it aims at a radical transformation of that power. Therefore, as in the theory of economic organization, the theory of political organizations must be supplemented by a new category. Physicists would probably call the category the antiparty inasmuch as the result of the process calls for the annihilation of parties. Then what are the basic functions of such a political organization among us today?

The fundamental task of the existing organization, the League of Yugoslav Communists, is undoubtedly to accelerate and protect the social transformation that has been begun, until the time when it itself will disappear as no longer needed. Actually, the League of Communists will be successful in performing its task to the extent to which it will have succeeded in doing away with itself as a political organization. The League of Communists does not have (as was once inferred on a more primitive theoretical level) a ready-made formula for socialism, which now only needs to be put into effect by crushing the resistance of various hostile forces. In today's complicated situation it is no longer clear who the enemy is or where he is, or what is resistance and what is a socialist orientation. It is the job of social practice and science (we are speaking of *scientific* socialism) constantly to revise, correct, improve, and construct that socialist formula. As far as I can see, the League of Communists would have four basic functions, or two pairs of complementary functions: the function of overcoming historically inherited contradictions and morally-politically integrating Yugoslav society, and the function of overcoming political conflicts against the background of socialism and the construction of a democratic culture.

Overcoming Historically Inherited Contradictions and Conflicts

Yugoslavia is a highly heterogeneous country, culturally and economically. Per capita income is several times higher in the most developed districts than in the undeveloped regions. The difference in development between Kosmet and Slovenia is as great as, e.g., between Nigeria and Greece. The differences in economic development condition equally great differences in the standard of living, labor productivity, education, educational level, etc. Yugoslavia is at the top of the world scale in relative number of students; yet at the same time one-fifth of the population is still illiterate. The differences between city and country, between intellectual and manual work, are likewise great. Further, the Yugoslav economy has one of the highest growth rates in the world. This produces a rapid transformation — not only economic, but also social. One of the signs of this process is the mass exodus of peasants to the towns. Another is the constant change in the economic system.

In this situation of great potential and actual tensions, of incomplete construction of the institutional system, and of rapid and intensive changes, the country requires an organized social force that will have a stabilizing action and be in a position to control and direct all those complex processes.[28]

Moral-Political Integration of Yugoslav Society

Whereas the first function is confined to establishing mere social equilibrium as the basic condition for the functioning of any social or, more narrowly, political system, the issue is now the establishment of permanent social integration, which is the basis for social self-continuance. It is known that morality has an integrative function of this kind in every society. It is also known that morality is a historical, or social, category, and hence that in a heterogeneous society like ours, several moralities, possibly even conflicting ones, may coexist. At the same time, morality, however important, does not exhaust *social action,* to which, for want of a better term, we may give the name of "political." Social action is a complete system of social reactions of individuals and groups conditioned by inherited and acquired systems of evaluations and prejudices, or ethical and existential components of human life, personal experience, and mode of interpretation of symbolic communication. Even when the interests of the individual social groups are not in opposition, it is easy, in a

211

heterogeneous society, for the possibility of communication to be lost, a condition that may then be exploited in various demagogic ways. This is a possibility that predominates by far when the interests are actually contradictory, or when their groups think they are.

Social behavior is determined by social character. "For any society to exist," E. Fromm observes [15: 229; also 16: 94-95], "it must mold the character of its members in such a way that *they want to do what they have to do;* their social function must become and be transformed in them into something that they perform out of an internal need, and not by compulsion." Special character internalizes external needs and thus orients the physical, intellectual, and emotional energy of man in such a way as to satisfy the needs of the given socioeconomic system [17: 259]. In analyzing the fundamental types of social behavior, we may employ Riesman's [18: 8] typology of social characters, adding that Riesman evidently made use of the results of Fromm's analysis [17]. We shall, however, give this typology a different theoretical basis, and somewhat alter the terms and content of the various categories. Social character is that part of the character that is common to the various groups of society and is a product of the groups' experience. Riesman distinguishes three historical types of character, which we shall call the traditionally oriented, the individualistic, and the collectivist,[29] and which in my schematism correspond to the precapitalist phase of slow development, liberal capitalism, and organized or state capitalism.[30]

In precapitalist and, in general, economically undeveloped societies, the dominant social character is marked by the fact that it is in every respect formed by rigid traditions, precisely dictating the external forms of behavior. Thus, social conformity is attained by having people simply observe tradition in everything.

With economic development, society becomes more and more complex and changes fundamentally. Tradition, as the predominant integrative force, becomes an obstacle to development and must therefore be dissolved. The development of a money economy breaks down the previous primary groups and forms the family as the basic social unit, while market competition creates individualism. This individualist character is formed by training in the family, on the basis of values that correspond to the class character of the family. Thus, the new citizens, from their earliest youth, receive a specific class attitude that helps guide them throughout their lives. This turning inward, toward the self, toward a group of values and goals internalized from early childhood, is the basis of the force of social conformity in the individualistic societies of classical capitalism.

However, economic development not only goes forward more and more, and more and more quickly, but along with it the complexity of society and the tempo of social changes also increase. The reckless competition and class unscrupulousness of classical capitalism become dangerous to the social system because they evoke fierce reactions in the form of revolutions. It becomes necessary to think of people, as well as production and profit. Further, the extremely complex division of labor makes the cooperation of different individuals of decisive importance, and a new type of social character begins to appear in the most developed industrial societies, a type that is directed outward, toward others. Behavior is determined by what others think and by their evaluations and preferences; it is determined by collective, mass prejudices, by conceptions. Conformity is now not the indirect effect but the direct goal of behavior, and from that comes the well-known phenomenon of conformity, without ideas and without morality, in societies — what is called mass culture.[31] In such a situation it is only natural that the inward-directed view becomes useless and is replaced by a "radar" sensitive to even the weakest signals in the behavior and attitudes of those around me, thereby enabling me to make rapid and suitable adaptations.

At first glance the collectivist character seems to be a dialectical negation of the other two modes, and hence a turn to a society on a higher level, on a level of cosmopolitanism as compared with the previous primary group. Actually, however, the collectivist type of man is not socially integrated. In the competition for the good graces of others, he tries immeasurably harder to win the favor of those who decide than the favor of those dependent on him. He is deeply imbued with the feeling of hierarchy and, when circumstances permit, shows himself as an unscrupulous bureaucrat. He is in a state of "antagonistic cooperation." He represents total alienation of the personality.[32] He remains, wretchedly and helplessly, an isolated individual in the crowd. That is the point to which the regimes of social existence of modern Western man have come, as expressed in the title of Riesman's book, *The Lonely Crowd.*

Here it is important to note that the lonely crowd, as a social phenomenon, is not characteristic only of highly developed capitalism. It is also characteristic of the Stalinist systems, which imitate that capitalism not only in the productive aspect but also in the aspect of social organization. Therefore we can by no means regard the collectivist mentality, which is often made such a show of, as an indication of socialism. The standard theoretical expositions of it are deeply anti-Marxist, in their terminology and their content. Thus, e.g., the basic Stalinist theory of the "party" as leading the "masses" by "transmission" is nothing more than a variant, with a time lag from Plato and Pareto, of the ancient elitist theories of social organization.

It is not a long distance from the elite to the "cult of personality." And in point of fact we could, with the necessary modifications, apply Fromm's authoritarian character as one variety of the externally oriented, collectivist character. When for various reasons the social system does not function as it should, when the divergence between expectations and reality become too great, when the feeling of national or social danger goes beyond certain limits, then within the individual there is a heightening of the feelings of anxiety, bewilderment, personal insignificance and worthlessness, and a specific mechanism is developed of escape from this psychologically intolerable reality. It is a mechanism of rejection of personal freedom, of merging with the crowd, and a longing on the part of man to submit to an absolute authority, the authority of the party and the chief, which offers complete certainty. And therefore the party, that is, the Central Committee, *can* never go astray, and in fact never goes astray, as is seen from the *Short Course of the History of the Soviet Communist Party (b).* And therefore the leader, from the day he was born, must exhibit extraordinary revolutionary qualities, as is seen from the same *Short Course* and the published biographies of Stalin. Here it is important to note that it is not very relevant that the books in question totally distort the facts and that Stalin was an evil man, as Lenin saw. The essential thing is that the social situation produced the authoritarian character,[33] and it was therefore necessary to find a corresponding leader, and any expressions of skepticism and criticism had to be treated (even without the fabrication of the Moscow trials) as counterrevolutionary activity and treason. One can hardly say that the CPSU(b) consciously and infallibly guided the transformations of Soviet society, as was generally believed; indeed, both the CPSU(b) and Soviet society went through violent convulsions of a disorderly development, with the sacrifices that are now generally known.

After these explanations, we must now return to our situation. We find a traditionally oriented social character in the country, in those small settlements where everybody knows everybody else, where the level of education is low, contact with the outside world weak, and people still live in primary groups. The brief development of capitalism in the regions of Yugoslavia took on an individualistic character. Administrative socialism and the

214

relatively prolonged political monopoly of the leading cadres, with formation of conformity from the side of the social security service, led to the development of the collectivist character and the corresponding mentality. In this connection we can stress three important facts.

1. The transition from one morality to another or, more broadly, from one social character to another, does not take place all at once. During the interval there is a period of anomie, in which the previous standards have ceased to apply but the new system of standards has not yet taken hold or is not yet constructed. These are the very dangerous periods of "declining social morality" and "loss of social discipline." They are periods that are all the more dangerous, the more tempestuous the social transformations. And social transformations are functions of the rate of economic growth, which in Yugoslavia was one of the most rapid in the world.

2. Evidently, none of the three analyzed types of social character can serve as the basis for construction of a socialist society. We must examine our actuality to see whether it provides indications for the formation of an adequate, fourth type of social character, which has not yet been historically realized, but which can and, therefore, must be realized.

3. Insofar as social development takes place anarchically in this area, as has been the case for the most part up to the present, it is to be expected that the collectivist character will be enhanced. What that means is depicted by Riesman and Fromm in their books.

As a desirable alternative character, with a different orientation, Riesman gives the autonomous character. The autonomous personality is able to adjust to the behavior standards of his society; however, he does not do so mechanically but is free to choose whether and how he will do so. But Riesman cannot indicate what social institutions in the Western world produce autonomous personalities. It is evident that there are no such institutions today, and that autonomous personalities remain isolated individuals and as a social type represent an unattainable ideal.

The alternative I should put forward is the associative character, which represents a positive definition of the autonomous character. The associative personality achieves full integration with the social community — not in an unconscious, unthinking, and hence enforced way, as individuals do in the primary groups of undeveloped societies, but as a free, autonomous personality with conscious choice, making possible the basic conditions of his

215

social adaptation. As the institution that spontaneously produces the preconditions for the formation of the associative character, I see the institution of self-government in all the fields of social, economic, and noneconomic activities.

In a sense, social character is only another name for social relations. The associative personality is only another name for the socialist personality. The formation of socialist social relations may be slowed or accelerated. Chaotic development is certainly not the fastest possibility. Development will be accelerated to the degree that society is able to form an avant-garde of associative personalities. Unlike an elite, the avant-garde is not called on to rule, but to act; it is not differentiated from the "mass," but includes the socially most mature individuals from the various clearly articulated social groups; it relies not on political authority, but on moral authority. In this sense the moral standards of the members of the League of Communists play a decisive role in realizing its moral-integrative functions. Similarly, this predetermines the policy of recruiting members of the League.

Overcoming Political Conflicts on the Basis of Socialism

Although the remnants of class society have not yet disappeared,[34] we have not had any serious problems with the class enemy for a long time. The only two really serious political crises that the country went through after the military phase of the revolution was won were crises within the governing party: the Cominform in 1948 and the police conspiracy in 1966. This shows clearly that *today the conflicts arise on a basis of socialism.* Organizationally and — even more so — conceptually and ideologically, the League of Communists was poorly prepared to overcome conflicts of this kind. Under the complicated conditions of having won power, formal unity proved to be quite inadequate. In order to protect itself from similar shocks in the future, the League of Communists had to construct certain mechanisms and to set them in motion (this is usually called the democratization of the party), mechanisms that had previously not existed or functioned weakly.

In order for the League of Communists to successfully perform its primary function, it must be a firm organization of political activists; in order to be firm, it must be essentially unified; in order to be unified, it must be deeply democratic. With this we come to the fourth function.

Construction of Democratic Culture

Yugoslavia does not have centuries of peaceful development behind it as a national state, in which the democratic culture of the citizens could be formed gradually and in a definite, I should almost say natural, manner, as was the case in France or England or in the Scandinavian countries. Nor can we permit ourselves the luxury of extending the process of constructing democratic culture over the coming centuries and thereafter. At the same time it is obvious that democracy cannot function if citizens do not use their democratic rights in a suitable way. It is an unpleasant fact that we do not have much criticism of the highest agencies of state and party, or of individual high officials. If criticism is lacking, the process of bureaucratization and hierarchical structuring of society takes place. The reasons for the absence of this criticism are of interest.

Opposition to criticism appeared very early in workers' parties. Characteristic in this respect is a reaction of Engels[35] almost eighty years ago: "The labor movement is based on the sharpest criticism of existing society. Criticism is its living element; how can it aim at avoiding criticism itself, forbidding debate? Are we to demand free speech for ourselves only to abolish it within our own ranks?" At the same time, a party, like every bureaucratic organization, necessarily generates resistance to criticism (explaining it by the general interests of the struggle); this resistance is intensified, the more the organization is centralized. This applies as well to a party in peacetime, such as Engels had in mind, but it applies even more to an illegal party, which objectively must reduce criticism to a minimum under those conditions. What happens then is that the habits formed under conditions of illegality are later carried over under conditions that are radically different. It is evident from the context, as from other letters of Engels, that his reaction would be even sharper because the party involved was not in opposition, but had power firmly in its hands.

The absence of criticism among us is usually explained by saying that the persons who are the potential objects of that criticism try with all their might to prevent it. It is well known that there have been interventions with editors and radio broadcasts, as well as through party channels. Although I would not dream of denying these empirical facts, their interpretation seems to me to be one-sided and naive. Those persons influence their milieu much less than they themselves are products of that milieu.

As far as I can see, the basic explanation lies in the general undemocratic atmosphere that we inherited and that we perhaps made even more undemocratic. Consequently, criticism of the central committee or of the government will generally be taken as an attack on the regime and on socialism. If the state does not react to the criticism, it will be believed that the person criticized has ended his political career and that the criticism actually came from official sources and is only the announcement of a replacement.[36] If it did turn out like that, the critic (and the editor of the means of communication involved) would get a corresponding entry in his police records and might even be called in for an interview. At the same time, criticism of our bureaucratic chiefs, of the chairman of a commune, or of the head of an institution would have even worse consequences, both for the critic and for the one criticized. It has happened that members of the League of Communists have been penalized even when they have not made explicit criticisms but merely expressed some unusual idea that differed from the standard stereotypes. And resignations, as the expression of dissent, have been as good as unknown in political life.

In such a situation criticism did not cease, but it was transformed: it became irresponsible or stayed behind the scenes, or both. If criticism is discouraged in the everyday relations of people, people have no chance to get used to hearing criticism. This is the source of those fantastic, destructive, unproved, and totally irresponsible criticisms of individuals and institutions that come into the open from time to time. Hence, too, the many intrigues, secret reports, and denunciations that took the place of the open democratic struggle of opinions. And hence, too, the perverted phenomenon of duplex man, a moral-psychological type totally contrary to the free creative personality of socialism.

In the last few years things have begun to change. The press, radio, and television have played an enormous role in the development of this democratic culture. Liquidation of the political police has removed the major obstacle to the further development of this process. We have reached the point where a local newspaper can, without major repercussions, criticize the management of a factory, and *Borba* can criticize the work of a communal committee. At the same time we have not yet established criticism on the same levels and, even less, criticism from below upward. In a patriarchal milieu, such as prevailed in a country that only recently emerged from its peasant huts, the latter is regarded as a subversion of authority that cannot be tolerated. The patriarchal milieu is not in the habit of evaluating

218

arguments; it is guided exclusively by personalities. In logic this is known as the fallacious *argumentum ad hominem*. "The lower the level of logical culture and logical discipline of a man's thinking," the Soviet logician Asmus explains [21: 373], "the less able he is to divorce the probative force of an argument from the feelings, sympathies, and prejudices it arouses in him. . . ." Unfortunately, it is not a matter only of a fallacious consequence of inadequate logical culture. The real social situation is such that the authority adds to argumentation such a factual and proved-by-experience weight that the logical content acquires only secondary importance.

There is still another aspect to democratic culture: initiative. The patriarchal milieu creates authorities in order to use them. To the same extent to which the bureaucrat desires power, the patriarchal milieu imposes it upon him. It is a closed and consistent system. Under it the citizen does not wish (or does not know, which comes to the same thing) to make use of his democratic rights. As he once did to God, he now turns to a "higher instance" for his beliefs and defense. "I am, for example, forced by environment to exercise power," journalist S. Djukić reports the Secretary of the Communal Committee of the League of Communists of Vranje as saying (*Borba,* October 9, 1966, p. 4). And since our administration is technically not the most efficient, as is the rule in an undeveloped country, our conservative citizen is in fact pretty much in the right. In order to put into effect the rights guaranteed by law, interventions are required. Interventions conditioned the mechanism of the VIP (*veza i protekcija,* which means "corrections and protections"), and this constitutes the greatest obstacle to efficient functioning of the mechanism of self-government.

It turns out that the question of criticism and that of self-governing initiative do not reduce merely to "allowing criticism" or "guaranteeing initiative by regulations," although these of course are crucial preconditions. Since we have to deal with a socio-psychological structure cemented by traditions, nothing will be accomplished by that passive permission. Again, criticism can do great harm in an uncritical milieu. And in a milieu that is not educated to criticism, even the most reasonable criticism may give rise to erroneous interpretations, making the criticism lose its meaning. Further, in a situation of this kind, insistence on self-governing initiative may be taken as hypocrisy (and this does happen). But the *withering away of the state is inconceivable in a milieu where the citizens have not learned to make full use, with complete responsibility, of their civic rights.*

Exercise of civic rights cannot exist in a milieu in which the cult of authority exists, in which there is no criticism. There can be no criticism in a milieu in which citizens do not exercise their rights. *The bureaucratic patriarchal ring can be effectively broken only by a political force that is at least in part outside it.* Therefore, in realizing the preconditions for formation of a democratic and self-governing society, the League of Communists can and must play the decisive role.

Hence, the furtherance of criticism and self-governing initiative, as the bases for the development of democratic relationships and the education of citizens in the exercise of their political freedoms, is one of the most important tasks of the League of Communists. Communists will accomplish this task most effectively if they first develop democratic culture fully in their own ranks.

Democratic Centralism

The function of the party, a league of political activists, is the source of its organization, as has been said. It is usually held that the basic organizational principle of the League of Communists is democratic centralism. But to say this is not to say much. Democratic centralism means the taking of decisions democratically and their centralized, i.e., unified, execution. It should be recalled that this principle is applied even in social democratic parties and that a centralized variant is applied in communist parties; in fact, we shall find several variants of the principle in many other organizations. The problem is whether the accent is on "democratic" or on "centralism," and how the two components are combined. The democratic centralism of the days of wartime or illegal struggle is obviously no longer suitable. Still less suitable is democratic centralism as Mao Tse-tung, for example, sees it: "The organization must be placed above the individual, the majority above the minority, the higher party functionaries above the lower, and the central committee above the entire party. That is democratic centralism in the party" [22: 84]. Let us see what kind of democratic centralism would correspond to today's conditions.

First of all, it is clear that decisions must be taken by majority vote. The minority must bow to the majority. Moreover, that minority must not organize permanently; that would be making a fraction, like founding a new party. At the same time, the withering away of the state implies the withering away of parties. Accordingly, minorities and majorities take form on an ad hoc basis for individual decisions, and their personnel composition changes constantly. In this way the ideas of the individual (and not, as previously, those of the chiefs of the party apparatus) come to expression. As regards all this, opinions are more or less in agreement. The disagreement begins with the question of how the minority should behave when a decision is being executed.

Four answers are possible: go along with it and hold your tongue; go along with it and start a discussion; do not carry it out; oppose its execution. Under normal circumstances the last two solutions are out of the question. As for the first two, it seems to me dogmatic to insist on one or the other; everything depends on the circumstances. If an important decision is adopted by a majority of a single vote, the majority will probably be wise to desist from carrying it out. But if 90% of Communists vote for a decision, the 10% should reconsider their position before reviving the discussion. If it is a matter of extremely important decisions, such as, for example, the struggle against national chauvinism or, in its time, the struggle against the Cominform, then, of course, full unanimity is an absolute necessity. But most often decisons will not be either so fundamental or so evident, and hence, I presume, it will be desirable to allow constant reexamination of decisions made while they are being carried out. Just what decisions come under this heading cannot be established in advance. That too is a matter of democratic culture. In the last analysis some qualified majority may have to decide in each case whether such reexamination can be tolerated or not.

The situation is most complicated when there are disagreements on principles, for example, with reference to the formulation of programs or statutes. The explanation usually given in this case is: membership in the League of Communists is voluntary; with it you accept all the obligations involved, especially the program and the statutes; if there is something you don't like about them, then resign from the League. I think this explanation cannot be accepted because it means retaining the party organization and implies a direct invitation to form other parties or organizations. The League of Communists is not one party among others, so that if you are not satisfied with it, you can enroll in another; it is the *only* organization in which the most active fighters for socialism register. Inasmuch as no one is in possession of the definitive formula for the construction of socialism, just as no one knows the absolute truth, the League must be broad enough to absorb a variety of thinking. This is not a matter of an abstract truth or an abstract freedom, but of the very real interest of the working man in avoiding unnecessary deviations and insuring the adoption of

221

the most effective solutions. When it is a matter of new ideas, a majority is not by any manner of means the best guarantee of their correctness. By the very nature of things, new ideas are advanced by individuals or by minority groups, who then try to convince the majority that their views are correct. To prohibit such activities would be greatly to impoverish the League both theoretically and ideologically, and to destroy its role as an avant-garde.

It would be interesting to know what position Marx and Engels would have taken on the question just raised. As scholars and political activists, they were often in positions where they had to fight for their ideas against the ideas of the majority. A characteristic case in this respect is the *Critique of the Gotha Program,* which is ranked today as one of Marx's classical political works. However, the party leaders at the congress for uniting the German Social Democrats at Gotha in 1875 did not accept Marx's criticism and did not find it advisable that the congress should know of the criticism. Marx expected that; in the letter of criticism that he sent to Bracke[37] he stated that he and Engels would disagree with the congress and added: ". . . it is my duty not to recognize, even by diplomatic silence, a program that in my conviction is completely unacceptable and demoralizing to the party." Fifteen years later, Engels came to the conclusion that the time had come to make that criticism public. However, the party leadership opposed it, even then. Engels stated his position unequivocally in a letter to Bebel:[38]

". . . since you tried to forcibly prevent publication of the article and allowed warnings to get to *Neue Zeit* that in the event of repetition it might be taken up by the party and censored, the takeover of your entire press by the party cannot but appear in a strange light to me. How do you differ from Puttkamer (Prussian Minister of the Interior — B.H.), if you introduce a socialist law in your own ranks? To me personally it is all one, more or less; *no party in any country can condemn me to silence if I have decided to speak out* (my emphasis — B.H.). . . the party *needs* the science of socialism, and that cannot live without freedom of movement. Unpleasantnesses have to be expected, and the best way to deal with them is with dignity. . . ."

In these citations, it is not a question of petty-bourgeois anarcho-liberalism, as Stalinists or Maoists would say, but of the only possible position proletarian scientific workers could take.

Some might think that so great a divergence between science and the party is no longer probable today. Such an idea would be a dangerous mistake. Here is an illustration. Let us go back fifteen years and consider a scholar, or a group of scholars, whose investigations led them to the conclusion that in the next decade it would be necessary to give up central planning, develop the market, make banks independent, introduce interest, liberalize foreign trade, and put into effect everything that today is characteristic of the Yugoslav economy. Those people would undoubtedly have been denounced as bourgeois ideologists, class enemies, and antiparty groups, and would have been unceremoniously expelled from the party.[39]

A similar lack of understanding may therefore be expected today with the remark that, as it seems, the center of dogmatism has now shifted from the domain of economics to that of politics. There are definite reasons for this. At one time it was held that the quickest and most stable economic growth can be achieved by central planning; you simply issue orders and everyone complies. Then we found that administrative planning is not the most effective but the most primitive form of planned direction of the socialist economy. And today our neighbors' experience is that central planning means a steady drop in the rate of growth. Political centralism is based on analogous prejudices. The appearance of divergent thoughts is interpreted as a dangerous devastation of unity, a destruction of necessary authority, and an intolerable weakening of political organization. On the contrary, the open expression of ideas actually strengthens political organization, since all the problems are brought to the surface at once and adequate steps can be taken in good time to solve them; otherwise, they remain masked by a formal unity, while pressures accumulate, leading to explosions. There is a very definite, almost a functional, interdependence. The more a political organization is democratized, the fewer pressures there are toward setting up fractions or new parties, open or secret. And the fewer the pressures, the greater the possibility of democratization. The entire art of politics consists in effectively guiding this process.

Finally, mention must be made of the role of the party press in the problem at issue. Today that press operates pretty much under directives. As such, it leans toward conservatism, as is generally the case in the organ of a party in power. But if the League of Communists wishes to be an avant-garde, it must have an avant-garde press. In the situation as it stands today, the appearance of a new conception in a party organ would be regarded generally as a new directive, and not as the individual idea of the author (except for the "Letters to the Editor" department). Accordingly, party papers reject such work and divert them to other newspapers and magazines. But they are rejecting, along with those works, all the new and avant-garde ideas. Although the party press will have to have a partially directive character in the future too, there is no reason why great emphasis should not be laid on presenting and discussing new ideas, criticism, and polemics. In fact, it is an essential need. If the League members are to outgrow the level of ready-made directives and become political activists finding the most adequate solutions for their daily work, the party press will have to become a stage for the liveliest discussion of all the theoretical and practical questions of our societal life.

Some Organizational Problems

On the basis of our practice and our discussions up to the present, it would seem that some organizational solutions have definitively crystallized. We begin with these solutions.

1. Since the League of Communists of Yugoslavia is not a traditional political party, whose only concern is vote-getting, but aims at being an avant-garde that will transform social relationships and consciousness, its basic organization must be linked to the place of work and not to residence. Accordingly, party meetings will be open, as a rule. The Socialist League embodies the complementary territorial principle of political organization.

2. Since the LCY is against professional leaders, then in principle every member of the LCY must be a member of a base organization. The admission, disciplining, and expulsion of members are performed by the base organization.

3. Since the League of Communists avowedly aims at decreasing and, finally, eliminating the factors of power from its organization, a strict separation is made between it and the state apparatus; party leaders may not be government functionaries at the same time, and vice versa.

4. By virtue of 2 and 3, a system of rotation is practiced at all levels. The members of the leadership are responsible to their electors and may be recalled at any time, in accordance with an established procedure. But they may also resign on their own initiative, because of dissent or other reasons, without thereby affecting their party status.

5. The League of Communists is not an organization raised above society, nor does it propose to impose its ideas on society by force. It operates by persuasion, example, and organization. In particular, the LCY is not outside of nor above the Socialist Alliance of Working People of Yugoslavia (SSRNJ), but operates

within it. Some agencies, e.g., commissions, may operate jointly.

6. Since territorial decentralization (the communal system) has been proclaimed in the country, the League of Communists has not only vertical connections, influencing the government and the Skupština, but also suitable committees reflecting definite links at all levels of the organization of government. Up to the present, these have often been chains of command. From now on they would have to be converted into political consultations. Furthermore, local committees would have much more independence and exercise much greater initiative in analyzing the political situation on the scene and in taking suitable positions.

7. Until now the function of collecting and analyzing political information has been mainly performed by the security service. It has been found that this work was done in an extremely primitive and unreliable manner, and that the consequences were horrifying. This practice has been done away with. Obviously, this function has to be taken over by party organizations and committees, together with the SSRNJ, with full commitment on the part of the party and other press. In addition, I do not see any reason why most of this work could not be stripped of the conspiratorial atmosphere it has been cloaked in hitherto, and performed openly. In fact, this is essential if we are to educate politically mature citizens.

The next few propositions do not seem to have been generally accepted yet:

8. In collecting and analyzing political information, the committees must have an expert staff of professional political scientists, sociologists, economists, and psychologists. These functions, of course, are not subject to rotation. But the political functions of leadership would have to be gradually deprofessionalized.

9. Committees at all levels would have to have subcommittees embracing a wide range of members of the LCY, and nonmembers, with the necessary qualifications and a marked interest in working in the field in question. In particular, the committees would have to rely on scientific organizations as a whole, and not only on individuals who happen to be members of the subcommittees. Until now the opinion has prevailed that scientific organizations have to be financed by the state, and committees might sometimes get some services from them. As a result, systematic scientific work was not organized in a number of vital domains. Regular review of theoretical trends at home and abroad in the field of social sciences and art; research on the labor movement; investigation of political phenomena and social processes, and so

forth — all these could be financed directly, and in this way organized, by the Central Committee. But district committees could also have funds for scientific work. If for nothing else, these funds could serve to conduct inquiries from time to time into various local political and social problems. Actually, the possibilities of work are much greater — for example, finding out why self-government is not functioning in some enterprises; why there are tensions with some social, national, or religious groups; why the population reacts negatively or positively to certain measures; and so forth. In general, our society is becoming more and more complex, and under these conditions the League of Communists should rely much more on science than has been the case to date.

10. In order to carry out the principle of "the right man in the right place," we can no longer continue our previous centralized assignment of cadres. In addition, there can be no genuine intraparty democratization as long as leadership cadres impose their choices on the highest instances instead of being bound by their electors and the base organizations. Elections up to now have been co-optations ratified by voting rather than genuine elections. Naturally, if such was the case in the League of Communists, this negative practice was even more characteristic of government elections. If we truly wish to enact socialist democracy, it is absolutely essential that Communists be the first to set up their own organization on those principles.

11. The broad masses will judge the League of Communists mainly by what sort of people from their own milieu enter the League. Hence, the surest criterion for recruiting new members is to insure that the candidate is outstanding in his own milieu. If he is a worker, is he an innovator or rationalizer? Does he go over the norm? Is he outstanding in governing agencies and an example to his comrades? If he is a peasant, is he a model producer? For students, grades are important; for artists, talent; for a scientist, creativity. Of course, all these people must have, in addition to their professional ability, a definite moral quality if their milieu is to look up to them. In the present situation, in fact, the moral quality of the candidate is of crucial importance. In the previous policy for admitting members, the crucial criterion was his sociopolitical commitment. That criterion expressed orientation toward a "political society," toward the government of society by force. Immediately after the revolution, in the days of the CPY, that orientation was functional; today, in the period of the LCY, it is dysfunctional and leads to loss of prestige and significance by the League of Communists. An inquiry by Kilibarda, with 775

subjects, showed that about half of them thought that the criteria for admission into the LCY were lower than they should be. Inquiry into political admissions in two large firms in 1965 showed that 29% of the new members were admitted on the basis of sociopolitical activity, 22% on the basis of their work and zeal, and 13% on the basis of moral qualities. An inquiry into the opinions of members and nonmembers of the LCY as to what the policy on admissions should be gave inverted criteria, with moral qualities in the first place, work in second place, and sociopolitical activity in last place [27: 198-203]. The results of this last inquiry are a good expression of the requirements of the new situation. If the League wishes to be the social avant-garde, its members must exercise that function in their milieus. That is still another aspect in which the League of Communists differs from classical political parties, which do not try to enroll the best people in the country, but only the best politicians in the country. If this is so, then the cadre policy of recent years was rather unsuccessful. Good people's leaving the League, [40] and the refusal of very positive elements to join on the grounds that the League was joined either by people who did not enjoy the respect of the public or by those who had lost it — these are indications of this phenomenon.

12. In order to insure that elections will really be elections, all elections to party leadership must be secret, with the number of candidates at least, say, 50% higher than the number of places to be filled. There must be at least two candidates for the post of secretary. Candidacies with platforms must be entered at a stated time in advance in order to enable the voters to choose the best fitted. In order to make possible initiatives from below, candidacies may also be proposed by lower instances and basic organizations. All election results must be made public.

Finally, new possibilities:

13. In a system of self-government, the initiative must come from below, and for solving not only local problems but *all* social problems. If it is alleged that self-government and direct democracy are not functioning most efficiently today, once again the explanation is, at least in part, that *mutatis mutandis* they have not been present in the League of Communists. There, the basic organization only received directives, worked out their details, and executed them. The base organization had no initiative, and in general it had no influence in forming the policy of the League; that was done at the center. If the center did not continually send down directives (as happened in recent years, which is clearly positive), there was disorientation and passivity "on the spot," and all work came to an end. To my way of

227

thinking, the base organization must take a most active part in the sociopolitical life of its milieu and of the country as a whole. It will be in a position to solve some problems itself, directly. Some problems will go beyond its sphere of action and there must therefore be possibilities of passing them on for solution, in an organized way, by the next higher level in the district. Similarly, some problems will be of the scope of the republic or all-Yugoslav. For example, a base organization may take note of the emigration of scientific and professional cadres from the country and have some indication that the reason for this is irresponsible pressure by the security service, or an incorrect political relationship to those people, or an incorrect cadre policy. Or the organization may feel that in its commune, or in the country as a whole, the political course with respect to individual producers is incorrect. Or it may be the opinion of the base organization that the provocations of the West German Government[41] can no longer be tolerated and that sanctions must be applied. Or, on the basis of the experience of their members and friends, it may conclude that the legal system does not meet the needs of the country. These attitudes and conclusions may be objectively right or wrong. The essential thing is that they have appeared and must be dealt with. First of all, the base organization will present its problem to the district committee. If the district committee regards it as justified, it will send it on; if not, *it is obliged to submit it* for consideration to a district party conference, most likely the annual conference, where the delegates of the other base organizations will have a chance to evaluate it. If the conference adopts the resolution of the base organization, it will send it on to the next higher instance, where the procedure will be repeated, with a representative of the base organization having an opportunity to give an oral explanation. In this way individual resolutions may reach up to the party congress.

14. But party congresses are held every four years. For the above-mentioned system to function properly, meetings would have to be held more frequently — say, every year. We already have such meetings on the level of the base and district organizations in the form of annual (or biennial) conferences. It will now be time to introduce annual general party conferences as well. It should be added that the order of this ascending line of initiative from the base organizations could be linked to the work of subcommittees at all levels. In this way the meetings of the subcommittees and the annual conferences would be transformed into genuine political tribunes (instead of the former soporific monotony), in which every important sociopolitical problem

228

would be taken up and which would politically activate the broadest party — and not only party — masses. That too, naturally, is a precondition for the League's fulfilling its avant-garde role and for citizens being prepared for responsible political life.

The foregoing fourteen problems evidently far from exhaust the organizational problems of the League of Communists. They have been so chosen as to present the basic organizational preconditions for enabling the LCY to perform its functions, as analyzed above.

FOOTNOTES

1. Cf., e.g., A. Rumiantsev [1: 11-34]. He was quite right from his point of view: worker self-government weakens the dictatorship of the *bureaucracy* and the consequences of any dictatorship. It likewise eliminates *administrative* planning.
2. This need was underscored by V. Bakarić at the first session of the Commission on Reorganization of the League.
3. See his address at the Sixth Plenum of the League of Communists of Montenegro.
4. A recent inquiry into the opinions of students at the Institute of Social Sciences clearly brings out the implications of the fact that social origin is quite secondary as compared to differences in national culture. "Social origin is almost an irrelevant factor in the levels of evaluation of the sociopolitical system, whereas major variations in ideas can be seen in students from different national-cultural milieus." Further, the more developed milieus have higher levels of aspiration: "Students from centers that are weakly developed socioeconomically (Skopje, Sarajevo) usually have rather positive attitudes toward this society, while students from the more developed sociocultural milieus (Slovenia, Croatia) are more critical." Finally, nationality plays an outstanding role: " . . . it was observed that nationality . . . conditions the greatest variance in attitudes toward ideals, or influences the structure of the student's ideals much more than other characteristics of his personality. Second place in the order of importance of characteristics is membership in the League of Communists and the nature of the faculty. After that come sex, religious beliefs, social origin, etc." (Broćić *et al.* [5]). As students are more culturally mobile than other cateogries of the population, it may be expected that these observations would be seen even more markedly in other social groups. We add one more bit of statistics: illiteracy is 1.8% in Slovenia, 41% in Kosmet. There are similar spreads in other indices of economic, cultural, and health standards.
5. E.g., the decisions of the Sixth Plenum of the Central Committee of the League point out that "the structure of the League of Yugoslav Communists has been outstripped in many respects by the democratic and self-government development of society" [24: 19].
6. "Normally," says M. Marković, "those will be the leaders who have, to the greatest extent, the personal qualities required for successful leadership and who can most successfully interpret and apply the party program. Hence the tendency to regard the directives as *their own,* and the conscious identification of the individual with the collective will of the organization to which he belongs" [6: 10].
7. At least one empirical inquiry has been made in this area; K. Kilibarda finds that the reputation of the LCY has declined systematically from the time of the war of liberation to the present [27: 216-217, 234]. At the same time, no serious empirical investigation has yet been made of what the League of Communists and its members *actually* represent in the people's consciousness and in our actuality. One surprising datum, which calls for further study, emerged from a routine preliminary questionnaire of the Workers' University on the occasion of a lecture of mine at a large business firm in Belgrade: half of the fifty Communists questioned declared that members of the LCY are a separate social stratum, just as workers, peasants, artisans, intellectual workers, and leader cadres are. In answering the next question, only 8% of those questioned regarded LCY members as the most highly esteemed "social stratum," while workers received 32% of the votes.
8. The ethical problem is raised most often among us by philosophers; their professional interest is probably also a factor. "As if it were sufficient," D. Grlić asks, for one, "that the same man, who was once ready to give his life for the truth, need only imagine how bold words may prevent him from becoming an academician,

an ambassador, or the head of an institute, and these small social privileges become a sufficient reason for conformism on his part, for silence or skillful camouflage of ideas, perpetual shifting, ambiguous investigation, or shrewd temporizing" [7: 40]. Although the posing of the problem seems just to me, the solutions that have emerged from philosophical discussion do not always seem realistic. Although individuals may influence social processes, and personalities of high moral qualities may help raise the general moral level, there are many more relevant ways in which social processes form personalities, including their ethical qualities.

9. I still have a vivid recollection of an event some years ago, at a meeting of a territorial base organization. Corruption was under discussion. "Why is this point raised at all?" one speaker said (incidentally, an official of the security police)."We all give bakshish to get things done." What impressed me at the time was not so much the fact that one degenerate bureaucrat had lost the feeling for basic moral distinctions, but that none of the fifty Communists present reacted to his statement and that the same man was later elected to the secretariat of the organization. After the Brioni Plenum, he was expelled from the League of Communists and the Security Service.

10. The danger arising from the merger of party and state leadership was noted relatively early. In 1950, E. Kardelj warned in the Skupština: "The question of organization is at the same time a political one. We have a situation on the local level where the rule is for the secretary of the party committee to be elected as chairman or secretary, at the same time, in the local people's council. The result was that the party committee was merged in his hands with the apparatus of the local people's council. Thus, there was no social factor, or at least a greatly weakened one, that could control the government apparatus, that could criticize it in the name of the people, in the name of the party" [24: 388]. Although it was not stated explicitly, it may be presumed that there was an awareness of the negative consequences arising from the merger of government and party apparatus, and on higher than local levels.

11. This fact, and the existence of a clear awareness of it, are well illustrated by a case cited in 1964 by S. Kavčič. On the occasion of the reception for some new members, the secretary of a base organization of the League in Slovenia said: "Now you are no longer what you were before; now that you have joined the League of Communists, you will have to leave outside a part of the freedom you had up to now." In his commentary, Kavčič remarks that such cases are obviously no rarity [24: 459]. That they are not rare is confirmed by an empirical investigation by K. Kilibarda in another part of the country (Kraljevo region). The author is surprised himself by his findings, and tries to find a justification for them: "The investigation indicates the existence of inaccurate and incomplete views, and even prejudices (sic!), such as the state of initiative in the League of Communists. On this question, members and nonmembers of the League of Communists differ; e.g., nonmembers rarely cite initiative as a quality most needed to be a member of the LCY and to be a leader in it. Even more, the opinion exists that qualities contrary to initiative are requisite to be a member of the League of Communists, and still more so to be a leader in it. On this basis, it is held that a certain obedience, even in the classic sense of the word, is required" [27: 50].

12. V. Bakarić notes significantly that careerism and orientation toward mediocrity tend to begin in youth organizations [24: 176].

13. J. Schumpeter, after citing historical examples, remarks: "As every political leader knows, it is only in mediocrity that loyalty can be counted upon" [8: 281].

14. The following instance is illustrative. It relates to American government bureaucracy, but *mutatis mutandis* could apply to any other nation's bureaucracy, including ours. C. Wright Mills quotes J. Halle, a member of the political planning staff at the State Department: "We hope that the American public will finally realize that the words 'reliable from the point of view of state security' have become a euphemism. This personnel policy accounts for the primitive policy in the last five years of eliminating from government service those who are intellectually and morally eminent and filling their places with politically acceptable people, that is to say, with those who cannot be suspected of being intellectually or morally superior" [9: 275].

15. "Linking the two peaks," says V. Rus, in analyzing an article in *Delavska Politika,* "is of special interest to those leadership groups in enterprises who lack sufficient professional ability and sufficient success in running the enterprises. Their authority cannot be justified on either professional or working lines; they therefore try to legalize it on political lines. Entering into association with the leaderships of sociopolitical organizations is a crucial means, in such cases, for consolidating positions of domination" [11: 1091].

230

16. Immediately after the Brioni Plenum, Tito, obviously with Ranković in mind, observed on one occasion that "the conditions under which a man is situated and works sometimes lead him to be false to himself and to enter on a path that he would not even dare to think of. This is not a question . . . of one man. It is a question of people who arrived at responsible positions and were not equal to them" [24: 139]. "Subjectivism in the cadre policy of the LCY," V. Vlahović concludes concerning the same problem, "brought it about that those cadres who are incapable of coping with the battle of opinions, who cannot rely on their own knowledge and ability or fail to understand the course of social development, set up the logic and mechanism of closed groups, a sort of political underground, insulated from the judgment of publicity" [24: 732].

17. Reacting to Hegel's thesis that hierarchy is protection from the abuse of power, Marx gives an excellent description of the bureaucracy: " . . . as though the hierarchy is not the *main abuse,* and as though the few personal sins committed by employees can be compared with the sins that essentially emerge from that hierarchy; the hierarchy punishes employees if they sin against it or if they commit a superfluous sin for the hierarchy; but the hierarchy protects the employee if it sins through him; in other words, it is hard to convince the hierarchy of the sins of its members . . . [12: 72].

18. When a positive determination of the rules of living is socially blocked, and utilitarianism has become the basic criterion of activity, then moral barriers are down and abuses become a constituent part of everyday life. In this context, K. Crvenkovski observes: "An enormous number of citizens' complaints and petitions have come to the attention of government agencies, the League of Communists, and state and party functionaries, and have been discussed by the highest representative bodies. We encounter this problem everywhere today; people complain of the Communists and the Communists complain of the violation not only of their civic rights but of their rights as members of the LCY" [24: 221].

19. The first statistical data on the development of the LCY were made public only in 1967, which in itself is symptomatic. The analysis below is based almost exclusively on these data, which were prepared by S. Filipi [24: 746-788].

20. In that year a check of the social structure was made; previously, registration according to occupation was made when the candidate was admitted to the LCY. As a result, the number of workers and peasants shown decreased by 45,000 and 93,000 respectively, and the number of employees and others increased by those amounts.

21. The factor of more rapid growth relates to the 1954-1966 period, since there are no data for 1953.

22. For a correct interpretation of the results of the analysis, it should be remembered that it is not subjective desires that are involved but objectively conditioned facts.

23. Admission of workers reached a maximum in 1959 with 43.0% of all admissions, and a minimum in 1966 with 30.1%. Expulsions rose from 24.5% in 1951 to 57.1% of all expulsions in 1965.

24. Ž. Vidaković gives an interesting explanation of the opposition to collectivization: ". . . the mass participation of the peasant in the armed phase of the revolution and in the establishment of revolutionary power contributed to the failure of the governmental-administrative nationalization of agriculture, for the sociopolitically active peasantry did not passively and submissively accept administrative methods of collectivization" [26: 42].

25. V. Cvjetićanin has published an interesting empirical study on Communists in a Croatian village. At the end of the article he cites, without comment, the statement of peasant Bradić at a party discussion in Velika Gorica. The following excerpt from his statement succinctly sums up the situation in the village: "Well, I was an activist for ten years in all the sociopolitical bodies and leaderships; I have a high position and am a leader in the village. But up to the present, in Donji Hruševac and its surroundings, no one has given a report on the Eighth Congress of the LC, on the Fifth Congress of the Croatian SSRN, on the Communal Statute, or on the Yugoslav Constitution. We do not know what the Statute is, just as we do not know what the economic measures are. I do not know; nor do the others. Nothing happens there. Nobody gives a talk on health, veterinary questions, animal husbandry, care of pigs, agriculture, etc. No tractor has ever plowed a furrow in Donji Hruševac, and we learn for ourselves what has to be done to improve animal husbandry, wine making, farming, and everything else. . . . We have a cooperative that sells coal for 80 dinars, and we sell it for 40 dinars. . . . That is exploitation of the agricultural producer . . . All of us see that and are well aware of it. And then they say, 'They're ours, let them work,' but this peasant has 10 acres of land and you stick a tax on him . . . .

And the cooperative cheats the peasant. That's the way to be a Communist.. . . I have 50 people that would want to be Communists, and don't I know why? I have apples but they are rotten and the pigs eat them. You have plums and can't sell them. Not only in Donji Hruševac but in Strezevg and other places. We have a school, but it has gone to the dogs; our children go out to pasture, when they should go eight years to school.. . . You go to buy fertilizer at the cooperative, and they cheat you in every way.. . . If you want the fertilizer for the spring, they'll give it to you for the fall and tell you it's good for the spring.. . . But the farm expert I went to see told me one kind was for this, and the other kind for that; at the cooperative they sell it for everything. So we are cheating the farmer. What kind of League of Communists organization are you going to have, how can you organize in the villages . . .?" [25: 13].

26. It might be asked: just what would a proper village policy have been like? It is easier to give an answer after the fact than before. Probably, the basic elements of such a policy would have to be: building on the political capital derived from the war, to carry through an agrarian reform limiting the size of holdings and employment of outside labor (which was done); converting the former large holdings into state property, provide them with mechanized equipment, make them nurseries of modern technology, and form cooperative relations with individual peasants (this was done only in part); and taking advantage of existing traditions, stimulating spontaneous forms of cooperative economy. This was not done; not only that, but even today the spontaneous formation of cooperatives is called "wild cooperative" and is persecuted. Also required are: by clear directives and economic means, stimulating the expansion and transformation of individual production to cooperative production in enterprises; eliminating illiteracy (after a quarter-century of socialist construction, one-third of the peasantry is still illiterate) and organizing a specific program of mass education and study in the villages; systematically introducing into the LCY the progressive peasants, producers who have won social respect in their communities; liberating and stimulating economic initiative, and considering the results of productive labor as socialist, and not kulak.

27. The situation in which the LCY was after the Brioni Plenum inaugurated the reorganization as described by M. Hadži Vasilev: "If we except the activity of the developed organizations of the League, which adjusted to the new conditions, the social practice of most organizations is characterized as follows: (1) a thin layer of Communists is working in the old bureaucratic way, because from such positions they will be able to usurp self-government action or continue to be identified with power; (2) the mass of Communists . . . *are rallying around their organization* . . . from a deep feeling that they are giving up the old relationships, that the actual social action of the organization is inadequate and the problems remain open, inside and outside it; (3) *passivization* of a large number of Communists . . ." [24: 358]. I have no way of establishing scientifically how true this evaluation is. The personality of the author and the publication in which it appears call for taking it as highly significant.

28. An interesting public opinion inquiry in 1964 showed that three-quarters of those questioned, in every social stratum, felt that the influence of Communists in the work of agencies of self-government should be reinforced, the primary aim of this being to improve their work and to create better relations in enterprises and establishments. The region with the smallest proportion of persons calling for increased communist influence was Slovenia, where it was only 60.2% of those questioned (Džinić [14: 259]).

29. In contrast to the terms "individual" and "collective," the terms "individualistic" and "collectivist" have a pejorative meaning in our language, which is what I meant to express.

30. Comparing this typology with, for example, Gurvitch's typology of morality, it will be seen that the first type corresponds to "traditional morality," the second to a combination of "imperative" and "utilitarian" morality, and the third to a combination of utilitarian morality and the "morality of later-made judgments" (G. Gurvitch, *Problems of the Sociology of the Moral Life* [19]).

31. Describing this kind of conformity, E. Fromm says: "I have to do what everyone does, so that I have to agree, I dare not be different, I dare not 'go off on my own,' I must be ready and willing to change as standards change; I dare not ask whether I am right or wrong, but only whether I am approved, to make sure that I am not an 'exception,' not different . . . Nobody has power over me except the crowd of which I am a part and to which I submit" [16: 158].

32. "To the extent that 'man is as they want him to be,' man is not a personality; he is

uneasy, depends on the approval of others, constantly demanding their permission. An alienated person feels inferior whenever he is afraid he is not in line. Insofar as his feeling of his own value depends on the approval he gets for conformity, he naturally feels threatened in the consciousness of his 'ego,' in his own self-respect, when any feeling or thought or action is involved that could be interpreted as deviation. But insofar as he *is* a human being and not a robot, he cannot avoid deviation and therefore always fears disapproval. . . . The feeling of strength and security does not break through into his consciousness, but the feeling that he has lost them is always there" (Fromm [16: 201]).

33. We know these "characterological" traits from our own propagandists of the "policy of the firm hand," required to keep order. To the degree that this is not a matter of bureaucrats fighting to keep their positions, it involves disoriented individuals, confused by the constant changes brought to them by our social development, individuals trying to overcome their insecurity by means of the certainty of dogmatism, and the alienation of their personalities by a symbiotic relationship to infallible authority. Duverger also gives a good description of this authoritative type of man [2: 29]: "This kind of political behavior is particularly characteristic of insecure personalities, who never succeeded in creating their own personalities, in getting stabilized; of personalities who doubt their own 'egos' and their own identities. They grope spasmodically for the external milieu because they find no resources within themselves."

34. This is a fairly slow process. For example, the bourgeois revolution in England took place in the seventeenth century, but remnants of feudalism have survived down to today. Yet no one would think of regarding England as a feudal country or fear that feudalism might be restored there.

35. Letter, Engels to Gerson Trier, December 18, 1889.

36. "It seems to me," observes K. Crvenkovski, "that we still . . . believe that an open remark by a functionary, a person in the ranks of the League of Yugoslav Communists, relating to his views and conceptions . . . is the beginning of the end for him, that a remark concerning his position is the process of his removal. We do not have the habit of free dialogue, of coming to agreements.. . . I should even say that the 'higher' we go, the more explicit is . . . this mentality, although it cannot be said that it does not exist 'below' " [10; 131-132].

37. Marx, Letter to Bracke, May 5, 1875.

38. Engels, Letter to Bebel, May 1-2, 1891.

39. Even today, in fact, dogmatists both at home and abroad hold that open blasphemy is being committed by us, and they state, in the Fichtean spirit of "so much the worse for the facts," that socialist commodity production is a *contradictio in adjecto.*

40. This serious condition has not yet been systematically studied. Three data shed some light: workers leave the LCY most of all (more than half of all resignations); the highest percentage leaving is from the most developed republic, Slovenia (2.1% of the membership in 1966, or three times the mean for Yugoslavia), and resignations of members of long standing (66% with over five years' standing) [24: 784].

41. The West German government broke diplomatic relations with Yugoslavia and refused to pay war reparations.

REFERENCES

[1] A. Rumjancev, "Socialist Reality and the 'Theories' of Comrade E. Kardelj," *Komunist,* 1956, No. 18.

[2] M. Duverger, "Sociology of Political Parties," in *Sociology,* Book II, Naprijed, Zagreb, 1966.

[3] *Political Parties: A Sociological Study of the Oligarchical Tendencies of Modern Democracy,* Free Press, Glencoe, 1949, translated from the 1911 original.

[4] R. T. McKenzie, *British Political Parties,* Heinemann, London, 1955.

[5] M. Brocic *et al.,* "Students and Socialism," *Godišnjak* [Annual], IDN, 1965.

[6] M. Marković, "Moral Integrity of Personality in Socialist Society," *Filozofija* [Philosophy], 1965, No. 1.

[7] D. Grlić, "Personality and Courage," *Filozofija,* 1965, No. 1.

[8] J. Schumpeter, *Capitalism, Socialism, and Democracy,* Harper, New York, 1950.

[9] C. W. Mills, *Elite Government,* Kultura, Belgrade, 1964 [originally published as *The Power Elite].*

[10] K. Crvenkovski, "Democratization of Society and Democratization of the LCY," in

Current Problems of Reorganization and Further Development of the LCY; VŠPN, Belgrade, 1967.

[11] V. Rus, "Cliques in Working Organizations," *Gledišta,* 1966, No. 8-9.

[12] K. Marx, *Critique of Hegel's Philosophy of Right of the State,* V. Masleša, Sarajevo, 1960.

[13] E. Redžić, "Contradictory Tendencies in the Social Structure of the League of Communists," *Pregled* [Review], 1966, No. 3.

[14] F. Džinić, "Public Opinion on the Influence of Communists on the Work of Self-Management Organs," in *Social Management in Yugoslavia,* Yugoslav Sociology Association, Belgrade, 1966.

[15] D. T. Suzuki and E. Fromm, *Zen Buddhism and Psychoanalysis,* Nolit, Belgrade, 1964.

[16] E. Fromm, *Healthy Society,* Rad, Belgrade, 1963.

[17] E. Fromm, *Flight from Freedom,* Nolit, Belgrade, 1964.

[18] D. Riesman, *The Lonely Crowd,* Yale University Press, New Haven, 1966.

[19] *Sociology,* Book II, edited by G. Gurvitch, Naprijed, Zagreb, 1966.

[20] *Second International,* Rad, Belgrade, 1951.

[21] V. F. Asmus, *Logic,* OGIZ, Moscow, 1947.

[22] Mao Tse-tung, *Speeches and Articles,* Trideset dana, Belgrade, 1949.

[23] K. Marx, F. Engels, *Critique of the Gotha Program; Critique of the Draft Erfurt Program;* Kultura, Belgrade, 1959.

[24] *League of Communists of Yugoslavia in Self-Management,* edited by M. Nikolić, Kultura, Belgrade, 1967.

[25] V. Cvjetičanin, "Communists in the Village," *Sociology of the Village,* 1967, No. 16.

[26] Ž. Vidaković, *Changes in the Structure of Yugoslav Society and the League of Communists,* Sedma sila, Belgrade, 1967.

[27] K. Kilibarda, *Self-Management and the League of Communists,* Sociological Institute, Belgrade, 1966.

234

CHAPTER VI

Evolutionary Perspectives

The analysis of the fundamental components of our present social situation has been made in the framework set by this essay. The time has come to cast a glance into the future.

It is highly unpopular in the social sciences (with the exception of economics) to engage in prognoses. This situation is probably conditioned by the fact that those sciences (once again, with the exception of economics) are so far from being exact. Nonetheless, consideration of the prospects for development is of crucial importance for the rational conduct of social tasks. For my part, personally, there seem to be the necessary elements for considering these perspectives. It is not impossible that, in taking this long view, I am projecting the possibilities of my own narrow specialty, economics, too uncritically onto the other social sciences and the phenomena of society in its totality. However, until someone proves the contrary, I am convinced that it is possible to program not only industrial production but also, *mutatis mutandis,* social development. Without such possibilities, after all, *scientific* socialism loses its meaning.

We begin with the best-known factor, the economy.

For over a decade the social product of Yugoslavia increased at the rate of almost 8% annually per capita. This growth means doubling per capita production (and hence economic development and the standard of living) every nine years. In 1965 the per capita social product of Yugoslavia was $588; that of the United States was $2,700. [1] This means that with unchanged expansion in the

235

future, the Yugoslav economy will in the next 19 years approach the level of development of the country that is today the most developed one in the world. It means that the present generation of Yugoslavs may expect to reach the American standard of living. At first glance this might seem only an arbitrary exercise in arithmetic. But the calculation is much more than that; it is a real possibility. At one time it was generally believed, and many insufficiently trained economists still believe so, that the rate of growth must decrease as the stage of development rises. This thesis is refuted both empirically and theoretically. The argument, based on theory, showing that the alleged retardation is a fallacy is fairly complicated and specialized, so that it falls outside the scope of this survey.[2] But the empirical verification is very simple. We need only compare the rates of growth of all developed countries in the postwar period with the corresponding periods in the last one hundred years to see that present rates are markedly higher even though these are well-developed economies. Further, if we draw up a list of the thirteen most expansive economies in the world, we find that they are all developed economies, with a lower limit of development represented by Yugoslavia, Bulgaria, and Romania [1]. It is possible, therefore, that the economic expansion of the decade will continue over the next two decades. But *possibility* is not *necessity;* this distinction must be taken into account in discussing the prospects for development.

Rapid economic development is desirable in and of itself because it makes possible a rise in the standard of living. But economic expansion is also a key precondition for the solution of other social problems. One of them is also a national question. It was emphasized earlier that great differences among the various republics and regions are a constant source of social tensions. It was pointed out that the extreme differences between Kosmet and Slovenia are as great as those between Nigeria and Greece. If we wanted to eliminate these differences during the lifetime of a single generation, then, with the high rate of general expansion, the Kosmet economy would have to develop at twice the rate of Slovenia. That is a difficult but not impossible task. But if the Yugoslav economy developed at a low rate, Kosmet would have to attain a growth rate some thirty times that of Slovenia [3]. Of course, that is quite impossible. Accordingly, slow development would result in prolonging the differences in economic development for *several generations.* It does not require much imagination to see how far the feeling of nationhood would be strained by such an endless continuance of the economic (and hence the general social) process of equalizing the positions of our

236

peoples and nationalities.

The next question relates to changes in the stratification structure of society. It was shown previously that economic development converts the pyramidal structure into a spheroidal one and thus diminishes intrasocietal distances. This process is a direct function of economic development and can be accelerated or slowed down as economic development is accelerated or slowed down. Closely connected with this is the problem of education. It has been shown that the hierarchical nature of social strata in our society is essentially dependent on degrees of education. The higher the education a given individual achieves, the greater his chances of reaching the higher social strata. Obviously, therefore, making education universal is a key precondition for increasing social mobility and decreasing social differences. But for all the degrees of education to be made equally accessible to every member of society, much greater resources would be required than are available to our society. Therefore, economic expansion is the crucial, although not the only, precondition for making education universal and thus creating the presuppositions of a classless society. The importance of education for the development of socialist society is so great that we must devote some comment to it.

In the section on social stratification, I adduced Milić's coefficients of association, from which it appears that a worker's child has one-ninth the chance, and a peasant's child one-twentieth the chance, of reaching the professional and leadership category that persons whose parents are in that category have. The extent to which these social inequalities are reduced in the future depends on what chances for education the children of various social strata have today. According to the data of V. Tomanović for the 1961/62 school year [4: 678], among children of secondary school age virtually all children from the families of employees go to secondary schools, only a third of children from workers' families, and one-seventh of those from the families of peasants.[3] If we except schools for skilled workers, leaving only the secondary schools for training children for nonmanual and intellectual occupations, and if we exclude assistant and lower functionaries from the category of employees, then workers' children have one-fifth as much chance as employees' children of getting a secondary education. On the university level the differences, naturally, are still greater. A youth of worker origin has one-eighth the chance, and one of peasant origin one-thirteenth the chance, of getting into a college or university that a youth of employee origin has.[4] It will be seen that these probability indices are very similar to those based on Milić's association coefficients. If we add to this Tomanović's observation that the social structure of secondary school youth has not shown any changes in a positive direction since 1959, and that the inequalities in accessibility to universities from various social strata have very probably increased [4: 679], we shall have to agree that it is time to sound the alarm. Instead of abstract talk about the leading role of the working class and assertions of the rights of working people, the workers and other laboring people have to achieve *real* possibilities for raising their social status and, by emancipating themselves, emancipate society as a whole. It should be added that the period for which Tomanović points out a stagnation in positive changes in the social structure of students coincides with a period of slowed-down economic growth and certain anarchic tendencies in the domain of noneconomic activities, including education.

If there is any theme that keeps recurring in our survey, it is beyond doubt the thesis that self-government is the crucial principle in the organization of our society. Actually, Yugoslav socialism will stand or fall with self-government. As regards self-government on the initial level, in the factory, I think we may say we have come a long way from the autocratic one-man rule of capitalist and Soviet factories. But there is still a long way to go to the realization of genuine self-government. Today we are probably somewhere between the start and the finish, with an influence structure that V. Rus, on the basis of empirical studies, describes as oligarchical [5: 209]. Further development of self-government will depend in large measure on the tempo of economic growth. In this connection we may list the four preconditions for realizing self-government, as are well formulated by M. Marković [5: 66]:

1. *Technical.* Automation associates individual workers, whose individual effects can no longer be measured. I should like to add the classical observation that mechanization and automation of dirty and hard physical work increasingly eliminate the category of unskilled physical labor, and hence those workers who are not objectively in a position successfuly to participate in self-government.

2. *Economic.* "Self-government can develop successfully only in a relatively wealthy society, in which the elementary living requirements of people are already satisfied and in which every individual has attained such a degree of economic security that he does not have to worry about possible economic reprisals because of his social commitment." It may be added that with the increase in economic development there is also an increase in the free time needed for social commitment. Further, economic development

diminishes the discrepancies in personal incomes and thus equalizes the socioeconomic position of self-governing people.

3. *Cultural.* "Only educated, cultured workers, aware of their historical role, can successfully take part in the leadership of social processes." And culture requires, among other things, resources.

4. *Political.* The withering away of the state is a prerequisite. This precondition calls for further consideration.

However incompletely, self-government is already functioning on the initial levels. If we are to be able to speak of a self-governing society, self-government must develop to higher and higher levels of social organization. It is pretty clear that this is one of the fundamental tasks of the next stage of our social development. And it is also pretty clear that the construction of self-government upward is not an immediate effect of economic growth. In fact, the direct functional link between the tempo of economic growth and certain strategically important social changes disappears at this point. It is true that economic growth reinforces self-government in the factory and thereby heightens the social pressures toward the establishment of a self-governing society as a whole. But if the process is not stimulated and controlled in some other way as well, it can take much longer and be much less effective than is objectively possible. This other way is not economic, but political; hence, the crucial importance of the political precondition. And in our society this precondition comes down, in the last analysis, to the efficient functioning of the League of Communists.

The functions of the League of Communists have already been analyzed in detail, leading to conclusions that need not be repeated here. For the LCY to be able effectively to lead the process of constructing a self-governing society, it must not only have an internal structure that is in accord with that society but it must also be at least one step in advance at all times with respect to democracy. To be left behind would have disastrous consequences. If intraparty democratization lagged behind the currents of self-government in the society, a tendency for those currents to cease flowing would appear. In fact, we did go through tendencies of that kind in the period just before the economic reform. If this happened, it would mean that the interests of the LCY, and of the state apparatus as the executive agency, would clash with the interests of the society as a whole. Such a clash could then be resolved in one of two ways. Either the apparatus would impose its will on society by means of the power of the state, or pressures would appear for the founding of a new party or parties. In the first case, we should have a form of restoration of the Soviet type of state capitalism and, in the second, a form of restoration of bourgeois formal democracy; and in either case, an essential revision of the path Yugoslavia has taken thus far on the road to socialism, and an essential slowing-down of socialist construction.

In referring here to the concrete Yugoslav example as evidence that the development of the forces of production is the basic vehicle of social progress, which can be accelerated or delayed by the political factor, we have of course not made a new discovery. It belongs to the ABC of Marxism. It is also well known that the conditioning is not merely one-dimensional, but operates in both directions. A more universal and effective educational system,[5] a more rapid and better thought-out development of self-government, the absence of national conflicts, social stability, and a progressive political system — all these will assist in rapid economic expansion. In the equation of economic growth, the available material resources constitute only one of the independent variables; the other variables are those enumerated here [2: 232]. The above-mentioned reciprocal link between superstructure and base becomes much more important in a social system in which there is a definite possibility of programming the superstructure that should characterize socialism. This observation leads at once to the conclusion that the 8% growth rate per capita we have reached is not the maximum that can be obtained. Even higher growth rates are objectively possible, as can be proved very exactly, even on the basis of analysis of purely economic phenomena. Thus, economic research has discovered that the Yugoslav economy goes through more or less regular cycles [6]. These business cycles and their mechanism have remained unknown to those who shape economic policy. As a result, faulty measures have been taken, or intervention has been made at the wrong time and in the wrong way, all of which diminished the objectively possible rate of growth.

However, our problem is not exhausted by the observation that the rate of growth *could* be higher. It is much more complex. In contrast to the possibilities of accelerated expansion, there is the reality of a slowing-down of economic growth. This retardation began in 1961 and assumed drastic dimensions in 1967. In our economy, as in every other, industry is the vehicle of economic growth. The long-term growth rate of Yugoslav industry comes to something like 13% per annum. That rate fell to 4.5% in 1966, and to less than zero this year, something that has not happened since the time of the Cominform blockade. What is happening to Yugoslav industry? Have the forces of growth dried up? Are

240

unexpected or unpredictable surprises in question? Was that retardation objectively necessary? The answer is that it was not necessary, that it could have been avoided, that it was not unexpected and, in fact, was foreseen. From 1952 on, the Yugoslav economy has been the scene of a continual process of decentralization, the formation of market relations, and the reinforcement of the independence of economic persons. This process was accompanied by definite adaptations on the part of the state apparatus. However, changes in the apparatus, technical preparation of cadres, alterations in the methods of planning and controlling economic processes, study of the functioning of the self-governing economic mechanism and, as a result, the possibility of predicting and directing economic movements — all these lagged behind the needs of the economy. This backwardness was intensified by the rapid economic growth (the result of freeing the initiative of the self-governing producers), which doubled total production in eight years and almost tripled industrial production. The gap between the capacities of the agencies of economic policy and the needs of the economy widened and led to the first break in 1961, on the occasion of the inauguration of the new economic system, which functioned poorly and disabled three versions of the medium-term plan. Scientists warned of the danger of allowing such a condition to continue and proposed definite measures,[6] but the responsible agencies and instances did not give these warnings proper attention. They continued with the practical man's approach to the construction of the economic system and to the introduction of economic policies; economic movements got beyond the conscious control of society; business cycles were prolonged, unemployment increased, growth slowed down. It is true that the 1967 stagnation of industrial production will not last. There will be a revival of the upward cycle, but the mean rate of growth will be lower than before, and considerably lower than was objectively possible, unless the planning and conduct of economic policy are managed in a more scientific way. But the fact that we know the basic mechanism of the movements, that we were in a position to predict some of the factors in those movements, and that we can predict the further movements shows that we are in possession of the fundamental presuppositions for more efficient conduct of the economy in the future.[7] Once again, the mere possibility does not signify realization.

It follows from the foregoing analysis that we shall have to cope with great difficulties in our social development if we do not succeed in reaccelerating economic growth. Even if we should reach the previous tempo of growth, or even a higher rate, that would still not signify that we would solve our social problems in a satisfactory manner. The connection between economic growth and a well-organized society is not at all simple. There are countries in the world that are much more economically developed than we are, but we should not wish to copy the outlines of their societies. Therefore, it is not only important to bring about economic growth; how it is realized is equally important. In the very long-range view, there can be no contradiction between these two goals: the most progressive society will also make the greatest economic progress. Conversely, a country that is economically retarded will have to change its social system. That is one of the laws of socioeconomic development. But it is easy, in everyday life, to lose perspective, and immediate effects often obscure long-term damage, which is hard to make good later on. Thus, for example, M. Marković warns, "If the merit of an enterprise were *always* evaluated only by its success in obtaining revenue and if it were fully established that the basic interest of the worker will be arrived at by increased wages, that would have grave effects on the mentality and morality of the worker and of all other laboring people. The type of people such a society would produce would not differ essentially from the type of people that capitalism produces. They would be people whose entire activity would be motivated by the acquisition and possession of material goods. They would be people who aspire to *have* more, and not to *be* more. They would thus be reflecting the poverty of spirit that is characteristic of capitalist society, and whose elimination, according to Marx, is one of the aims of communism" [5: 70]. Fortunately, it is in no way necessary for commercialism to be made the supreme principle of social organization in order to obtain economic stimuli and distribution according to work. Both are possible by giving commercial relations the place they deserve in the organization of the *market*. The market, of course, is not only not identical with society, but is only one of the many institutions that society employs to organize its life. But it does not follow from the fact that there is no need to commercialize the morality of our society that no tendencies in that direction exist. In point of fact, those tendencies are very well marked, a significant element being primitivism in the approach to socioeconomic phenomena and ignorance of the functioning of the mechanisms of social and economic life; and Marković is thoroughly justified in sounding the alarm. Socialism does not consist of the standard of living, nor of the power of the state, nor of the nationalization of the means of production. Above all, socialism is a society of free, developed, autonomous personalities, who are in a position to control their social relationships. And therefore anything that leads to the alienation of the individual signifies, directly, destruction of socialist construction.

We have considered the strategic factors of the future construction of our society. It is time to conclude. Obviously, nothing is predetermined. There are laws of society that act autonomously and cannot be ignored. We know a good deal about them. But, in addition, there are the most diverse of possibilities that are open. It is up to us to take advantage of those possibilities intelligently. In this respect the task of the present generation is in no way less than that of the generation that made the revolution and brought the country to the door of socialism. The task is probably more complicated, since the society is more complicated. But our knowledge is greater. And thus there lies before us a fascinating struggle to convert possibility into reality, for the conscious construction of socialist society.

And then what, in the further perspective?

New problems will arise. We already discern one of them quite clearly. Our present efforts are directed at equalizing the starting possibilities of every member of society and at judging everyone by the results of his work. In this way we shall avoid the class differences. But we shall not avoid all social differences among people. Actually, it is just as fortuitous and unjust for one to be born intelligent and another to be born mediocre as it is for one to be born rich and another poor. Psychologically the former may be much more damaging. In a class society, those who are oppressed find a psychological outlet in explaining their position by the injustice of the social order, and in fighting against those injustices and that society. But what sense does it make to accuse nature of injustice and to fight against it? This new privileged group in a classless society, a group that does not rely on its origins but on its abilities, has already got its name, *meritocracy*.[9] Society will have to react to the phenomenon of meritocracy just as it has reacted to the phenomena of bureaucracy, plutocracy, and aristocracy. We can already discern the form this reaction can take. Differentiation of income is necessary in a poor society, where it helps produce stimuli to increased social production. As the wealth of society increases, economic stimuli become less and less operative, and this makes possible and is the condition for decreasing the gap in individual incomes. This process is definitely established empirically. Socialist society, in which class barriers have been removed and social mobility approaches the theoretically possible, is by its very nature a rich society. Accordingly, the income gaps will be small. The next phase of development may consist in eliminating all such divergences and making all the members of society economically equal. Here we recognize Marx's higher phase of communism. With the removal of economic differences, the social position of the meritocracy takes on quite another dimension, which will make it likely that the problem of meritocracy will cease to be socially significant. Its place will certainly be taken by the new, even more subtle problem of social, or merely interpersonal, diversity. That will call for new solutions, evoke new developments, and so on *ad infinitum.* At this point the possibilities of scientific analysis come to an end, and the realm of dreams begins.

FOOTNOTES

1. In 1961 prices, and social product according to the definition of the National Statistical Institute. The calculations were made by my colleague, S. Stajić (at the Yugoslav Institute for Economic Research), whom I thank.
2. The interested reader will find the solution to this problem in my book [2: Ch. 9].
3. It is hard to see the living people behind these statistical data. It is a great drawback of scientific writing (as compared to literature) that its numerical abstractions (which are required for rigor of analysis) actually destroy the content of the phenomenon under investigation. As it happens, on the same day that I wrote the above text, I read a letter in *Borba* (July 23, 1967), which I cite below, to the youth division of Radio Belgrade, a letter that gives content to the datum "every seventh child": "This year I completed the 8th grade in the 'Vuk S. Karadžić' elementary school in Konak, where I live with my parents. My parents are poor agricultural workers. They have twelve acres of land, but all the land in our district is poor. In addition, the crops are subject to natural calamities. Sometimes the year has a drought and nothing grows. Sometimes the year is rainy, and again nothing grows. Last year the Tamis overflowed in Romania and flooded those near the border. This was in the lands of Boka, Šura, Konak, and other villages. Many farmers and state farms were ruined last year. Nine acres of our land were flooded.
   "I have a sister who has turned five this year, and a brother who finished the 1st grade in elementary school. I ardently want to continue school, but it would be a disaster for my parents. I always had excellent marks. During my eight grades I got only four 'upper second' marks, and that in the Serbo-Croatian and Russian languages in the 5th and 6th grades. I attended the first four grades in the Magyar school, and in the 5th grade I went into the Serbian school; it was harder for me than for my friends and the other girls who went to the Serbian school from the beginning. Even though there was little chance that I could go on with my schooling, I took the entrance examinations for the Institute of Chemical Technology in Zrenjanin. On June 20 I was notified that I had been accepted. I was overjoyed that I had passed the entrance examination. I could only go to school if I received a stipend. Help me! I will be eternally grateful to you. I hope you will not disappoint me. Thank you in advance."
4. The differences from professional and leadership families would be still greater, since Tomanović includes routine and assistant employees in the category of employees.
5. In cities today, every child completes the eight-grade school; in the countryside, not even half the children [4; 676]. We have already referred to the great divergences in schooling, depending on social origins. At the same time, talent and mediocrity are equally operative in countryside and town, in worker and employee families. This reveals what a waste of the nation's talent is brought about by unselective education.
6. In 1962, for example, the Division for Economic Research and Methodology of Planning of the Federal Institute for Economic Planning mimeographed a memorandum containing this warning: "With the growth of productive forces, the economy becomes more and more complicated; initiative is decentralized; the final

resultant of the freely arrived at decisions of thousands of economic persons is not evident in advance; economic policy contains a whole arsenal of undifferentiated instruments, but the methods of guiding the economy remain indirect and the criteria for arriving at decisions are extremely complicated. The complexity of the economic mechanism and the delicacy of its functioning without interruption call for intensive scientific research and analysis on all levels, in the most diverse economic institutions. And this will require the training of specialized cadres. . . ."

7. I tried to point this out in my book *Ekonomska nauka i narodna privreda* [Economic Science and the National Economy]. It gives an exhaustive analysis of the mechanism of economic movements in the 1960-1965 period [7].

REFERENCES

[1] B. Horvat, *Note on the Rate of Growth of the Yugoslav Economy,* Yugoslav Institute for Economic Research, Papers and Monographs No. 4, Belgrade, 1963.
[2] B. Horvat, *Economic Theory of a Planned Economy,* Kultura, Belgrade, 1961.
[3] M. Bazler, *Classification of Yugoslav Regions by Degree of Economic Development, with a Special Look at Underdeveloped Areas,* master's thesis defended at Yugoslav Institute for Economic Research, Belgrade, 1967.
[4] V. Tomanovic, "Social Inequalities in Educational Conditions," *Gledišta,* 1967, No. 5.
[5] *The Meaning and Perspective of Socialism* (collection of papers at Second Session of Korčula Summer School, 1964), Praxis, Zagreb, 1965.
[6] B. Horvat, "Economic Cycles in Yugoslavia," *Ekonomist,* 1967, Nos. 1-4.
[7] B. Horvat, *Economic Science and the National Economy,* Naprijed, Zagreb, 1968.
[8] P. de Wolff and K. Härnqvist, "Reserves of Ability: Size and Distribution," in *Ability and Educational Opportunity,* edited by A. H. Halsey, OECD, Paris, 1961, pp.135-175.
[9] M. Young, *The Rise of Meritocracy,* Penguin, London, 1963.